No Regrets

The Wire was founded in 1982 and is the leading international magazine devoted to contemporary sound and music.

Rob Young is a former editor of *The Wire* and the author of *Electric Eden, Unearthing Britain's Visionary Music*. His writing has appeared in the *Guardian, Uncut, Sight & Sound, The Word* and more.

No Regrets
Writings on
Scott Walker
Edited by Rob Young

Contributors:

Richard Cook
Stephen Kijak
Biba Kopf
Damon Krukowski
Brian Morton
Ian Penman
Amanda Petrusich

Nina Power
Anthony Reynolds
Chris Sharp
David Stubbs
David Toop
Derek Walmsley
Rob Young

WIRE
thewire.co.uk

An Orion paperback

First published in Great Britain in 2012 by
Orion
This paperback edition published in 2013
by Orion Books Ltd,
Carmelite House, 50 Victoria Embankment,
London, EC4Y 0DZ

An Hachette UK company

3 5 7 9 10 8 6 4 2

A CIP catalogue record for this book
is available from the British Library.

ISBN 978-1-4091-2018-6

Printed and bound in Great Britain by
CPI Group (UK) Ltd, Croydon, CR0 4YY

www.orionbooks.co.uk

In memory of Richard Cook (1957–2007)

Acknowledgements

Thanks to Ian Preece at Orion, Neil Taylor,
Tony Herrington, Chris Bohn and all at *The Wire*,
and Charles Negus-Fancey.

Contents

This Is How You Disappear

Rob Young

Scott Walker: An Introduction

On 4 January 1965, a famous American died at home in London. He had left his homeland in his early twenties, drawn to the historic culture and literature of Europe, and had, in many observers' eyes, become more stereotypically English than many natives of his adopted land. Perhaps more than any other, TS Eliot had made a reputation as the voice of modernist fracture, a poet of the disjointedness of contemporary life, shaping a diction of 'the horror'. *The Waste Land*, his great 1922 poem, and its close companions *The Hollow Men*, *Ash Wednesday* and the later, elegiac meditation on memory, *Four Quartets*, described a world in ruins through a medium of shattered stanzas. Difficult language and syntax betrayed a wealth of cultural reference points, from the high-flown cantos of Dante and Elizabethan tragedy to the street slang he picked up in the tea rooms and fashionable salons of twentieth-century London.

One month after Eliot's death, an aeroplane carrying Scott Walker and two companions touched down at London Airport. It would be too fanciful to state that Walker provided a direct replacement for Eliot, but there are remarkable similarities between the two men. Misfit Americans who adopted England as their home. Socially awkward and scrupulously defensive about their private lives.

No Regrets

Possessed of a dry, even sarcastic humour if pushed, and stern critics of the work of their contemporaries. Each of them, too, spent a portion of their artistic careers essaying more popular forms than their honest selves might have otherwise allowed. For Eliot it happened later in life, in the dramatic verse and theatre works he wrote following his embrace of the Church of England. For Walker, who has shown no obvious religious leanings, though he has talked of 'spiritual' elements in his later songwriting, his trajectory has spanned a long and bizarre arc that began in the glare of pop music and light entertainment, but which has evolved over a lifetime into the composer of some of the most serious and uncompromising music of his time. By putting each of these phases under the microscope, this book aims to map out and understand that development and to give the most convincing explanations yet about how and why Walker's career, and his art, have turned out the way they did.

The shape of Walker's professional career raises disturbing questions about what's expected of a star, an artist in the public eye, what demands an audience is entitled to make of him, what he is entitled to do with that idolisation. Faced with unusually intrusive, even violent, invasions of his private life while still in his twenties, Walker quickly converted idolisation into isolation, but that exacted a toll on his public persona. His art now takes a long time to produce; the intervals are routinely interpreted as 'reclusiveness'. And in the fast-turnover media industry, being a recluse in society is viewed as a negative trait. And yet Walker does not rise to the bait, but fields these questions calmly and with quiet dignity. He is empowered to address these problems because he has embodied them; has lived through them, has negotiated them. The sheer contrariness of the career, that the man who intelligently side-stepped the 'underground' and psychedelic whimsy, citing its insubstantiality, yet spent the first half of the seventies trotting out middle-of-the-road scurf. In the beginning, he followed the logic of showbusiness at a time, the mid-sixties, when no one truly understood the potential of pop and rock music; when most of the money was made by songwriters and publishers rather than the performers themselves, who were treated as little more than labourers on a musical production line. The Walker Brothers were part of this world of single takes, seat-of-the-pants orchestral sessions and sneaky after-hours floutings of Musicians' Union rules to get the perfect take. The perks and pitfalls of being a public figure, with London's nightlife a disorienting mixture of glamour and sleaze. The search for quality and meaning in an atmosphere of trivia and superficiality. The requirement to express one's opinions via a music press that had not yet developed useful critical tools or discourse other than a reinforcement of commercial agendas. Walker's looks and existentialist charisma suited him perfectly to the mid-sixties hit parade; his artistic temperament and avant garde tastes were incompatible.

He was born Noel Scott Engel on 9 January 1943, in Hamilton, Ohio. His father, Noel Walter Engel, was serving in the US navy at the time, but soon took up a new post as a geologist with the Superior Oil Company, which was based in Texas. In fact, until Noel Sr rose to become Vice President of the company in 1967, his job ensured the family remained itinerant and home life was relatively unsettled for much of the time. The family was comfortably off and prosperous, but Noel, an only child, never made long-lasting friendships, and his parents' divorce when he was six did not help matters. With his mother, Elizabeth Marie, he moved to Denver, where Scott first discovered the solace of the cinema. At ten, he suggested to his mother they move to New York, which they did. In the big city, Scott got in trouble, running on the fringes of local gang culture even as he received his first taste of showbusiness, when he bagged a part in a Broadway musical called *Pipedream*. This supplied him with a weekly wage over its one-and-a-half-year run, during which period he also appeared on a TV talent show billed as 'Scotty Engel, the baritone from Denver'. These flirtations with the entertainment world led to the release of a teenage single, 'When Is A Boy A Man'/'Steady As A Rock', on RKO in 1957.

But his itinerant lifestyle continued, and he and his mother relocated to California when he was sixteen. On the West Coast he joined the orchestra at his school, Hollywood High, as a double bassist. After he acquired an electric bass, still an uncommon instrument in the late fifties, he began picking up session dates at various Los Angeles studios. He was developing a talent for insinuating himself quickly into the local scene of wherever he found himself; the evidence is the EP he released in 1959, *Meet Scott Engel*, on which he was described as 'the gonnest gasser of all gassers'.

According to Mike Watkinson and Pete Anderson's biography, *A Deep Shade Of Blue*, Scott was nevertheless leading a turbulent life on the edge of small-time crime and public nuisance, spending nights driving round the streets of LA with a youthful gang, vandalising street furniture and covertly invading the gardens of the rich and famous in Beverly Hills. One anecdote has Scott involved in pushing an outside toilet off the edge of a cliff. Although he was destined to be a massive international star in less than a decade, this image of needling the establishment from the inside is attractive and pertinent.

At the end of the decade he enrolled in Chouinard Art Institute, where he was finally able to apply himself with dedication, and he obtained good grades. The college was part-owned by the Walt Disney corporation and Scott even briefly worked on some designs for Disney. These were the days of freedom and discovery, in which Scott was imbibing Beat literature, watching his first Ingmar Bergman pictures in LA's movie houses, and soaking up the West Coast jazz of Barney Kessel and Victor Feldman.

As the sixties opened, Scott was doing odd jobs in the metaphorical backroom of the entertainment industry, driving a van for Liberty Records and performing menial tasks at Phil Spector's

Gold Star Studios. But he had found himself a full-time manager, a man called Eddie Fisher who had been a 1950s popular music idol himself, and was married to none other than Elizabeth Taylor. Scott's main musical partner during these early sixties years was his high school friend John Stewart. In one of their groups variously known as The Moongooners or The Newporters, they plied the local gig circuit and occasionally were used as a pickup band when the likes of The Righteous Brothers or Ike & Tina Turner were in town. In those days, Scott kept bumping into another young man popping up in various rock 'n' roll combos, John Maus. They had first set eyes on each other at an audition for a TV play in 1960, so the story goes, and though they didn't hit it off at first, whenever they found them-selves thrown together on stage in impromptu engagements – Scott still playing the bass, Maus as a vocalist and guitarist – they always gelled musically. In early 1964 they officially tied the knot and became The Walker Brothers, by which time they had already started grow-ing the shaggy hairdos that would become their signature look. Their musical tastes immediately set them apart from the prevailing zeit-geist – they weren't into the folk-rock and garage punk of The Byrds, Love, etc, but preferred the loungey, laidback showmanship of Jack Jones and Frank Sinatra. Their single 'Pretty Girls Everywhere'/'Doin The Jerk' was recorded after they received a break from Nick Venet, an executive at Mercury Records. Around the same time the group made a cameo in the lamentably poor surf movie *Beach Ball*, queuing up in their sports car during a parade at the end.

When The Walkers secured a twenty-six week residency at Holly-wood's Whiskey A Go Go club, they needed to tie down a regu-lar drummer. Enter Gary Leeds, a larger-than-life character who'd just finished a British tour with PJ Proby. What he had seen of the UK scene convinced him that the three had the potential to make it big there. A plus: being abroad would be a good way of avoid-ing being drafted to fight in the newly declared Vietnam War. They made plans to pack up and leave, but not before recording 'Love

Her', produced by Jack Nitzsche, a single that properly ushered in what we now think of as The Walker Brothers sound. Venet wanted a baritone lead vocal, and so Scott was promoted to vocalist. And so they were ready to make their acte gratuite, their leap into the dark.

They finally departed from Los Angeles on 17 February 1965. Within four months, the group had sorted a record deal and were interviewed by the *New Musical Express* in a flat they had just moved into in Chelsea. At the end of the interview, a man from the electricity board arrived to cut off their power.[1] By the end of 1966, he told an interviewer, he was forced to move address every couple of days and had even had to leave a monastic retreat early because of the intrusive pursuit of girl fans.[2]

Anthony Reynolds's overview of the frenzied activity that lasted throughout The Walker Brothers' career in this book emphasises the provisional, fictive nature of this supergroup: the fact that nearly all its recordings were studio constructions way beyond the capacity of the three nominal 'Walkers', and even their brotherhood was a stage-managed conceit. Early, phenomenal success came within a few months and proved as exhilarating as it was traumatic, leaving Walker with a lifelong mistrust of celebrity, and a wariness of involvement with both live performance and journalistic proping. Even so, a perceptive, occasionally caustic critical judgment often shines through interviews he has given, right back to circa 1966, when he was being courted by the music journals of the day, so attuned to bubblegum and hype that Scott's burgeoning interest in 'serious' musics and film went largely overlooked (or lightly mocked).

Perhaps the first register that he was unsuited to the mass exposure of pop stardom came in February 1966, when he entered Quarr Abbey on the Isle of Wight, in order, as the rumour mill churned it, to find some peace and solitude as well as to study Gregorian chant. For two of the three weeks he still had to field the attentions of his most persistent female fans and later made his apologies to the Abbott. Immediately following this retreat, he was making openly cynical pronouncements in the press about his 'celebrity' status. Reporter Keith Altham, who appears to have been an unusually trusted media confidant to Walker during these early years, recalled Scott even having to run a gauntlet of admirers and autograph-hunting technicians and executives on the way in to the Philips Studios in Central London. He signed his name with one hand, calling himself 'the fastest biro alive'.

' "You know I've always thought it would be a laugh to do the big time bit," smiled Scott. "Get myself some gold printed visiting cards and just hand them out to people. Don't speak, just hand out a card. Then I'd get on to the phone to one of my friends and say, 'Hi there, this is Scott Walker.' Then I'd play one of my records immediately and follow that with 'You've been listening to Scott Walker – you can read all about me in the following magazines and papers this week. We are appearing at the following halls and signed photos can be obtained from our fan club secretary in London.' Then you follow that all up with 'By the way, how are you?' Can you imagine the guy's face the other end?" '[3]

The ennui in these remarks is palpable, and we sense the fatigue with generic repetition that Scott would sum up many years later in the comment, 'All that guitar-based rock stuff – I just feel like I've heard it before so many times. It goes on and on and never seems to end. It's just the same narrow ground being worked over. It would drive me mad to have to work within those parameters.'[4] His response to this condition was to embark on the most productive (in terms of rate of recorded output) era in his life, during which he got a taste of producing and orchestrating his own material for the first time.

*

An existentialist, Walker once informed a journalist, is 'A person who needs no other people – a world in himself. He lives for the moment. A belief in existence rather than essence.'[5] That world unto itself was amplified when Scott went solo at the end of the 1960s. If he had retired in 1970, his run of four albums, *Scott 1–4* (1968–69), would have left him with a strong and lasting reputation. Now the artisan who was attending a couple of classical concerts a week, and was immersed in the orchestral music of Beethoven, Brahms, Shostakovich and Sibelius, began to write songs that he couched in imaginative and vivid orchestral arrangements that owed more to the lustrous soundtracks of Michel Legrand and Ennio Morricone, or the Dion of 1968's *Abraham, Martin & John*. Even more crucial to this development, though, was Jacques Brel, introduced to him by a *Playboy* bunny girlfriend, who provided the key here, gifting Walker with Gallic pizzazz, a sense of flinging caution to the winds of fate. Less often noted but equally important was his discovery of Léo Ferré, the bohemian balladeer from Monaco who made a speciality, in the 1950s and sixties, of Mediterranean anarchist songs and settings of poems by Apollinaire, Baudelaire and Rimbaud.

Convincingly separated from anything currently fashionable in psychedelia or proto-progressive rock, these solo albums were vehicles for Walker's first serious attempts at songwriting, and their mix of themes refracted the experience of the young, lonesome hipster, a mix of bedsit romanticism, late-night surrealism and seedy bohemiana, outlined in Nina Power's overview of *Scott 1* and *2*. Many of the songs are character sketches. As a lyricist he was developing a surprising breadth, delivering a mixture of imagined characters and lowlifes – 'The Amorous Humphrey Plugg' (an uncomfortable modern parallel of Eliot's Prufrock), the ageing transvestite 'Big Louise', 'The Girls From The Streets' – or stranger visions like 'Angels Of Ashes', in which he pleads, *'let the great constellation of flickering ashes be heard'*. In all this, the sheer size of the voice pushed the material way beyond parody or pastiche. 'Montague Terrace (In

Blue)' on *Scott*, when it briefly picks up pace, drives all before it in a wave of emotion that elevates its kitchen-sink scenario into something verging on operatic.

Walker sounds at home in these albums, making free with the vast studio and instrumental resources at his disposal courtesy of Philips, fully engaged with producer Johnny Franz and his arrangers Wally Stott and Ivor Raymonde. There's a clear desire to orchestrate each flutter and nuance of feeling, each peak or trough of sentiment. 'Big Louise', for instance, features a staircase effect in the violins that descends down, down, down behind the principal melody. It's an early example of a desire for aural equivalence that Scott would continue to explore at the end of the century, with vastly different resources and results. As Derek Walmsley points out in his piece on *Scott 3* and *4*, even on these albums Walker managed to reach certain tonal regions that still elude all analysis, to profoundly unsettling effect. 'It's Raining Today', the track that leads off *Scott 3*, is at some level a faint pre-echo of his later avant-garde work, underpinned with a layer of discordant droning strings, like an itch that refuses to be scratched.

But all the while Walker was labouring under the expectations set up by The Walker Brothers' commercial triumph (his fanclub membership was still 16,000 strong at the end of the sixties). The first two albums sold well, but the increasingly rarefied or (as some perceived it) middle-of-the-road aspects of the later two, allied to his problematic public persona, caused the audience to thin out considerably. At the same time, his reputation was enough to secure a contract for a six-part BBC television series, titled simply *Scott*, which aired for the first time on 4 March 1969. The idea of a 'celebrity'-hosted variety show was common at the time – Dusty Springfield, Julie Felix and Tom Jones all had high-profile small-screen extravaganzas around the same time – and from the surviving audio tapes of several episodes, Scott made a reasonably good fist of playing the host with the most, bounding down a grand looking, but in reality flimsy staircase made of wooden crates covered with blue and white crepe paper, introducing guests such as Dudley Moore, Salena Jones, Gene Pitney, Jackie Trent and Tony Hatch. (At the other end of his career, in 2006, he would write a song about a washed-up TV presenter, 'Hand Me Ups', that features pants-wetting children and ends with a gruesome cameo from Donald Duck.)

Ian Penman discusses and rehabilitates this curious interlude at length, and, via a work of imaginative projection, speculates on the fractured consciousness at work behind the dark glasses at the time. Penman rounds up all the splendid contradictions and conflicts ruling Walker's house in the years comprising the accompanying album, 1970's *'Til The Band Comes In* and *The Moviegoer*, and makes a more persuasive case for the music in these underrated records – and for the entire notion of Scott as capital-e Entertainer – than ever before. A telling anecdote from a fan who was in the audience for one taping speaks volumes: 'Scott lingered on stage once the show was complete, talking to musicians or technicians and was deep in conversation when he suddenly looked up, shielded his eyes, and frowned as realisation dawned upon him that he was in the spotlight. He moved away into the shadows, still intent in conversation, the spotlight operator once more swung the light on Scott, who again stepped into the darkness. Once more the spotlight followed him and Scott laughed, seeing the joke the operator was playing on him. He started to fool around, much to the appreciation of the audience, running to dodge the spotlight for a few moments before chasing off to the wings. Scott then stuck out his arm from offstage and the spotlight illuminated his final gesture – a wave goodbye to the audience.'[6]

If Scott had disconnected from the soundworld of his pop contemporaries, he was also distancing himself physically. By 1969 he was living in a flat in St John's Wood and making frequent trips to the continent, many of them to visit his Danish girlfriend Mette

Teglbjaerg in Copenhagen. Various tours and live dates took place in the same year, and he produced a jazz album by flautist Ray Warleigh, a member of the band that accompanied him on a summer tour of that year.

There were further signals that he was moving on: in 1969 he lost his manager and changed his name. Maurice King had taken The Walker Brothers under his wing back in 1965, and played the classic managerial role for the time. Walker was his principal protégé, but after Scott caught him slipping bungs to New York lawyers in an attempt to help him evade the Vietnam draft (a story told in *A Deep Shade Of Blue*), Walker fired him. Meanwhile, in a further instance of cleaning out the closet, the songwriting credits on the label of *Scott 4* read 'Noel Scott Engel', which speaks volumes about the need to emotionally reconnect with his pre-fame identity. It lends a certain double resonance to lines on one particular track, 'The Old Man's Back Again', on which Walker sings, *He'd like another name/ The one he's got is a curse these people cry* ...

As an artist, Engel soon reverted to Scott Walker, but in 1970, with his TV commitments over and tours wound up, he moved to Amsterdam, stamping a clear separation from the world of London showbiz. Living in and exploring the continent with Mette, as well as writing the original material that would end up on that year's *'Til The Band Comes In*, he was nevertheless reported to be considering working as a session bassist again, naming the likes of Georgie Fame and Alan Price, and even claimed to be interested in joining the supergroup Blind Faith. In the light of what had gone before – and what was to come – these seem like surprising impulses, but the 1970s would be characterised by all sorts of decisions and career moves that appear, now, to be counter-intuitive and ill judged. The interlude between 1970 and 1978 has been habitually abandoned by the majority of critics, finding the ground far too fallow: a watered-down mix of show tunes, Easy Listening balladeering, saying yes to too many smoky working men's club gigs and a weirdly cool-hearted, refried Country rock; a period of too much drinking, culminating in a Walker Brothers reunion that dragged on just that bit too long. As Walker himself said much later: 'I went into some kind of despair mode at that point and started drinking very heavily, more than I did normally, and that went on for a long time, and it didn't stop until [The Walker Brothers] did *Nite Flights*.'[7]

'*Til The Band* is a dislocated hybrid album of ten original numbers plus five covers, all running together on side two. The originals were all credited to Scott and Ady Semel, a fashionable, cultured Israeli who was also Walker's new manager – of a younger pedigree than Maurice King. Semel already looked after husband-and-wife duo Esther and Abi Ofarim, who had a chart hit in 1968 with 'Cinderella Rockefella', and what he actually did to Scott's new songs – written while on holiday in Greece – is still unclear, though Scott claimed 'He acts as my censor, vetting all my lyrics and striking out the words likely to harm old ladies.' Semel's sleevenotes to '*Til The Band* claim a kind of existential kinship: 'I've known Scott for over a year now, but can't really tell whether we think alike. We tend to respect, though, each other's idea of solitude and suspect, each in his own way, that "it might be lonelier without the loneliness".' There is humour in some of these songs, as treacherous as black ice. 'Little Things (That Keep Us Together)' lists war, starvation and a plane crash as comfort '*that keep us warm and close, keep us together and help us get by.*' Esther Ofarim appears on a solitary track ('Long About Now') but is credited with a 'guest appearance' on the album as a whole; it's hard to avoid the suspicion that Walker's spotlight was being hogged by lesser talents. In any case, this was the last time anything written by him would appear on record until *Nite Flights* in 1978. Income was an issue from late 1972, after his daughter Lee was born, and he married Mette on 18 December 1973, in Las Vegas. These events put different kinds of pressures upon his schedule; made it easier (especially in these years of UK recession) to say yes, harder to approach the more ambitious, less commercial impulses. Semel hooked him up with a new producer, Del Newman, and brokered a record deal with CBS which was to derail him, artistically, for several years, tying him in to a series of albums in which he had little creative or emotional involvement.

In her essay on the three Country-influenced records, Amanda Petrusich does not claim these as redeemable masterpieces, but her thoughts on this manifestation of American music – created in stilted laboratory conditions in Britain – shed new light on this greatly misunderstood period in Walker's life. At some subconscious level, she speculates, these could have been an attempt to reconnect with the home from which he was exiled, during the Nixon era, one of its more ignominious periods politically speaking. Despite the title of his 1973 album, in no sense do the tracks on these albums 'stretch' the form in any way (the title derives, apparently, from his colleagues' nickname for Walker), which is not to say they're not competently, even at times beautifully, arranged (check the funk of 'Use Me', the gospelised 'No Easy Way Down', the soul-food 'Delta Dawn', which you can imagine Elvis doing). At the same time, he was the father of a young child and, into 1974–75, most of his energies were taken up with keeping in touch with his family, who had moved to Mette's native Copenhagen. This was the period during which he was persuaded to undertake various well-paid gigs in working men's clubs and cabaret venues, and record albums of nothing but covers, a derailment which may well have retarded Walker's later breakthrough change of style by several years. Writing in the *NME* in 1977, Phil McNeill asked how 'the man who made some of the world's most powerful records should have subsided into feeble bleats? How the lion became a lamb?' Walker's sheepish answer: 'I should have kept pursuin' what I was pursuin'.'

Although Walker was prepared to smile and give positive quotes for his press releases in the mid-seventies, he had embarked upon this new deal in the belief that the label would be interested in new

material from him. 'New material' from Scott Walker, though, was
not generated in the conventional way, by first producing a demo
to be approved or rejected by the paymasters. Walker was nurtured
under Philips's almost unlimited budget, in a very different economic climate, and beyond that, he simply had no appetite to play
this game of rubber-stamping. As far as his own compositions were
concerned, Scott Walker didn't do demos, didn't audition new songs
in front of company executives, and needed much longer than a few
months to conceive and complete a whole new album. In the leaner
years of the mid-seventies, that attitude was largely incompatible
with music-business practice. No wonder a crash was looming.

These were strange years, in retrospect, during which Walker
appears not so much to have lost control, as to have ceded it to
immediate imperatives. Sunk deep in the bottle, living from one royalty cheque to the next appearance fee, all three ex-Walker Brothers
were in freefall eight years after splitting up. In 1975 John Walker,
almost destitute in California, returned to the UK and formed a New
Walker Brothers with a winner of British talent show *Opportunity
Knocks*. By then, Scott's marriage was on the rocks, and he was living
in a West London hotel, driving an orange Volkswagen Beetle with
a coathanger aerial. The pair of them got together again, and called
Gary, who was enjoying number-one status in Italy with cover of
The Easybeats' 'Hello, How Are You'. Ady Semel closed a new deal
with GTO Records and installed the threesome in a flat above New-
ton's restaurant on New King's Road. Marc Bolan, who lived nearby,
dropped into the restaurant one day and met the Brothers there, and
there are unconfirmed reports that the four of them took part in
at least one bluesy jamming session. Meanwhile the trio sallied out
on epic record-buying sprees, and listened to their purchases while
sunbathing nude on the roof terrace.

On the sleeve of The Walker Brothers' 'comeback' album, *No
Regrets*, released in autumn 1975, they look like tanned Californian gods; Gary and John's toothsome grins threaten to outshine

the whole image, while Scott, clutching a can of Newcastle Brown Ale, hides his face behind an outstretched hand. The Tom Rush single that gave the album its name was a surprise success, levering them on to several television appearances, including the *Vera Lynn Christmas Show* at the end of that year. They were given a deafening ovation at the end, prompting Gary to comment that 'this was the first time any of us had experienced that one magic moment when we knew we had done something really, really special'.[8] In the surviving clips of this brief Indian summer, they genuinely seem to be enjoying themselves. But they were working hard, too, touring using public transport, holding gambling sessions as they raced up and down the country on British Rail. The single reached number seven in the UK top forty by January 1976, but around this time Ady Semel fades out of the picture – and from the musical history books – after which the group was briefly managed by David Apps, who had come from looking after the likes of Tom Jones and The Bay City Rollers. Over the next couple of years, as they failed to match that single's success, Scott finally appears to have acknowledged that this was not the way forward, and their increasingly sporadic gigs saw him looking less and less committed to the task in hand. By 1977, he was refusing offers to tour, and turning down the potential of earning thousands of pounds from the cabaret circuit. As he entered his mid-thirties, his ambitions in more progressive directions welled up to the moment of truth. Difficult though it might have been, decisive steps needed to be taken in order, finally, to *'Let the great constellation of flickering ashes be heard'*.

In the early months of 1978, Scott Walker fulfilled the final live engagements of his career to date. By then, though, he must have already written the four tracks that appeared on The Walker Brothers' album of that year, *Nite Flights* – a quartet that Phil McNeill described as 'entirely untainted by MOR'. As he cranked out 'The Sun Ain't Gonna Shine Anymore' those last few times at shabby Northern nightclubs, it must have been a dislocating experience when he also had a song like 'The Electrician' under his belt, and had embarked on an entirely new way of lyric writing – oblique, avant garde, syntactically 'difficult' – at odds with the trite lines and rounded narratives of the songs he'd been singing in recent times. The full story behind these phenomenal tracks – which, Brian Eno has been quoted as saying, remain a ne plus ultra of popular music to this day – is told in Biba Kopf's chapter on The Walkers' seventies reunion. Some years later, the preoccupations of tracks like 'Nite Flights' and 'The Electrician' can be seen as part of a continuum of thought that has stretched across much of Walker's own output. That is to say, there is an interest in totalitarianism and its discontents; in the banality of evil and an insistence on portraying the perpetrators of cruelty as human beings. 'The Old Man's Back Again', on *Scott 4*, referenced Joseph Stalin, while 'Hero Of The War' jauntily described the civilian impotence of a crippled ex-soldier. Leapfrogging over the lost years of the seventies, the *Nite Flights* tracks are embroiled in the murky world of torture, hypocrisy and third-world corruption, and a straight line can be drawn from there to tracks such as 'Bolivia 95' (*Tilt*) and 'Clara' and 'Buzzers' (*The Drift*). 'Bolivia 95"s lines about *'The tiles speckling/ darker and/darker//around/my feet'* and enigmatic *'Lemon Bloody Cola'* refrain, point towards the shadow side of the Coca-Cola manufacturing process, involving the harvesting and covert processing of Bolivian and Peruvian coca crops in the US, while the fate of the byproducts are kept a closely guarded secret. The two tracks from *The Drift*, meanwhile, examine the direct effects of fascism upon the flesh: on the body of Benito Mussolini, who appears in 'Clara' as both lover and dictator; and upon the anonymous victim of Balkan atrocities in 'Buzzers': *'Polish the fork and stick the fork in him ...'*

These continuities with the early work have become more marked with each new release. There is the theme of disease, for instance, literally evident in the single 'The Plague' (1967), but also in the medieval endtimes of 'The Seventh Seal' (*Scott 4*), right through to 'Cue', which tracks the spread of a malevolent virus, and 'Darkness', the mutant gospel track – expressionistic, claustrophobic call and response – he contributed to *Plague Songs*, a thematic compilation curated by the 4AD label in 2006. There is also the insistent recurrence of angels throughout his songbook: 'Angels Of Ashes', 'Archangel', the *'Archangels in the city lights'* of 'Fat Mama Kick', to cite just three. The resonance with Walker's real surname is surely more than a coincidence.

Nothing flowed immediately from Scott Walker's *Nite Flights* quartet of songs, and the terminal disintegration of The Walker Brothers upon that album's release passed almost unnoticed. Despite David Bowie trying to approach him to produce an album, Walker remained under the radar and terminated his GTO contract at the end of the decade. The early eighties were lean years during which he sold off a large tranche of his classical LP collection to keep himself financially afloat, and saw most of his back catalogue deleted. A new record deal with Virgin was signed in February 1980, the label acting true to type by expecting him to begin work straight away on a new recording leading to a run of albums. But if there was any ghost of new material in Walker's head, it had barely gestated.

Meanwhile other, younger champions were keeping his beacon alight. Nineteen eighty-one saw the appearance of a compilation of Walker's late-sixties solo material put together by Julian Cope, singer with The Teardrop Explodes. The album, entitled *Fire Escape In The Sky: The Godlike Genius Of Scott Walker*, was released on the Teardrops' label Zoo, and was critically well received, even though its plain grey cover and tiny, almost illegible text didn't make it a particularly appealing prospect in the record racks. Still, it was enough to keep the momentum going. Shortly afterwards, Phonogram cherry-picked a collection of late-sixties tracks under the banner *Scott Walker Sings Jacques Brel*, the first explicit acknowledgment of his close musical relationship with the Belgian singer. Though far removed from the work he was gearing up for, the album sold reasonably well and maintained Walker's profile as a distinctive and imaginative interpreter.

And thus he entered what might be termed Walker's 'third phase' in his artistic life, in which he came to an acceptance that 'time and receptiveness fit together'.[9] In interviews ever since, he has stated that songs and lyrics come to him after long periods of waiting. Occasionally, though, he may need some external stimulus to get the job completed. Dire Straits' manager Ed Bicknell took charge of Walker's affairs in 1983, trying to revive his dormant Virgin contract by at first trying to broker Walker as a record producer for the label, then persuading him to buckle down and record new material of his own. To make it happen, Walker utilised the time-honoured tactic of retreating to a quiet place in the countryside. He rented a 'workman's cottage' near Tunbridge Wells, south-east of London, and over two months in the late summer of 1983 completed the writing of the album that became *Climate Of Hunter*. On his return, he almost straightaway began laying the songs down during a three-month stint at Sarm West Studios with Peter Walsh, a young producer chosen by Walker after hearing the work he had done on Simple Minds' *Sparkle In The Rain*. An odd gang of musicians were assembled for the sessions, including free improvisation saxophonist Evan Parker, guitarists Mark Knopfler and Ray Russell, trumpeter Mark Isham, and Walker's former GTO labelmate Billy Ocean. It also featured keyboardist Brian Gascoigne, who has remained one of Walker's core accompanists to this day. There were reports that players were required to record their parts with no knowledge of the rest of the track, nor the lyrics, while Walker himself hired a hall in Islington solely to test out his vocals, singing alone to backing tracks on a tape recorder. By the end of the year it was finished, and Virgin released it in the spring of 1984.

As Damon Krukowski explains, *Climate Of Hunter* marks a distinct evolution in Walker's lyric writing, and the texts of these seven originals (plus one cover, 'Blanket Roll Blues', authored by Tennessee Williams) stand up to literary scrutiny in their own right. Put under pressure by this entirely un-pop syntax, the musical arrangements are distended further to accommodate them, especially on tracks like 'Dealer' and 'Track Six'. Here, and progressively more so on *Tilt*, Walker's songs become a kind of modern parallel to the German Romantic Lied, where the musical settings are forced to enact the sense of the texts. In Schubert's *Winterreise* (1828), one of the definitive Lieder cycles, for instance, the piano was made to synchronise with the sung texts by evoking natural imagery such as winds, storms, water gurgling beneath ice, animal and bird cries and even a rusty weathercock. 'The idea is to make [the text] resonate,' explained Walker at the time. 'If you can find a polemic in there, good for you (chuckles). But it's to get this resonating factor going. I don't cut up, I'm not that kind of writer. I can just tell you that, uh, it's not easy. I have to work at it and, please, someone else work at it when they're listening.'[10] Walker had very distinct notions of the sounds required for his words, or suggestive of moods and emotional states. Sometimes this could take the form of sound effects: 'Rawhide' on *Climate Of Hunter* opens with the clanks of cowbells; by *Tilt*, he was asking percussionist Alasdair Malloy to create the scratching of claws trying to scrape their way out of an eggshell on 'The Cockfighter'. 'Psoriatic', on *The Drift*, opens with the hollow noise of an internally miked 'big box' being scraped with a breeze block with the intention of portraying the point of view of a pea being rolled around under a thimble. As Walker's vision has become more vividly precise, his sonic requirements have become ever more adventurously esoteric.

Climate Of Hunter contained its share of continuities with his previous work, too. Listen to the opening notes of 'Sleepwalkers Woman', then jump back fourteen years to 'Boy Child' – they are twins. The eerie string drone used on 'It's Raining Today' and 'The Electrician' recur on 'Rawhide', 'The Dealer' and, as an electronic buzz, on 'Track Three'. And an interest in evolutionary process, early agrarian civilisations and the open prairie, central to 'Rawhide', would reappear on *Tilt*'s title track and 'Buzzers' (*The Drift*). The dour 'Blanket Roll Blues', which closes the album, was a song Walker had heard once in a Marlon Brando movie, but he had to scour every Brando videotape he could find until he located it in *The Fugitive Kind* (1959), an early vehicle for director Sidney Lumet, written by Tennessee Williams.

A much-discussed sofa interview on Channel 4's live rock show *The Tube*, and a handful of press encounters were all that Walker was prepared to do to promote the album, but Bicknell did his best to keep things rolling, trying to arrange a modern covers album around 1985 that would feature Walker singing songs by Difford & Tilbrook, Mark Knopfler, Boy George, Joan Armatrading and others – which would have been an inappropriate throwback to the misguided covers albums of the mid-seventies. Walker didn't play ball on that one, and a more promising hook-up with producers Brian Eno and Daniel Lanois didn't get past the recording of a handful of backing tracks, with Robert Fripp on guitar, at Phil Manzanera's Chertsey studio. Walker reportedly didn't see eye to eye with Lanois and felt the sound slipping out of his control. These tracks are rumoured by several of the musician participants to have been of extremely high quality, but they remain locked in the vaults.

The perception of 'reclusiveness' which has shadowed every public move he has made since then begins here, even though as David Stubbs points out in his chapter on Walker's side projects and production work, he is not so much reclusive as conducting business with an extremely low profile, and not actively seeking any publicity. In the late eighties into the nineties he seemed to be relatively settled, living in South West London. One of the more surprising appearances for Walker watchers was a flitting cameo in a television advert for Britvic orange juice in 1987. In an era when the charts were full of revived rock 'n' roll numbers and sixties retro styles, this advert rounded up a number of pop idols from the era, including Eric Burdon and Dusty Springfield, and presented them in brief filmed vignettes. Walker is viewed through the glass window of a cafe, sipping his juice, but what's remarkable among this company is how far he had travelled, artistically, compared to his contemporaries.

Until the arrival of *Tilt* in 1995, *Climate Of Hunter* could conveniently be dismissed as a baffling addendum to an otherwise quantifiable narrative of superstardom > MOR > decline > irrelevance. The eccentricity of an album that was barely promoted and which included four tracks titled only with numbers meant that Walker could comfortably be written off as one of pop's holy fools. *Tilt*, which pushed the envelope a great deal further in all dimensions – lyrically, texturally, orchestrally, atmospherically – was also widely slated as a work of grande folie. Only with the appearance of *The Drift* in 2006 could a pattern be seen clicking into place. Now, it was clear that, although operating at a glacially slow pace (by the standards of quick-turnover pop music, anyway), the three records formed a continuum, which marked out a distinct late style, vastly more ambitious than anything he had previously tried. This impression is only confirmed by the fact that, as of early 2012, he was in the midst of recording a fourth album that, according to his manager, 'picks up where *The Drift* left off'.

The ideas for *Tilt* took a long time to brew, but when it finally appeared eleven years after *Climate Of Hunter*, it proved to be a confounding and entrancing experience. This was a music that managed to be big and psychologically intimate at the same time; all the more impressive for its small-scale, do-it-yourself origins. In a promotional interview CD released to the press, accompanying *Tilt*, Walker explained: 'I have a Telecaster at home, and a little five-octave keyboard – not a synthesizer, it's just a piano – so I keep things simple, and before I prepare I get together with whoever I'm working with and notate it all, the top line.' In the early nineties, as the album was being written, he completed three years of an art course at Byam Shaw, an art college in South London, and talked about Francis Bacon – who hymned the fragmentations of TS Eliot in paint – in relation to the music on *Tilt*, which reached new heights of expressionistic power in its inventive use of orchestral textures, a massive church organ, and extended instrumental techniques.

There was the orchestral song 'Farmer In The City', an epic paean to the dead spirit of Pier Paulo Pasolini, speaking from beyond the grave to his former lover, the child actor Ninetto Davoli, side by side with 'The Cockfighter', with its locust-like pattering of bows rapped on hollow bodies, and 'Bouncer See Bouncer …', where Walker's signature continuous string purr was replaced by a sampled loop of guitar harmonics that sounds like the rattling of a chain. 'We don't know what the names of the chords are but you just grope around until you find the appropriate sounds for that. And that's why you have to pick players that are … an extension of your psychological sound.' Later he added, 'I want to catch this terrifying moment as much as possible, the impact of this feeling as much as possible. That's just the way I work.'

At the same time, Walker's lyrical content became even leaner, stretching syntax, testing signification to its limits and using cross-historical cut-ups. 'The lyric dictates everything on these tracks … even down to the cover of the record … If it tells me to change the time or whatever, I will obey the lyric, 'cause that's where all this came from. So I will be listening very carefully to what that's saying to me.' In the same interview, answering the accusations of 'difficulty' of his lyrics, he cited the unquestioning respect shown to both James Joyce and Michael Stipe of REM: 'Nobody seems to give him much of a problem about it … but I think I'm lucidity itself by comparison.'[11] Brian Morton's commentary on this album, which proved that the approach on *Climate Of Hunter* was no one-off, reinforces how Walker's late music seems destined to remain deliciously problematic, irreducible to a single interpretation. 'This isn't anything new,' he has commented. 'I've always done this. It's just a way to talk about the unsayable things of existence, the unnameable. You're working around it, it's a lot of edge work. You're using language to discuss things that are beyond language.'[12]

This 'edge work' continued, virulently, on Walker's last completed opus as of early 2012, *The Drift* (2006). Artistic ambition on Walker's scale could no longer be accommodated on a major label, and he found a new sympathetic home at the longstanding independent label 4AD, who nevertheless exhibited huge faith in investing in the orchestral and studio resources this project required. The songs here inhabit a series of thresholds – between death and life; between a sense of connection and disconnection; sanity and madness; waking and dream states; dissonance and harmony; time past and time present. The antique, candlelit home of the thimble rigger, '*Neath the bougie*' in 'Psoriatic', or the braying donkey on the streets of Galway in 'Jolson And Jones' – this is the raucous, earthy world Walker originally heard in the songs of Brel, Brecht/Weill and Ferré, made deeply uncomfortable and strange by musical arrangements that frequently seem to be lurking, liminal presences rather than written-out scores. As he did with 'The Electrician', so he continued to confront barbarity, suffering and pain – the sharp end of brutal ideologies – head on in his lyrics, which resonated across a wide temporal range, from the final days of the Second World War to recent conflicts in the Balkans and the September 2001 attacks on Manhattan. In fact Walker's late-style is one of very few examples in a popular music idiom (however tenuous that connection has remained) to acknowledge the presence of war as a real, ongoing geopolitical fact lying behind the veneer of Western liberal democracy. At the end of *No Regrets* we approach this monumental achievement from several angles, with David Toop supplying a cultural context for the manifold themes addressed; Chris Sharp, who commissioned the record for 4AD, reminiscing about the circumstances of its construction; and a full transcript of an interview Walker gave to this writer shortly before the album's release. At the same time film maker Stephen Kijak was piecing together his biographical tribute, *30 Century Man*, and his memoir, included in this volume, sheds extra light on Walker's unconventional studio practice.

A pattern emerges in the various interviews Walker has given over the past thirty years or so: he generally claims to be contemplating some kind of return to live work, which never materialises; he also promises to work faster (a claim that similarly, rarely holds water). The nearest he has come to performing was at an event in November 2008 at London's Barbican, entitled Drifting And Tilting: The Songs Of Scott Walker. Here, various vocalists including Damon Albarn, Dot Allison, Jarvis Cocker and Gavin Friday performed selections from Walker's last two albums in a semi-operatic multimedia staging that included a forty-two-piece orchestra, choreographed dancers and back projections. Walker did not perform, although he was manipulating the sound mix from the auditorium. The work he undertook in the first decade of the twenty-first century placed him closer to the role of an auteur composer, following commissions for film soundtracks (Leos Carax's *Pola X*), art song ('Scope J' and 'Lullaby (By-By-By)', written for Ute Lemper) and contemporary dance works such as the four instrumental movements he wrote for CandoCo in 2007. Walker's comments on *And Who Shall Go To The Ball? And What Shall Go To The Ball?*, which was choreographed by Rafael Bonachela for disabled and non-disabled dancers, give some insight into the obliquity of his musical conceptions: 'The music is full of edgy and staccato shapes or cuts, reflecting how we cut up the world around us as a consequence of the shape of our bodies. How much of a body does an intelligence need to be potentially socialised in an age of ever-developing AI? This is but one of many questions that informed the approach to the project.'[13]

While this book was in the closing stages of production, it was announced that Walker was at work on a new recording project, again with his regular 'band', an orchestra, and figures like pedal steel guitarist BJ Cole who had worked with him on his mid-seventies 'Country' LPs. At the same time, work was ongoing for a composition as part of the Royal Opera House's OperaShots series in 2013.

TS Eliot found faith in the last years of his life, a belief which sustained him through difficult times and which fed his poetry, inspiring its changing phases and its mutation into dramatic pieces. While his songs occasionally hint at unattainable states of grace, and of religious imagery, there is no evidence that Scott Walker has found any faith, though he remains acutely aware of the role religion has played in the history and culture of the Europe he has adopted as his home. Rather, he offsets the exalted with an existentialist's sense of the absurd.

If there's any line at all that can be drawn between 'The Sun Ain't Gonna Shine Anymore' and 'Jesse', it's the fact that both songs are responses to irrevocable changes of state: ways of 'going on', of coping with tragic events that offer no hope of ever going on. That is the thread that holds true over Walker's extraordinary, ongoing half-century career, and which only appears to be intensifying with each new project. Like Eliot, Noel Engel, whose name may even be a derivation of Angle, the Germanic race that populated the British Isles, has left America far behind and adopted Europe, specifically Britain, as his permanent home. And like Eliot, he has worked his way steadily towards a language – textual and musical – that confronts the horrors of the age. Whatever audiences and critics may make of Scott Walker's recent output, it is clear that this is music made out of necessity, not out of any other commercial imperative. After half a century, he is now in full control of his art and has negotiated a long and difficult transition from a popular music milieu based around ephemerality and fashion to a precarious position between fringe rock, contemporary composition and avant-garde sound art. The writings in *No Regrets* cumulatively celebrate this singular achievement.

1. Altham, Keith, 'American Walkers Love Wild Wild Fans' in *New Musical Express* (11 June 1965).
2. Jopling, Norman, 'The Reluctant American: Some Interesting Opinions From Scott Walker' in *Record Mirror* (31 December 1966).
3. Altham, Keith, 'Scott Smarts After [Eric] Burdon's *JBJ* [*Juke Box Jury*] Slamming' in *New Musical Express* (11 March 1966).
4. O'Hagan, Sean, 'Interview: Scott Walker' in *The Observer* (9 November 2008).
5. Altham, Keith, 'Walker Hostility On The Wane' in *New Musical Express* (15 April 1966).
6. Pountain, Chris, 'Scott At The BBC' in Scott Walker/Engel Collectors Page (http://147mark.tripod.com/scottwalkercollectorspage/index.html).
7. Reid, Graham, 'Scott Walker: An Interview' in *Rock's Back Pages* (rocksbackpages.com, May 2006).
8. Walker, Gary & Walker, John, *The Walker Brothers: No Regrets – Our Story* (London: John Blake Publishing, 2009).
9. A Bangs radio interview.
10. Cook, Richard, 'The Original God Like Genius' in *New Musical Express* (17 March 1984).
11. Scott Walker quoted on *Tilt Interview CD* (Fontana/Wizard Radio CD, 1995).
12. Irvin, Jim, 'That Francis Bacon, In-The-Face Whoops Factor' in *Mojo* 18 (May 1995).
13. 4AD press release, 2007.

The Hollow Men

Anthony Reynolds

Take It Easy With The Walker Brothers (1965)
Portrait (1966), *Images* (1967)

It is early 1965. The record company office is in central London, a city approaching the pinnacle of its own swing. The A&R man is harassed, edgy and ex-military service. Prematurely middle-aged with thinning, greased-back hair, he is impeccably clad in old-fashioned pinstripes. There is a bottle of scotch and a soda siphon on the upright piano in the corner. Behind a cluttered desk holding reams of contracts, mail, chits, memos, teacups and two bulky telephones, the A&R man is chainsmoking. Everyone in Britain is smoking. As the ashtray fills, the A&R man is being pitched a group that in a few short months will rival, in the United Kingdom at least, the popularity of both The Beatles and The Rolling Stones.

The pitch goes something like this:

'Full orchestra. Brass section, woodwind, strings. The lot As for the rhythm section – the piano, the drums, the bass, the guitars – electric *and* acoustic – the rhythm section are jazz players. And we'll get some extra percussion in. On top of the drums Maybe we'll even have *two* drum kits. Yeah. To go with the double bass *and* an electric bass. You know that Phil Spector in America is using two of everything now? "Wall of Sound" he calls it. Big sound and big hits. Maybe we'll even hire *two* pianists. Throw the odd choir in there.

Not on every song. But have one on hand. Just in case. Yeah, The Mike Sammes Singers will do.

'OK, that's your instrumentation. We'll have top arrangers bringing the whole lot together. Song-wise? We're gonna have a mix of material – mostly Yank. Some of that Bacharach & David stuff. Those boys are writing up a storm at the moment. Plus a few standards, Gershwin, Legrand, quality tunes. Nothing *overly* familiar. But catchy tunes. *Quality* tunes. Something for the mums and for the little girls. OK. That's the backing.

'And who'll be fronting this lot? This is the best bit. Three American kids. Californian. Two blondes and a brunette. Good-looking lot. I'm talking movie-star handsome. Not like our lot over here, all that lank-haired, spotty Herbert, boy-next-door with broken teeth Freddie And The Dreamers crap. These kids are *seriously* good looking. But can they sing? Ha, ha – let me put it this way. The one guy sounds like Tony Bennett. He's got that jazzy, sexy, smooth smoky thing going on. The other guy? Two words: Frank Sinatra. I'm not kidding you. He's a young and sexy Sinatra. Sounds twenty years older than he is. Sings like an angel and looks like one, too. How old? Early twenties. Can you believe it? The third guy? He's the drummer. Not bad looking. He'll do. Right mouth on him. Every group needs a Ringo, right? The kid's got personality. But, er, he won't actually play drums on the records. Hell, we got Ronnie Verrell, best drummer in the business to do that, right?

'So ...What are they called? They're called The Walker Brothers! You know, like The Righteous Brothers? But no. In this case they're not actually related. None of 'em. Not to *each other*, anyway. It's a gimmick. They do *look* like brothers, mind. But then again, none of them are actually called Walker either, come to think of it ...'

Sadly, such a phantasmal pitch never took place. By the time The Walker Brothers were signed to the UK branch of the Philips record company in early 1965, the label already had in its possession a handful of Nick Venet- and Jack Nitzsche-produced Walker tapes recorded in California the previous January. Philips, through a licensing deal with America's Mercury Records (the arrangement was actually with Venet's and Nitzsche's own subsidiary label Smash), were thus free to release 'Pretty Girls Everywhere'/'Do The Jerk' with a minimum of investment and risk. This was just as well, as the least impressive Walker Brothers single in their entire catalogue was thus able to disappear on release. Under pressure from the increasingly desperate Walker Brothers themselves and their imposing soon-to-be manager Maurice King, Philips tried again, casually releasing the two remaining Nitzsche recordings, 'Love Her'/'The Seventh Dawn', in the UK that spring.

By May, the much more majestic, agony-in-aspic mini-symphony of 'Love Her' was a top twenty hit. The Walker Brothers were now appearing in every UK music paper and on television; the female record-buying public was falling in love, and a deal was hurriedly done by the top brass at Philips to buy The Walkers' contract wholesale from Venet. John, Scott and Gary had arrived. As far as most of the public were initially concerned, The Walker brothers *were* actual siblings who had magically appeared, fully and perfectly formed, overnight. They had materialised in Britain with a gloriously downbeat single in which the architecture of their own particular melancholic splendour was both splendidly obvious and exquisitely consummate. Yet as the imaginary pitch illustrates, nothing about The Walker Brothers was ever as it seemed.

It is hard, even now, to define the enigma of The Walker Brothers. During their fourteen-year on-off existence, Noel Scott Engel, Gary Leeds and John Maus released a catalogue of music that, even at their commercial height, embraced everything from light MOR jazz ('Come Rain Or Come Shine') to Bavarian beer-hall polkas ('Experience'). You didn't even have to look beyond the hits to recognise a constantly changing musical identity that was less about a group evolving exponentially, as The Beatles did, and more to do with the group's personal taste and the market forces of the day. The Walker Brothers of 'The Sun Ain't Gonna Shine Anymore' are not The Walker Brothers of 'No Regrets', yet both hits are instantly recognisable as The Walker Brothers. Then again, both versions are light years away from the image projected by their first and final single releases. Between the sunshine and bubblegum of 'Pretty Girls Everywhere' and the charred, coked-out throbbing husk of 'The Electrician', on 1978's *Nite Flights*, lies the testimony of a journey as expansive, intriguing and fragmented as Scott Walker's own psyche.

It's important to remember that in his initial tour of duty as a Walker Brother, Scott was a young man. Although constantly hindered and blessed by a more contemplative and serious side than many of his peers, he still operated along the same ley lines. He was vain ('He was obsessed with his hair,' remembers The Walkers' first drummer, Tiny Schroeder). He liked girls, enjoyed a drink and was as curious about the world as any other fledgling adult. He had been singing professionally since before his voice broke, and was no stranger to the very cheesiest aspects of showbiz, having been 'adopted' by the Eddie Fisher TV show during the late fifties. (The patronage was scuppered when Fisher's wife, Elizabeth Taylor, absconded with a certain heavy-drinking Welshman.) So although Scott was technically young when The Walkers broke big in 1965, in showbiz years he was middle-aged. Compared to his pseudo-siblings, he was also troubled to the point of neurosis. As their fame and earning ability increased, the pressure was on for Scott to become simply an entertainer. And yet it could be argued that as far as his psyche was concerned, he was not even equipped to be a singer. Blessed with a beautiful voice, Scott only came to be lead vocalist of The Walkers by accident, via an off-the-cuff suggestion by Nick Venet during the recording of 'Love Her'. Until then, he had been content as the group's bass player. As a vocalist, compared to Sinatra, Andy Williams, Tony Bennett, Dusty Springfield and even his 'brother'

John, Scott never truly seemed to derive any pleasure from singing. Indeed, one only has to watch the remaining television clips to see that the act was sometimes agonising for him. He could never be casual about the process, no matter how much scotch he drank.

Scott himself was unsure of the medium his muse was best suited to, and the pop success he experienced, while seductive, would only confuse the issue (and it was a real issue) for years to come. In some ways, Scott was a Swedish film maker trapped in the life of a pop heart-throb. This was a ridiculous position to be in during the UK music industry of the mid-sixties. Perversely, it was this reluctance that made him appear even more vulnerable and thus attractive when compared to the relatively happy-go-lucky personae of his bandmates. And artistically, as far as his role in the group went, if The Walkers were The Beatles, Scott was a composite of John *and* Paul, with John Maus as George and Gary as band assistant Mal Evans. Scott was by far the most intellectual and conceptual of the three, but unfortunately for him, he was also deemed by many to be the most talented and attractive. Faced with the everyday ordeal of having to make a living, and later (from 1972) with a family to support, Scott would coast along in such a role as long as it was fiscally viable, despite the protest of his conscience. Only when the public totally lost interest would he seem to find the wherewithal finally to be true to himself, and by then the 1970s were almost over.

June Clarke was a young, self-described 'dolly bird' who worked as secretary for The Walkers' live agent, Harold Davidson, at their peak. (In 1968 she was privy to an insider's view of Scott's massive solo success when she switched to work as Maurice King's secretary.) She was a close witness to the sheer aesthetic impact of The Walkers, which most people only glimpsed fleetingly on a Friday night TV show. 'They were so good-looking in real life. Not merely photogenic,' she recalls. 'I couldn't take my eyes off John and Scott. They were these American male gods who looked perfect. Scott was very aloof. There was a certain amount of arrogance ...' With Scott's and John's uncommonly exquisite voices, the wealth of material available to them and the booming pop market, The Walkers could hardly fail.

Even during the spring of 1966, at the summit of their enormous fame, when 'The Sun Ain't Gonna Shine Anymore' was a huge hit on both sides of the Atlantic (number one for four weeks in the UK; peaking at thirteen in the US), The Walker Brothers appeared even more amorphous than their contemporaries. Up until 1965's *Rubber Soul*, The Beatles had still presented themselves as four Scousers recorded playing live in a room together with overdubs added after the fact. Over at Decca, the 'anti-Scott', Tom Jones, sang in the studio exactly as he did in concert. With Jones, you just made sure there were more proficient musicians in the studio with him than there were on stage. But in the case of The Walker Brothers – the group my own mother and a million other mothers-to-be fell in love with – summoning a mental image of the group, when accidentally hearing any of their 1960s hits, is much harder. They were neither a Monkees boy-band, nor the studio boffins which The Beach Boys had lately become. The Walker Brothers were cut from the cloth of both while never resembling either. The trio only definitively existed for a two-year period, between the early summers of 1965 and 1967 – the timeframe within which The Walkers' most enduring, immortal pop image was minted. Yet like the spider-egg-web memory cruelly programmed into the replicant's memory in *Blade Runner*, The Walker Brothers *felt* real, but did not actually exist in any recognisable reality. Gorgeous, seductive and occasionally surprisingly strange – what other number one pop groups in the sixties were referencing Orpheus and Sartre alongside Gershwin and Phil Spector? – they nevertheless did not adhere to any accepted notion of authenticity as a group, either on stage or in the studio. With a drummer who barely played on any of the records, and a bassist and lead guitarist who let session musicians play all the parts (frequently the norm back then), The Walker

Brothers were essentially two solo singers sharing a b(r)and name. Augmented by orchestras and the cream of the era's session musicians, and abetted by sympathetic and imaginative arrangers, John and Scott fronted unique and increasingly schizophrenic albums. These huge hit LPs were the works of a mythical beast, spawned and constructed under the laboratory conditions of the Philips Studio in Stanhope Place, near Marble Arch. Ultimately The Walker Brothers only truly existed in a 'fourth dimension': within the actual grooves of the millions of vinyl albums, EPs and singles pressed worldwide in their deceptively plain name.

As iconoclastic as they were, when it came to the actual recording process, The Walker Brothers followed the same methods as any other act who passed through the Philips Studio. Johnny Franz was both head of A&R and the label's in-house producer. An accomplished pianist who had signed Shirley Bassey, Dusty Springfield and Harry Secombe to the label, the elegant Franz also formed an immediate bond with the twenty-two-year-old Scott Walker that extended into a rare friendship beyond the boundaries of the workplace. They regularly ate together, both at the Lotus House Chinese restaurant on Edgware Road, and at Franz's own home near Hampstead Heath – where Scott first heard Frankie Valli's version of 'The Sun Ain't Gonna Shine Anymore'. Their partnership would endure up to the time when Scott was eventually dropped by the label less than a decade later, but while their collaboration within the Philips studios survived, it thrived.

The studio itself, situated above the heart of London (the Central Line tube below would sometimes interrupt meetings, and even sessions, with a faint rumble), was held in much less mythological regard than its Abbey Road rival, but was easily as industrious as its west London counterpart. Visitors approached via a stairwell from the street and then entered the actual building through a kind of stage door, turning left and up another set of dimly lit stairs. This would bring you to its main space, Studio

One, which was used by every UK Philips artist (and occasionally by 'outside clients' such as Serge Gainsbourg and The Who). Situated up on a raised platform and measuring sixty by twenty feet, with twenty-five-foot-high ceilings, the room accommodated everything from three-man beat combos to full orchestral and choral sessions with every permutation in between. The Walker Brothers sessions, being a combination of both extremes, were among the largest. Alan Parker, an ascending session guitarist from an accomplished jazz background, remembers the studio during the very first Walker Brothers recording session being 'a little bit confined. Long and narrow. The control room [where the mixing desk, producer and main engineer were situated] had a narrow walkway at the back, where we [the musicians] used to stand and listen. So it was a bit restrictive, with all the orchestra and brass, percussion and singing groups – it was really crammed in.'

Roger Wake was the tape operator at almost every Walkers session ever recorded. Still a teenager at their debut session, he remembers the recording space with undiminished clarity, calling to mind the conditions of a small crew aboard a modestly sized oceangoing boat: 'There was the studio, then the control room and then a separate machine room, where the tape machines were. The control room had big windows so that Johnny Franz and Peter [Olliff, engineer] could look out and see into the studio. From where I was in the machine room, we had a little window about three feet square so I could see into the control room.' Monitors were in use so that Franz could speak and listen to both recording artist and tape operator, although, in the unofficial hierarchy that reigned in the studio, the latter waited to be spoken to before voicing any opinion. Working in the sonic equivalent of a boiler room, Wake was responsible for the multi-track tape machines, the glowing amps and the oversized patchbay that allowed the machines to communicate with one another while channelling and capturing the enormous noise in the studio. 'It was all valves back then,' Wake points out. 'The first time

The Walker Brothers recorded in England, it would have been on an old German valve console. On four-track tape.' As such, there was little scope for mixing once the recording was complete. Any effects required would be applied during the actual recording, and these were limited to whatever pedals the guitarists were using and the enormous in-house spring reverb that was seemingly applied to everything ('The Holland Tunnel effect', Gary called it. Occasionally the actual tape was manipulated with a pen, causing a primitive but effective phasing effect). Time was tight and the tyrannical Musicians' Union was inflexible regarding everything from tea breaks to the actual length of the sessions. This could result in extreme frustration for perfectionists such as Scott: 'Just as we get a nice atmosphere and feel on the disc, everyone gets up as one man and off they go for a tea break. The feeling is completely lost.'

The scores of musicians were usually paid during their lunch break, their fees being handed to them in small paper envelopes by a charlady who simultaneously took orders for refreshments. What records were retained of such transactions and personnel were later trashed, and as a result no individual records remain of which musicians played on what sessions. Once the (usually three consecutive daily) three-hour sessions were over, there would be little opportunity for meticulous mixing or editing of the tracks. The balance of instruments was arranged prior to recording by sound engineers who were as meticulous as particle physicists in their duties. The correct positioning of microphones was paramount, depending on the effect desired. Incredibly, at the earliest sessions John and Scott would record their vocals live, actually sharing one microphone. 'It was a pretty frightening experience,' remembered John; 'you had to be in the position of knowing what you were going to do ... Scott and I, as a duo, didn't work on separate microphones. Any of the balances and things between ourselves came from ourselves.' High and low frequencies for the track as a whole could be added at the mastering stage. But essentially, accounting for the variables of playback, the sound you hear on any Walker Brothers record is exactly how it sounded in the control room there and then, as it happened. In the case of singles, the songs could be in the shops as soon as one week later.

The bulk of actual material was usually chosen a few weeks in advance. John and Gary maintained that the choice of songs was down to the group, although undoubtedly any song proffered would have to be approved by Franz. 'I suggested "Make It Easy On Yourself", states John. 'It was an old Jerry Butler hit back in the States … it was one of the best Bacharach & David songs ever written.' Indeed, much of The Walkers' chosen material had already been recorded and released by other acts and many had already been hits, albeit only in the United States. John and Scott would often run through potential hits in Franz's office above Studio One, where the chainsmoking producer, who was also an accomplished pianist, kept an upright Steinway piano. Appointed arrangers – Reg Guest, Ivor Raymonde and Wally Stott – would usually begin to score the material a fortnight in advance of any recording session, working to either acetate or tape demos (if the material was previously unrecorded) or already existing commercial recordings. Until the results of Scott and John's own songwriting began to surface, it was usually the latter. ('Lonely Winds' and 'There Goes My Baby', both of which appeared with 'Make It Easy On Yourself' on the group's debut album, *Take It Easy With The Walker Brothers*, released in November 1965, were almost identical in arrangement to the versions already recorded by The Drifters. 'We would embellish the original arrangements,' explained John.)

There would be no chance of previewing the huge orchestral arrangements before the recording date. Everyone heard the score played for the first time on the very day it was recorded. A few run-throughs would be indulged, mostly for the engineer's benefit, and critiques could be made during the brief Musicians' Union-regulated time, but essentially this would be the first and last time such arrangements (or 'accompaniments', as they were credited) were ever played. The result was a form of widescreen, magisterial surround-sound, even in mono. The songs sounded massive and yet were intricately bejewelled with detail. The vocals were clear, upfront, titanic yet intimate. Such factors were all vital trademarks of The Walkers' sound and identity. And although John and Scott's sole contributions to the recordings were the vocals, working with such a large number of personnel on each track, in the truest sense The Walker Brothers' records were a genuine group effort.

The chosen arrangers at the sessions would also conduct their scores, usually in view of the vocalist. Work was plentiful and the arrangers were in high demand. As such there was little outright competition between any of them. The individuals were seasoned professionals who treated each assignment – be it a Peter Sellers or Dusty Springfield session – with equal commitment. Stott, Guest and Raymonde were different personalities with diverse backgrounds who worked toward the same goal of excellence. Ivor Raymonde was the dominant arranger during The Walkers' earliest UK sessions. His son Simon, the former Cocteau Twins bassist, sometime solo artist and head of the Bella Union record label, recalls that 'Whilst all three [Raymonde, Guest and Stott] knew each other and worked together on different records, I got the feeling they were all very different characters with different influences and backgrounds. Ivor was a brilliant accordion player and had busked in the East End of London, but also studied music at one of London's music conservatories, Trinity College of Music in Greenwich. He worked as a pianist in a jazz band on the Queen Mary cruise ship after leaving college, and they used to sail from Southampton to New York, where he and his fellow musicians would head straight to Birdland where they could hear amazing jazz sets from his favourite musicians like Stan Getz and Miles Davis. Must have been quite an inspiration! Then he and Wally Stott worked together at the BBC as music directors. Ivor was always someone who was happy trying his hand at anything … He then moved over to Philips Records, which of course led to the development of the solo career of Dusty Springfield … this in turn led him to working with The Walkers. His arranging during this period was for sure certainly informed by Phil Spector.'

John Walker would not necessarily agree: 'The Spector sound wasn't really a consideration. Everybody – Jack Nitzsche, Sonny Bono, even Brian Wilson and Nick Venet – was simply trying to see how big they could make a record sound. Spector did it adding layer after layer of overdubs. We got that big sound in one take.' Whatever the precise influence, the arranger 'loved working on those tracks with them', as his son affirms. 'They were among his favourite arrangements to do. Putting a band together and working out the right combination for that band, or a singer, was something he loved to do, and I know he was very proud of those tracks and that period.' This was a boom time for pop music and no expense was spared, as Ivor Raymonde himself would recall. 'Never, never, never ever worried about money, ever. Nobody ever said to me, "Look, we can't afford to have ten violins and four violas and two cellos." You know, if I'd say, "Well, I think we ought to use sixteen violins", they'd say, "Go ahead and do it." Providing the money from a recording point of view didn't seem to be a problem.'

Once the potent Scott/Franz/Raymonde chemistry had alchemised, the results were instant, and Philips's investment was repaid immediately – with interest. The very first song of the very first Walker Brothers UK recording session was a triumph both aesthetically and commercially. 'Make It Easy On Yourself', released in the dying summer of 1965, was an instant classic, reaching number nineteen in the US and number one in the UK singles charts (the *Take It Easy* album made the UK top three).

The Walker Brothers – their songs, image and sound – were in demand. From the perspectives of their label, agent and management, John, Scott and Gary were a walking, talking licence to print money. Touring was the most immediate source of cash, bypassing the convoluted administration thrown up by royalty payments. Live, The Walker Brothers were yet another proposition. John, the 'shining presence' who sang beside his buddy Scott night after gruelling night of their mid-sixties tours, explained the dichotomy between their live and studio incarnation with typical Californian understatement: 'You're not gonna do "Make It Easy On Yourself" with drums, bass and guitar. We had this huge orchestra. So what are you going to do when you're playing live? We need a huge orchestra. So [live] we at least needed to have a seven-piece band.' Even this statement was paradoxical, as The Walkers would rarely perform ballads live as part of their stage show (George Gershwin's 'Summertime', included on the Brothers' follow-up album, *Portrait*, was a rare exception). Their live set was geared much more towards uptempo numbers, and escorting the boys in and out of the venue as quickly and safely as possible. Completely different personnel were used live. The Quotations were a beer-sodden, pill-popping, roadbroken outfit, and much rougher around the edges than their studio counterparts. Rehearsals took place at Maurice King's grotty Starlite Club in Soho, just off Oxford Street. Anyone privy to these sessions would have been among the very few ever to hear what The Walker Brothers sounded like live. The Walkers' actual tours were a deafening carny show. The noise and screams from the audience obliterated the sound before it had a chance to leave the stage. As such, Walkers concerts were less about the music and more about playing out a ritualistic ceremony where the blond American gods appeared in the flesh before their braying worshippers. Dave Cash, a popular pirate radio DJ and early friend of The Walkers, recalls, 'I saw them live four or five times. I stood at the side of the stage. No, of course you couldn't hear anything. But when you're a pop star that's not the point.'

The only official document of The Walkers' live performance is a recording from a batch of concerts in Osaka from their Japanese

tour in early 1968. This tour of the Far East was undertaken for con-
tractual reasons after the group had officially ceased to exist. The
recording and set list is untypical of The Walkers' usual live sets, as it
was staged for simultaneous television and radio broadcast. Having
moved on from the group by this point, Scott and co obviously had
no interest in the performance other than as an ephemeral event
that paid some pocket money and afforded a free trip to the East.
Apart from John, Scott and Gary, all the players are sight-reading
local musicians, and the results are irreverent and sake-soaked.
Scott's voice is never less than beguiling, but the general performance is so sloppy that even getting to hear ballads that were rarely
played live – 'In My Room', 'Make It Easy On Yourself' – is hardly
enough to sustain repeated listening.

Outside the venues, The Walkers' own management sold bootleg
posters of the revered trio, the resultant cash bypassing both The
Walkers themselves and their record company. Fraught with riots,
injury and mayhem, ill served by the archaic British road system
and woefully inadequate sound systems in inappropriate venues
(civic halls, cinemas, working men's clubs, even church halls), such
tours would serve to put Scott Walker off public performance for a
lifetime. 'Things were so primitive when I was performing,' Scott
would recall, decades later. 'I simply could never achieve the results
I was after. It was all quite traumatic for me as a young man.' Scott's
problems with live appearances were far from mere affectation or
an advanced case of nerves. During the height of 'Walker mania',
the group was under constant physical threat. All of the Walker live
appearances were overshadowed by the insanity that hordes of hor-
mone-high females brought with them. 'They were ripping your hair
out and everything,' Gary would recall. 'John's head was cut open
about three times.' This was no exaggeration. John was actually hos-
pitalised during a riot following one concert. Scott often had to run
for what felt like was his life, seeking sanctuary in a backstage toilet
cubicle while hysterical fans attempted to batter their way in. The

threat was visceral and real for all concerned. 'I remember one incident with a girl about half the size of us,' remembers Gary. 'I guess
she must have been twelve years old. She grabbed hold of John's hair.
I was screaming, "Let go! Let go!" Because the whole crowd was
surging and it was getting to the point where everything was going
to collapse … So I finally hit her in the face – she screamed but she
still held on. There was nothing else for it but to hit her … I just felt
the end was coming … and … we were going to get killed.'

Peter O'Flaherty was bassist with Simon Dupree And The Big
Sound, a 'happening' group at the time, who found themselves
slotted in on The Walkers' final tour. 'Most of the audience were
girls,' he remembers (stating the obvious). 'The area was in complete chaos when we arrived … surrounded by screaming girls who
were after The Walkers. It would have been easy to lose an ear, a
leg or a more private part. Looking down from the window of our
dressing room, we could see the chaos below. The police … called
in the mounted police. A few of the girls had bags of glass marbles.
They'd throw a handful of these under the horses' hooves. These
could make the horse buck and throw the rider off …'. The scene
he goes on to describe inside the venue is more akin to something
by Bosch or Milton than a happy-go-lucky swinging sixties pop
panorama: 'I wandered around the theatre, [and] around the stage
area I saw a hysterical girl being pursued by the security guards.
Her face, hands and legs were covered in blood. Later somebody
told me that to get to the theatre she'd crawled through a small broken window and cut herself to pieces on the broken glass … When
The Walkers did their act … there was so much screaming, we
never heard a thing they did. It was a bit pointless.' At the very epi-
centre of this carnage and mayhem was Scott Walker, the reluctant,
existentialist pop idol who would rather be at the pictures or settled
at home with a book. 'It was like a great hands and mouth coming
out of the dark at you,' he would recall decades later.[1]

As Scott matured into his solo career and the audiences became

less savage, his fear of live performance morphed into an actual pho-
bia and one he treated with self-medication, downing scotch and
Valium before taking the stage. The most disastrous result of such
poly-pharmacy was when he sang the same song twice during a solo
1968 gig.[2] His saxophonist at the time, Ray Warleigh, commented
sardonically, 'Surely, you'd think that with two versions of "Black
Sheep Boy", the audience would be happy at getting more than their
money's worth.'

Live TV sessions entailed yet another version of the group. Again,
due to a mixture of Musicians' Union rules and BBC policy, John
and Scott would often be playing with yet another line-up, rely-
ing on the anonymous in-house studio musicians who played to
score sheets and chord charts. Very occasionally the riotous, rowdy
group The Quotations would also muster an appearance. During the
earlier TV performances, Scott still looked like he was having fun.
Meanwhile, Gary Leeds was having it for real.

'Gary couldn't play drums. When they played live there was
another drummer behind the curtain, and Gary Leeds used to
have paper sticks.' Ralph Gurnett, the self-styled 'Scott body-
guard' who was besotted with the group's lead vocalist, used Gary's
mediocre-to-average musicianship as the proverbial stick with
which to beat the hapless non-drumming drummer. Gurnett was
not alone in his disdain. Billy Bremner was lead guitarist in The
Walkers' touring band and would go on to play on Gary's debut
solo single 'You Don't Love Me'. 'Gary was useless,' states the
Glaswegian Bremner, 'and he knew that. [Live] he could do whatever he wanted, because there was another drummer sitting behind
him ... so Gary could fuck around, and do what he wanted.' Prolific session drummer Bobby Graham offered a more reasoned
observation. 'As far as drumming went, he wasn't a player as such,
not really. He may well have asked to play on the records, but
[Philips producer] Johnny Franz decided who was gonna do what.

He was the boss. The producer always was ...' Kim Fowley, Gary's old Los Angeles pal, summed up popular opinion: 'He couldn't play the drums worth a shit.'

Throughout his musical career, Gary would only ever be credited as an instrumentalist once on a pre-*Nite Flights* Walker album, playing 'salt shaker' on 'Lines'. Retrospectively, he would claim that this was due to stringent Musicians' Union rules, but at the time it was an open secret that Gary was less a drummer and more somebody who merely owned a drum kit. Up until his own (mysteriously over-rated) Gary Walker And The Rain album, released in 1968, he would not even play drums on his own solo hits. And yet it didn't matter. Gary was as much a Walker Brother as either Scott or John. He was a brilliant pop star while his time in the sun lasted, and in a fecund era that boasted more than its fair share of stars, Gary was for a while a bona fide face around town. The fact that he never came close to contributing directly to any of the massive Walker Brothers hits is as irrelevant now as it was then. Without Gary's drive and ambition, it's probable that John and Scott would not have moved to Britain in the first place. Gary's most notable talent was for instigating the very expedition that ushered in The Walkers' destiny. Using $10,000 borrowed from his stepfather, Gary brought John, Scott and himself to the ultimate right time and place: London, in February 1965.

'We had the long hair, the different look. And having heard "Love Her", I knew we had the sound too,' reckoned Gary, correctly. 'He was the catalyst,' affirmed John. Not only was it was Gary who singlehandedly engineered the move from California to London, it was Gary who hustled their case incessantly on arrival. He also convinced John and Scott to stick it out when homesickness, alienation and disillusionment took their toll. As a result, within months The Walker Brothers had a deal with a worldwide major label. Some talent. From this point on, Gary may not have been necessary in any muso-like capacity but he fitted the bill exquisitely in every extra-curricular role that pop stardom proffered. Throughout their brief, white-hot phase of success, Scott would continuously look to his friend, a persistently good-humoured practical joker possessed by an ancient jester's spirit, for solace and laughter. 'He took something from Gary,' observed the group's press agent Chrissie McCall. 'Gary was the perfect buffer and a constant source of comfort and distraction to Scott.' 'Gary was Gary,' reasoned John, when asked yet again what it was exactly that Gary brought to the group. 'He was a Walker Brother. And he stayed.'

Thus, Gary Leeds the non-drumming drummer, constituted the beating heart of The Walker Brothers, a peculiarly quixotic and gilded American enigma.

For such a massively successful act, beholden so relentlessly to the road and the studio, little personal downtime or privacy remained. The trio's promo schedule alone – interview after interview for radio, TV, newspapers and magazines, charity events, appearances on *Thank Your Lucky Stars*, *Top Of The Pops*, *Ready Steady Go!* and numerous awards ceremonies – was punishing. What little time survived was mostly spent on recovery, and maintaining a regular human life: replying to letters, phoning family, keeping a flat, and simply catching up on sleep.

Retail therapy was allowed. John and Gary splurged on sports cars while Scott was fond of the occasional shopping binge at Foyles bookshop. The irregular hours entailed by touring were already short-circuiting the three young men's body-clocks. Uppers such as amphetamines and Dexedrines were common, and consequently sleeping tablets were used to control any unwanted after-effects. Like so many of their peers, all three dabbled in hash; John, true to his Californian breeding – the drug was much more prevalent in his hometown than in London at this point – would also occasionally snort cocaine. (Until the seventies, coke was a rare and exclusive commodity, available to only the elitist of the elite.) Booze was a much more convenient stimulant/depressive. Both John's and Gary's main vice was scotch. Scott's favoured tipple as a Walker Brother was vodka, and he increasingly used it to wash down the prescribed medication which he took in order to regain a sense of calm. Thus began Scott's valium habit, something he would not kick cold turkey until the early 1980s.[3]

(By the mid-seventies this dependency would reach its apex. '[Scott] and I were now very dependent on valium,' Gary Walker would later state, speaking about the seventies reunion era. '[We were] taking the highest permitted dose. Everything was fine until that tablet started wearing off and then we became very, very edgy … as in the sixties, he was terrified of the Valium wearing off on stage and had panic attacks while performing.')

Women were another obvious indulgence, and Gary took to the 'band birds', as they were then known (the term 'groupie' was not yet in common use), with particular relish. Scott affectionately called him 'Casa' (as in Casanova) for a while. And yet all three were still in their early twenties. They were young. They could take this punishing speed of life, and somehow, even at their most wrung-out, there was still energy left for more cerebral pursuits. By the recording of their first album, both John and Scott began to seriously pursue their own songwriting. Scott, who had already published a number of originals back in America, was perhaps being disingenuous when he explained the genesis of his writing. 'I was writing some very strange songs as B-sides,' he would explain years later. 'Because you get the publishing [royalties]. They [Johnny Franz, Maurice King and the Philips executives who in a few short years would insist on "No more of this Scott Walker shit"] didn't care what I wrote. That's how I got started, you see. They said, "Well, you can write anything and no one's gonna hear it 'cause it'll be on the B-side".'

None of these early attempts were A-side material. The lilting, lyrical and insubstantial likes of 'I Can See It Now', 'You're All Around Me' and 'Turn Out The Moon' were sweet-sounding stepping stones towards work that would soon become astonishingly affecting and profound by comparison. ('Orpheus', 'Archangel' and 'Genevieve' were also solo Scott Walker in all but name.) Perversely, although Scott would co-write with colleagues such as Franz and Raymonde, and even sing a John original ('The Saddest Night In The World'), neither he nor John – nor Gary – would ever co-write a song. This seemed to go unremarked upon at the time. On the one rare occasion when John was questioned about the discrepancy, he replied simply, 'We [Scott and I] have different minds and can't write together.'

While no acid head, Scott, by mixing booze with Mogadon, was bending that mind in his own idiosyncratic fashion. He began writing from his own altered state. 'Everyone was either drunk or stoned. I was a very heavy drinker for years ... it was crazy that whole time, because we were taking sleeping pills to sleep at night ... we were drinking so much. I was writing off that ... I was emotionally fuelled by all sorts of things, booze included ...'.[4]

In the minute spaces left to them beyond their musical activities, nature prevailed and the boys would have to find time to indulge love affairs, cultivate friendships and partake in the thriving social scene that broiled around them. The Bag O'Nails, the Ad-Lib Club and the Scotch of St James were famously popular Soho haunts of the day, and the trio also frequented their manager's own Starlite Club, where presumably they enjoyed an open bar tab. Incongruously, Scott would also become a regular at London's first Playboy Club when it opened on Park Lane in 1966. It was here that he met at least one (and, as it turned out, Jacques Brel-obsessed) girlfriend. Fashion-wise, The Walker Brothers were a law unto themselves. The haircuts that had originally been modelled on the early Astrid Kirchherr Beatles cut were now more refined; chic constructions affecting the look of mini-pompadours. John himself was an early client of the hugely fashionable Vidal Sassoon. June Clarke points out that 'even at their most popular, The Walkers never really fitted in, visually. I mean, compare them to Hendrix, the later look of The Beatles or even The Stones. They were a certain *kind* of American, you see. And God, everyone was so thin then. I have pictures of Scott on holiday, on the beach in Spain, and my God. You could count his ribs. It's almost gross.'

Away from the fleshpots of the West End, the cinema was increasingly a place of refuge, with Scott still actively satiating his appetite for foreign movies. And yet, while Scott's tastes were avant-garde compared to his 'siblings', he was nowhere near as interested in the burgeoning 'underground' scene as someone like Paul McCartney was. McCartney was already exploring other forms of contemporary music beyond pop and rock, incorporating the philosophies and methods of composers like John Cage and Karlheinz Stockhausen within his own musical endeavours as well as in his work with The Beatles. Scott's interest and autodidactic pursuits would remain for the most part private and personal. Scott was never *seen* to be part of the underground. His listening habits, particularly toward the end of The Walkers, embraced mostly classical (Beethoven, Shostakovich, Ravel) and 'progressive' or modern jazz (Miles Davis, etc). He seemed to listen less and less to other singers for pleasure, although, post-Jack Jones and Sinatra, he became fixated on Charles Aznavour and, most famously, Jacques Brel for a while – the latter being more of a chanson/vocal stylist than a straight singer or even crooner. It's fair to say that Tom Jones rarely graced Scott's state-of-the-art hi-fi.

'I get pleasure out of [modern classical composers],' Scott explained to the *NME*. 'I am not competing with pop writers or Brel ... what I do is polish up an antique, so to speak ... classical composers have made huge leaps but have progressed without becoming unmusical.'[5]

In his reading, from day one Scott was talking Sartre, Yevtushenko and Camus. His lifelong love of 'foreign' cinema – especially directors like Tarkovsky and Bergman – would remain a constant throughout. Yet for all his leftfield tastes, Barry Miles, chronicler of London's subterranean pop life, points out: 'Scott was *not* part of the underground scene. I saw him sometimes in the Scotch of St James, but from my perception he was part of the pop world. A very different thing.'[6]

Increasingly, The Walker Brothers' lead singer was following a cinder path through life and a London of his own. The Philips Studio was conveniently located for late-night excursions into the West End, and by the second album Scott and Franz would cheat the Musicians' Union rule of having to sing live with the orchestra by creeping back into the studio late at night to overdub vocals. Scott almost always did this alone. John was either attempting a domestic life with his wife and dogs at home or propping up a West End bar with PJ Proby. (That said, John could be as moody as his more famously temperamental buddy. 'I used to go over to John's apartment,' remembers June Clarke. 'He would phone me in the middle of the night: "June, come over, I'm lonely."') Gary was a more reliable personality, in that on any given night he might be found raving it up somewhere in the capital, a quintessential Austin Powers figure. Driven by work above all else, Scott Walker, heart-throb, pop pin-up and one of the most lusted-after males in Britain, would leave a midnight recording session and head out into the West End alone.

'Me and my mate would turn up at Ronnie Scott's,' remembers Beryl McKee, a Walker fan more bold than most. 'We'd often end up sitting at the same table as Scott. He was obsessed with [jazz singer/ pianist] Blossom Dearie. He always came alone around one-thirty a.m. Never with anyone. He'd get us drinks. "Same again?" he'd ask. "Same again?" He didn't talk much. We'd ... just nod and smile back, as I was so shy of him.' 'Scott didn't need company when he went to a gig,' explains June Clarke, reasonably. 'He went to listen to the music.'

As the group's success began to tail off (after the supernova of 'The Sun Ain't Gonna Shine Anymore' in 1966, The Walkers would never score as big again), Scott became increasingly obsessed with the work in hand, and in serving his own personal vision, to the exclusion of his hapless 'brothers'. From an employee's point of view, Clarke believed that 'He wanted everything done for him. He wasn't tolerant of anything that wasn't done his way. He seemed serious about not only his work but himself. He was not going to waste his time in conversations that weren't constructive. He'd sooner sit there and say nothing.' His behaviour now seemed to follow extremes, following a pattern of periods spent alone writing, time which led him directly to strenuous and extended sessions in the studio with his staunch ally Johnny Franz. He then indulged in relaxing time-outs, amply abetted by alcohol. 'When he went out, he'd have a good time,' says Clarke. 'When he'd had a drink he was fun. And he and John did go out. In all the time I knew them they weren't "recluses". They had their favourite clubs and their favourite restaurants. Or maybe they'd go to a friend's apartment and we'd listen to music and talk. Music was so important then. There was so much new, exciting stuff coming out weekly, it seemed. I mean … The Beatles alone could keep you busy! *Everyone* was waiting to hear what they were going to do next, from my boss Maurice King to the blousy spinster-ish music teacher at my old Victorian all-girls' school. *Sgt. Pepper* blew us all away!' Scott was publicly appreciative of The Beatles, on one occasion expressing his admiration for them on an episode of the television show *Juke Box Jury* and covering 'We Can Work It Out' during a Walker-devoted episode of *Ready Steady Go!*. But unlike so many of The Walkers' contemporaries, he was never in thrall to The Beatles. 'He was so complex,' confirms Clarke. 'I found him such a contradictory character at times … he was often at odds with himself. I never felt Scott was influenced by commercial music or his peers. When I knew him, in the sixties at least, with Scott it was classical and jazz that he measured his work against. But ultimately he was in competition only with himself.' Scott Walker's allegiance to his own particular, often perverse, aesthetic would eventually alienate him from both the public and the industry that enabled it. But in time, it would eventually reunite him with himself.

1. Peschek, David, '10 Questions For Scott Walker' in *Mojo* 80 (July 2000).
2. This story was widely reported in the popular press at the time. When I spoke to Chrissie McCall and June Clarke, two women who worked for The Walkers in the sixties and early seventies, both confirmed Scott's use of valium and sleeping pills as simply normal for the time, as anti-depressants were prescribed by doctors much less discriminately – and in generally higher dosages – than today.
3. Scott would discuss such issues in interviews up to the mid-nineties at least. He referred specifically to his own experiences with cocaine in the seventies in an unpublished interview with Joe Jackson (1995). John and Gary explore the subject of drink and drugs in explicit detail in their joint autobiography. Walker, Gary & Walker, John, *The Walker Brothers – No Regrets: Our Story* (London: John Blake Publishing, 2009).
4. Beauvallet, Jean-Daniel & Tordjman, Gilles, Scott Walker interview in *Les Inrockuptibles* 52 (winter 1994).
5. Logan, Nick, 'Scott Walker Sings Solo Release Of The Year' in *New Musical Express* (9 September 1967).
6. Miles, Barry, email to the author.

Black Sheep Boy

Nina Power

Scott (1967)
Scott 2 (1968)

What is the opposite of love? Cowardice? Loneliness? Hate? Should music 'about' love and its opposite (whatever that is) be lush, excessive, all-consuming, or should it be restrained, hurt, withdrawn? The romantic fascination, or rather the fascination with romance, that reached its zenith in the 1960s with pop's fixation on the boy band, was effervescent, uncontrollable. Female fandom, although not exactly without historical precursors, revealed the short circuit that exists between culture and desire, visual pleasure and ecstatic forms of identification. The boy-band became the focus of myriad modes of projection, bolstered by the groups' identikit outfits and assumed unities. The Walker Brothers were comprised neither of anyone originally named Walker, nor were they related to one another, but these facts are not important: what mattered was whether the assumed unity could hold, whether there was enough at stake in the game to want to continue playing it.

By the end of 1967, there no longer was. Scott Walker was a free, if far from untroubled, man, even as his name continued to bear the trace of a fraternity he would again return to before leaving once more. The frown he wears on the cover of *Scott* – his first attempt to be a boy without a band, a 'brother' without a family – says everything: *I don't want you to look at me, I just want you to listen*. But the hair, of course, is the same, and the shades and rakish scarf indicate a host of dark, or at least moderately dark, desires. But who is the Scott of the immediate post-boy-band era? What did he have to say about love (and its opposite)?

Scott was released in September 1967 and reached number three in the UK charts, hanging around for seventeen weeks. It was released in the US in the following year under the strange title of *Aloner*. Was Scott more alone than before? Was this title a fusion of two words that indicated Scott's life post-Walker Brothers? Scott's trajectory following the end of the first phase of The Walker Brothers (they were to re-form in 1975 with the album *No Regrets*) is indicative of the thoughtful, occasionally menacing and introverted path that he would continue to take overall, albeit with long, unproductive intervals and returns to less experimental waters along the way. *Scott* was also the beginning of a period of prolonged creative output, with five albums (*Scott 1–4*, plus the *Sings Songs From His TV Series* LP) appearing in the space of two years, followed by exhaustion and withdrawal.

The album itself came hot on the heels of his work with The Walker Brothers, appearing only half a year after the last collective effort, *Images*. It comprises a mixture of obsessions, borrowings, original tracks and extraordinary arrangements by Wally Stott, Reg Guest and Peter Knight. Although much of the record is clearly an attempt to introduce a version of English-language chanson with three Jacques Brel covers ('Mathilde', 'My Death' and 'Amsterdam'), it is also Walker's first real chance to break out of the group formation and write material for himself alone ('Montague Terrace (In Blue)', 'Such A Small Love' and 'Always Coming Back To You'). Other tracks on the record ('The Lady Came From Baltimore', 'Angelica', 'You're Gonna Hear From Me', 'Through A Long And Sleepless Night') were contemporary songs transmuted by Walker into heartbreakers without kitsch, a not inconsiderable achievement.

Walker was just twenty-three when he made *Scott*, a fact that seems scarcely believable. His voice somehow manages to be more magnificent than all the string arrangements, which would have buried any other singer in their furious bid for attention. But in a way, Walker's voice would always be too old for its human frame, cracking and straining on later records like the split-notes of a brass instrument played too hard, revealing the fragility of the whole. But here it is, confident, masterful even, despite or perhaps because of the content of the songs, which are all about love lost and regained, reciting female name after female name: Mathilde, Angelica, Joanna, a lady from Baltimore named Susan Moore, whose Daddy read the law. A wry exuberance and a series of what-ifs ('*There's so much you never knew*', he wistfully remarks on 'Angelica') make Walker a desperately attractive lover, though one gets the feeling that no single woman could compete with the attraction of his own finitude: '*a patient girl who knows the score*', he sings lustfully on the cover of Brel's 'My Death'. 'The Big Hurt' ('*Each time you go/I try to pretend/ It's over at last/And this time the big hurt will end*') mirrors 'Such A Small Love' in both size and sound, making the latter in fact sound like the largest thing in the world ('*Such a small love/Such a little tear/Is this all that's left/On your cheek so pale*'). That only serves to enhance the ironic framework of the song, which Walker asserted was written about a young man attending the funeral of a close friend, observing the disproportionate tears of a woman who only knew him for one night.

The strings that he would twist into experimental horror soundtracks in his later work are only saved from soupiness on 'You're Gonna Hear From Me' and 'Through A Long And Sleepless Night' by the hints of trouble in Walker's delivery and the uncanny vibrato of his voice. The fine line that separates schmaltz from shiver is barely breached before the triumphant finale of 'Amsterdam'. The covers that were later covered by others – particularly Marc Almond in his own Brel period – are somehow already encapsulated, hinted at, in Walker's roguish effusions.

*

The drunken, back-alley humour of numerous forgotten sexual encounters and debased poses flows seamlessly from 'Amsterdam', the final track of *Scott*, to the opening of *Scott 2* with another Brel cover, 'Jackie', which rushes in with such verve, humour and energy, albeit wistful, that you're inexorably swept up with the force of it all. The sleeve, too, hints at a kind of glorious expansiveness compared to the troubled loner of the first solo record: his mouth open in a roar, his hands raised as if conducting an orchestra at the back of a bar. Scott is at his sexiest here, his most aggressively humorous. His mention of *'authentic queers'* in the first track earned him a BBC ban in 1967, though you wonder if it wasn't the mischievous *'Spanish bum'* line that really upset them (*Scott 2* is really a record of asses, and ass-slapping). Beginning a long series of oblique reflections on fame and an ironic reflection on Scott's own practice, 'Jackie' talks of a time when *'My record would be number one/And I'd sell records by the ton/All sung by many other fellows.'* Walker's Brel obsession would filter down to many other contemporaries over the years, not only Almond, and provide his record company with at least one way of dividing up his opus into a more packageable entity, though it should be remembered that *Scott 2* was a number one album in 1968 and stayed on the charts for eighteen weeks, hardly an insignificant achievement.

On 'Next', another Brel cover, translated by Mort Shuman, Walker loses his innocence in a *'mobile army whorehouse'* where the hasty, affectionless serial sex causes the 'kid' of the song to suffer a trauma for ever after:

> *And since each woman*
> *I have taken to bed*
> *Seems to laugh in my arms*
> *To whisper through my head*
> *Next, next! [...]*

One day I'll cut my legs off
Or burn myself alive
Anything, I'll do anything
To get out of line just to survive
Never to be next
Never to be next

As much a reflection on the incidental brutalities of war as it is of the gonorrhoea contracted by the narrator, the processional horrors of *'the following and the followed'* could equally be seen as Walker's horrified recoil from the treadmill of fame and fandom. Commercially, and despite the sales of the early solo efforts, Walker was indeed to 'burn himself alive' in his inability to conform to the constraints of genre or faddishness, turning into the very antithesis of the boy-band pin-up, namely the cult outsider (though Scott was never as clean-cut as that demanded even in Walker Brothers days, with his slightly too long feathery hair and distant demeanour). But Walker's image from this point on is far less cynical than the dualism of boy-band/moody loner would indicate, because really Scott's dialectic plays out in the gap between overwhelming presence and total absence: the bigger the songs get, the louder he roars, the more he disappears as any recognisable kind of pop icon, the 'alienated' type or otherwise.

The work always dominates, and yet the work will never be enough … The gaps and the periods of silence, the air between walls of sound, will of course only increase in decades to come. Perhaps the hardest thing in the world is to sound convincing and at ease without betraying all the work that lies behind this impression. Scott confessed to the writer of *Scott 2*'s sleevenotes at the time of finishing the record, 'I'm afraid it's work of a lazy, self-indulgent man. Now the nonsense must stop, and the serious business must begin.' Despite his talk of girls from the streets (with their lips, thighs and *'sad and devouring eyes'*), or the ones that you eventually boot canine companions out for, despite their loyalty (*'And yet it's because of the girls/ When they've knocked us about/And our tears want to shout/That we kick the dogs out'* on 'The Girls And The Dogs'), or even Madeleine (*'White doves turned grey and flew away/And so did Madeleine'* on 'The Bridge'), *Scott 2*, for all its ribald sexiness, is not a romantic record. There is something post-romantic about Walker, which is perhaps why those of his fans who just wanted him to croon started to stay away in droves. The immanent demolition of schmaltz that Walker began on the first record continues here apace, the strings warping and lilting on 'Plastic Palace People', like a soundtrack to a sci-fi film. Composed by Walker himself, this is as psych-rock as he was ever likely to get. Of course it sounds nothing like the psychedelia that was actually around at the time, but it nevertheless owes something to the trippiness of the age, with gently surreal lyrics (*'Over the rooftops burns Billy/Balloon sadly the string descends/ Searching its way down through blue submarine air/The polka dot underwear'*). 'The Amorous Humphrey Plugg', another Walker-penned track, is similarly minimal, in part a reflective account of a mundane day (*'Leave it all behind me/Screaming kids on my knee/ And the telly swallowing me/And the neighbour shouting next door/ And the subway trembling the rollerskate floor'*), but because this is Scott Walker, after all, this is followed by the most extraordinarily Baudelairean phrasing: *'Oh to die of kisses/Ecstasies and charms/ Pavements of poets will write that I died/In nine angels' arms'*.

To return to the question of Walker's presence and absence, both musically and personally, it is here that Walker opens up an interpretation that further breaks down classical pop oppositions. Film maker Stephen Kijak, who directed *Scott Walker: 30 Century Man* (2006), said the following in an interview around the time of the film: 'I read an article once that said Scott Walker is Judy Garland for the gays who grew up writing poetry and wearing black turtlenecks,' which might confirm his status as an existentialist pin-up boy of sorts, but it is another statement by Kijak from the same interview which really touches on what Walker's work and periods of withdrawal might mean: 'That gap in our culture, the one that exists outside the mainstream – that's where you find artists, gay people, all the outsiders. "Queer culture" is bigger than most people think ... I feel like the alternative I belong to isn't a sexuality thing; it's your artistic pursuit, your point of view, your political, social and cultural beliefs, that set you apart.'[1] 'That gap in our culture': a perfect way to describe the uncomfortable space where Walker placed himself, impossibly, in this period withdrawing from what would otherwise have been all of the things we and he are supposed to want – money, sex, fame – in the name of what, exactly? A gap: a place to experiment, a place to be nobody, a place to work, or to not work. In the lyrics of Tim Hardin's 'Black Sheep Boy', covered on *Scott 2*: *'If you love me, let me live in peace, please understand/That the black sheep can wear the golden fleece'*. If Scott became the insider looking out, it may have been because he was never able to accept that there was an inside that was 'full' in the first place. The sweeping plenitude of his voice, the blossoming strings, are the antithesis of the hollow promise of 'success'. Walker's lack of interest in money has been well documented – possibly the most 'queer' position anyone can take and still remain alive under capitalism (although he might have done well to have had someone to manage what little he had rather than agree to participate in a Britvic advert in 1987, where he sits enigmatically for a few seconds wearing shades by a cafe window). There are many, fans and onlookers alike, who'll simply never understand why Walker turned his back on it all in the name of what his work could become, what it was to become.

But perhaps there are some who get it, even as they disagree with the ability of anyone to be able to bear it. His orchestrator Brian Gascoigne once said: 'He believes, and I take issue with this, that to convey a very strong emotion in the music, you have to be feeling it when you're making it. That couldn't be true, because the people who are playing Bruckner and Mahler every night would be basket cases ... after three of four hours in the studio, [Walker] is a basket case because he lives the thing with such emotion.'[2] If Gascoigne is right, then Walker cannot but preserve himself in a certain kind of withdrawal whenever he isn't living through his music.

Walker himself, in the same article, states that, 'Essentially, I'm really trying to find a way to talk about the things that cannot be spoken of.' Now this is, in many ways, the problem of modernism, one of the major questions of philosophy, poetry, the novel. And the response to this desire results in positions to which we have perhaps become accustomed: quietism (Wittgenstein's 'Whereof one cannot speak, thereof one must be silent'), the explosion of language (Joyce), ever-increasing minimalism (Beckett). But what of Walker's contribution to this need to say the unsayable? If you were going to outline a possible methodology, it's very unlikely to involve massive fame, art-house cinema references, the adoration of a Belgian singer, blocks of filmic strings, and a voice that moves over the years from dispossessed velvet to something that sounds like my grandmother in her final few months of confusion. Walker's trajectory is as improbable as the music he makes *because* of this trajectory, though this is not to say that it is easy to trace one from the other, either. Scott is a queer hero because he opens up this gap in culture and stays there, his magnificent voice at once familiar and strange. The first two records hint at what is to come in ways that make them both endlessly listenable on their own terms, but also crucial foundation blocks for a house that perhaps, ultimately, only one person could ever live in.

1. Stephen Kijak quoted in Kregloe, Karman, 'Documenting A Musical Outsider' in *After Elton* (www.afterelton.com/movies/2007/3/30thcenturyman).
2. O'Hagan, Sean, 'Interview: Scott Walker' in *The Observer* (9 November 2008).

Didn't Time Sound Sweet

Derek Walmsley

Scott 3 (1969)
Scott 4 (1969)

This was the point of cutting off. With these albums, both released in 1969 and separated by the money-spinning covers album *Sings Songs From His TV Series*, Scott Walker began a tactical retreat from the public life of the pop star. By the time of *Scott 4* he had sacked his old school manager Maurice King, given up on publicity interviews, and had his latest album obliquely announced on the cover of the *New Musical Express* with just the word 'Scott' and a quote from Camus.[1] These albums shoot philosophy from the hip, are enigmatic to the point of existential absurdity, and almost painfully beautiful.

Scott 3 and *Scott 4* were all his own work, except for three Brel songs tagged on to the end of the former. Around this time Walker had described Brel as a mere 'lyric writer', so the performances of three of his songs on *Scott 3* – 'Sons Of', 'Funeral Tango' and 'If You Go Away' – although stone-cold classics, also mark the end of that era, like memorabilia neatly boxed up to be stored in the attic. Around this time Walker was concerned with the relationship between the singer and the song to the point of neurosis. He specified that songs were to be sung 'in the right context and by the right people', and he was scared of others covering his own compositions, lest they were 'not being interpreted the way I want them to be'.[2] Searching for a more authentic life than just as another pop puppet on a string, he withdrew into the world of his own music.

You can still find a sheet music collection of his songs, along with others he made famous, published in 1968 by Carlin Music Corp of London's Savile Row. On the cover is the familiar image, smiling, photogenic, movie-star slim. The collection is titled *Scott*, but as so often, the first-name terms is deceptive, and glosses over the disconnect between the singer and the various audiences – teen pop, Easy Listening, rock vanguard – who wanted a piece of him. Any intimacy is punctured by a disclaimer, in small, angry capitals, that runs along the bottom of each of his songs in the book: 'THE USE OF THIS SONG WITH ANY OTHER MUSIC IS EXPRESSLY PROHIBITED.' Did he suspect that others might steal his labour? Or that they might water down his art by changing the music? The legal small print is defensive to the point of paranoia.

For Walker, art and money were inextricably linked. He brought up the latter in interviews time and again, as a corrective, perhaps, to the free mind/free love ideals of psychedelia. An interview with the *Radio Times* before the debut of his BBC TV show in March 1969 (publicity tagline: 'sings his own kind of songs') was typically forthright: 'No one ever believes me when I say I only work when I'm broke, but it's true,' he complained.[3] 'I feel most enthusiastic about writing,' he was quoted a couple of days later. 'I'm not enthusiastic about showbusiness in general.'[4] Writing songs offered him more money via publishing rights, more control over projects, and the chance to circumvent the endless, maddening grind of promotional gigs in provincial towns.

Since the collapse of The Walker Brothers, features in the weekly press on Scott had become perfunctory and formulaic, and underline how the press and star system were part of the same production line of consumption and fandom. They repeat the same old gags about his awkwardness; familiar myths are recycled about his beatnik past and his time as a bassist in bars and bands; to add some light relief, there's some music biz colour about managers, minders and screaming girls. Almost as frequent as the interviews were the photo splashes of Scott as centrefold; on the 5 April 1969 cover of the *Melody Maker* he was billed as 'Scott Walker in 3-D', the pop star as pure spectacle. Walker hated these trappings of pop, and countered journalists' questions by throwing back eloquent, self-contained, almost perfectly scanning aphorisms which break down the economics and illusions of the business: 'You may try and change the world but in the end the world will change you';[5] or 'I want people to face realities of life and not escape them';[6] or 'I am not concerned with international stardom.'[7] He seems to be talking with himself, and plotting how to set the world to rights. Taking control of his own songwriting on *Scott 3* and *Scott 4* was thus more than a solipsistic pastime, but a weapon with which he might recalibrate his economic, artistic and existential relationship with the wider world.

This elaborate game of give and take with the world outside is encapsulated by the strange case of his TV series, pilots of which ran in 1968 in advance of the series as a whole in 1969. Walker needed the money and the exposure, but had a distant relationship with the audience; he wanted to sing his own songs and feature his favoured artists, but BBC presentation and budgets meant he was often singing covers or introducing the Dudley Moore Trio. In an ironic twist, footage of the show no longer exists. But audio of the shows remains and can still be found online, and Walker comes across with a strange mix of easy American charm and frosty alienation.

The TV introduction to 'It's Raining Today', the track that would begin *Scott 3*, is like hearing a personality splitting right down the middle. 'This next one is one of mine,' he begins formally. 'It's sort of a reflection of my teenage years. And I came from the beatnik era in America ... I read Jack Kerouac, and I dug progressive jazz, and got kicked out of schools, hitch-hiked across America and the whole bit, you see. I met up with a whole lot of wonderful people.'

He's now talking in beatnik patter, but he checks himself and is suddenly cold and distant. 'The relationships were ephemeral but some of the best I've ever known. And this is a song about it.' At the end of the first show of the series, he signs off with a line worthy of Brel at his steeliest: 'You've been a wonderful audience. Now it's time for me to go away.'

As the opening track of *Scott 3*, 'It's Raining Today' makes a radical rupture with his previous work. It suggests a personality in a state of, if not crisis, then profound contradiction. An unearthly string section hums in the upper registers for a few seconds before some chimes, a bass and acoustic guitar gently begin to roll, and Scott Walker's slow, rich opening words – *'It's raining today ...'* – wrap around like velvet. Each line, each syllable, is drawn out and hangs languorously in the air: *'It's raining today/And I'm just about to forget/The train window girl/That wonderful day we met/She smiles through the smoke/From my cigarette'*. All the while, atonal strings linger, weightless, at the edges of hearing, like the zigzag lines in peripheral vision that preface a migraine.

The popular ballad of the 1950s and sixties is a triumph of audio ergonomics, where the singer can be as close as a whisper, while a string ensemble wraps around him in the stereo field. It's as if you could reach out and touch the singer and the instruments with your fingertips. 'It's Raining Today' shatters this mise en scène. The voice and the strings seem to inhabit separate worlds, with the string section warping the space and time of the song like a black hole. The strings have always haunted me. They form the introduction of the first album of Walker's own music, so these opening moments, where the conventional song-space of the ballad is shattered, suggest some kind of a challenge or code. Like the legal small print on the sheet music, it places a devilish question mark next to the relationship between singer and listener. Perhaps what follows is of uncertain provenance, with Walker as an unreliable witness.

I keep obsessively skipping the CD back towards this world within a world at the start of the opening song. Perhaps those strings are the sound of rain outside his window? As it happens, I can hear rain from the back door of my kitchen as I type away at the table. Countless sound events, splashes, drips, plinks, plonks, each one unpredictable, but you can intuitively grasp and attune to the rhythms. It's a window into a whole system of macro and micro climate cycles – clouds gathering, drips forming, rain falling, later to evaporate. These sounds are happening just a foot or two away from me on a warm summer evening, and it's comforting to feel so close to the world and its cycles of balance and continuity. The Greek composer Iannis Xenakis modelled these kind of physical processes – liquids, gases, Brownian motion – in his works, creating some of the most startling yet intuitively graspable music in all of twentieth-century composition. But the strings on 'It's Raining Today' are something else entirely – dense, opaque, uncanny.

To try to unlock their secrets, and to unburden myself of an obsession, I load a .wav file of 'It's Raining Today' into a piece of audio software called Melodyne. It's a program designed to take a sound waveform – a mass of frequencies, noise and other sonic detritus – and tease it apart into the notes, chords, voices and instruments that make it up. The entire song pops up in the centre of my window as a drab, thin sliver of sound. A grey progress clock begins to inch its way round the dial, and my laptop's fan chugs away to keep cool. After a long wait, chunks of waveform spring out of the original wave and separate into levels of coloured notes up and down the window. You can see the plucked guitar chords, the heartbeat electric bassline, and Scott's wandering vocal, with a scale on the left-hand side of the screen indicating the notes. Glancing eight seconds or so in, I can see the program has failed to figure out the opening string section. It guesses that there are long thin streaks of G and G sharp in the upper registers, while down several octaves, unruly tones are juddering between G, G sharp and

F sharp like a stock market readout on a bad day. These notes a semi-tone apart are what causes the discord – the small intervals means the harmonic overtones overlap unevenly. But looking closer, the screen is also filled with odd clusters, smears and ghost-notes, suggesting the technology can't tell where the notes are coming from. It has lumped strings and background sounds in together, and I can move these clumps up and down the scale, like trying to complete a jigsaw puzzle with pieces from two different sets. Faced with discord, the technology has drawn a blank. Listen closely, and the strings are certainly centred around G, but each instrument is locked into a hovering circle of vibrato, like bees moving in swarm formation, and the ensemble as a whole sends waves of discord rippling through the song. The arrangement suggests an uncanny alternative world, of impenetrable rain and unparseable sound.

The arrangements on *Scott 3* were entirely the work of Wally Stott, aside from a single Brel song, 'Funeral Tango'. Stott had a long association with Philips/Fontana reaching back all the way to the mid-1950s, and had also worked extensively in TV, radio and light entertainment. But his arrangements for *Scott 3* are bold, freeform structures. Glancing at the computer screen gives a visual sense of how sparse the arrangement for 'It's Raining Today' is. The string section is rendered as clustered, angular streaks, while Walker's vocal line is a thick wave of viscous liquid working its way up and down the vocal scale. It's like looking at vivid steel and glass architecture with paint oozing down the panes.

Walker distanced himself from the studio trickery of both pop music (with its superficial shallowness) and outward-bound psychedelia (an undifferentiated mush), so the arrangements on his records were vital. A fan of Sibelius and Bartók, he would hold forth on the virtues of various arrangers at length in interviews. *Scott 3* carries few of the trappings of rock – guitars, drum kits, electrification – that would time-stamp the album, and the voice and the arrangements are left to circle each other gracefully in free space. *Scott 3* echoes the sounds of ballad makers of the day but stands apart from them too, with songs that are untethered by percussion, and stretch out endlessly, as if moving in zero gravity.

The world of *Scott 3* is a ballet between Walker's voice and Stott's arrangements, and it's unmatched in his catalogue for its sense of blissful free space. Like 'It's Raining Today', many arrangements take their cue from ideas of movement and physical space. 'Butterfly' is a short tone poem led by a flute theme which seems to float on air currents; 'Copenhagen' evokes snowflakes through gentle pizzicato strings, harps and chimes; 'Winter Night' begins with chilling minor-key refrains like cold gusts of wind.

Walker's voice is at the centre of it all, thick, resonant with vibrato, echoed. An uncomplimentary assessment in *Melody Maker* at the time described Walker as 'an average singer with pitch problems' [*Melody Maker*, but sourced from *Scott Walker: A Deep Shade Of Blue*], but this is back to front; the voice is so strong and resonant, and the arrangements so mobile, that the notes sound in the right place even when they waver. On *Scott 3*, he sings off and around the beat like stretching a piece of elastic to breaking point. Sometimes, the songs almost reach a virtual standstill as you wait for him to sing the next word. This is how Scott Walker's voice seduces; he can sing anything – philosophy, trash, nonsense – and at his own pace, and the wrong always somehow sounds right.

As for lyrical themes, Walker described the album before release as 'songs of love and loneliness'. It's the same uneasy tension between intimacy and distance; he claims that the album is not as introspective as his previous works, but goes on to square the circle by declaring, 'loneliness is the most under-estimated thing in the world'.[8] The sleeves of his first run of solo albums, from *Scott* to *Scott 4*, encapsulate this game of hide and seek. All present a profile of his face, but on *Scott* and *Scott 4*, his gaze is lowered; on *Scott 2* he holds a microphone, eyes closed and lost in song; on *Scott 3* his face is only just visible reflected in a blue eye caught in extreme close-up, its purple-red lashes like alien foliage. The only eye contact you can make with these covers is with the beautiful, glassy, anonymous eye of *Scott 3*, and an enigmatic line in 'Butterfly' confirms the separation: *'Dark rivers your eyes/Belong to no one'*.

Several songs are in the third person, and feature loners, lowlifes, free spirits and outsiders (at one point the album was intended to be a series of stories of inhabitants of a tenement block). 'Two Ragged Soldiers' is about a pair of drunken bums, 'Big Louise' is a 'requiem for an ageing homosexual' (as Walker put it),[9] and 'Rosemary' begins with a young woman starting in horror from her nightmares. The strangest of these is the brief '30 Century Man', recorded with just an acoustic guitar, reportedly while stoned (which for Walker generally means drunk). It casts a cold, objective eye over human life from a thousand years hence, finding only eternal archetypes – *'See the dwarves and see the giants/Which one would you choose to be?'* – and the immortal old figure of Charles De Gaulle.

The songs are embedded with signifiers of distance and time. 'Two Ragged Soldiers' begins, *'They spoke transparent phrases to looking-glass women'*, as if other people are mere empty placeholders; each verse tells of seasons passing, marked only by the ebb and flow of fantasy and desire (drink again?) until the song slows, and they are left with memories, or a space where they used to be. 'Rosemary' begins with *'voices from a phonograph'* jolting her awake, before she steps to the window and glances at a photograph on the wall. She inhabits a limbo of endless evenings with *'mother's friends/pregnant eyes, sagging chins'*, where each strike of a clock drives *'nails one day further/in the coffin of her youth'*. The subject of 'Big Louise' is ageing, lonely and neglected; conceivably a gay man, as Walker intimated. He or she is now a mere shell, referred to in a cold metaphor as a *'haunted house/her windows are broken'*. Windows are everywhere in the songs – a screen on the world where time stops on 'It's Raining Today'; on 'Rosemary', the only way out of a nightmare.

Time passes strangely in *Scott 3*; it creeps by slowly, or years pass in a moment, or time seems to happen, somehow, elsewhere. 'Big Louise' ends with the ironic conclusion, *'Didn't time sound sweet yesterday'*. The memories of 'It's Raining Today' are introduced with the line *'I'm just about to forget...'*, and qualified by *'moments descend on my window pane'*. It's as if Walker can step back and perceive the passage of time from the outside.

Scott 3 concludes with the three Brel numbers. An exquisite reading of 'Sons Of' begins with a piano playing quick-time in a great hall somewhere far away, and the eternal iterations of *'sons of your sons...'* extend the idea of the passage of time. 'Funeral Tango' carries a bombastic arrangement by Peter Knight, while Walker calls out the *'crocodile tears'* of phony friends from beyond the grave in a caustic delivery completely at odds with the rest of the album. 'If You Go Away' is another Stott arrangement, which seems to halt the passing of time in some of its pregnant pauses – frozen moments before separation. The album is over in thirty-eight minutes, and seems to have turned time inside out. *Scott 3* emerged at the height of psychedelia, and while it eschewed its methods, ideals and its morality, it nevertheless makes ruptures in time and space that match any record of that era.

It's common to draw a narrative of Walker's solo albums getting more adventurous, and thus less successful, as he progressed throughout the series, but it's a misconception to make a connection between the two. *Scott 3*, released in March 1969, didn't match the commercial success of *Scott 2*, a number one album in the UK, yet it still reached the top ten. His profile remained high, and just four months afterwards, *Scott Walker Sings Songs From His TV Series* was released, a commercial tie-in with the TV show that Walker virtually disowned even at the time ('You must not consider this album in the same series as my first three albums'.[10] It again made the top ten, although it has long been out of print, doubtless with Walker's blessing.

By August 1969, there were brief mentions in the press of him writing eight new songs while in Greece and Portugal, probably the backbone of *Scott 4*, which would eventually be released in December. *Scott 4* was a commercial disaster on release, but would eventually be recognised as one of his masterpieces. The reasons for its commercial failure are primarily pragmatic rather than aesthetic. Most notably, the album's songwriting credits were printed on the LP label as Scott Engel rather than Scott Walker (a less surprisingly choice than it might appear at first glance – Walker's real surname Engel was mentioned frequently in the press even before *Scott 4*, with journalists perhaps happy to riff on the nickname of Engelbert Humperdink, a megastar at the time). *Scott 4* was also Walker's third album of 1969, and having sacked manager Maurice King, he did no publicity interviews at all for the album's release, after several years of giving reliably good quote in the press.

Scott appeared on the front of the 13 December edition of the *New Musical Express* in the image from the front of *Scott 4* – a white stand-up collared shirt, black jacket and a gold chain dangling, giving him a faint priestly air. But there was no album title, just a quote (uncredited) from Albert Camus: 'A man's work is nothing but this slow trek to rediscover, through the detours of art, those two or three great and simple images in whose presence his heart first opened.' The album is announced in perfunctory manner in a small Philips/Fontana advert inside, again under the name Scott Engel. For an album that was already a hard sell no matter what the content, these oblique announcements were the death knell for the record. It barely sold, and was deleted shortly after.

Scott 4 is an extraordinary record, yet it's worth considering what it must have been like to listen to for the first time. The opening chord of the first song, 'The Seventh Seal', is a flourish of minor-chord flamenco guitar, followed by a trumpet sounding something like *The Last Post*. There are echoes of Miles Davis's *Sketches Of Spain* from nine years previously, but the music could be from almost any era, with no studio fingerprints that might identify the year. By the end of the song, a tambourine is tapping out a cantering rhythm and a male Russian chorus is declaiming operatically. This must have alienated not only fans seeking Scott Walker the pop idol, but also those attuned to rock and soul and the urgent internal dynamics of, say, Led Zeppelin or James Brown, for whom the beginning of *Scott 4* must have sounded like shopworn exotica dressed up with cheap theatrics.

But Walker's vocal is even stranger still: *'Anybody seen a knight pass this way?/I saw him playing chess with Death yesterday/His crusade was a search for God, and they say/It's been a long way to carry on.'* The song is a relatively straightforward retelling of Ingmar Bergman's 1957 film of the same name – an allegorical struggle between life and death which starred Max Von Sydow as a Knight and Bengt Ekerot as the Grim Reaper himself, set in Sweden in the era of the Crusades and the Black Death. There are nine verses and no choruses (perhaps in the manner of the real hero of the film, a medieval minstrel); lyrics are crowbarred awkwardly into stanzas; and lines wander free with ad hoc rhyme-schemes: *'The Knight he watched with fear/He needed to know/He ran where he might feel God's breath/And in the misty church/He knelt to confess/The face within the booth/Was Mister Death'*. Written down, these lyrics read as a rather beautiful kind of blank prose, with the awkwardness of *'Mister'* perhaps intended as a Brechtian shock to the system. But Walker's voice is shackled by the lines, and hearing it for the first time, 'The Seventh Seal' must have seemed an ugly vessel for Walker to inhabit. The lyrical allusions would surely have bamboozled Walker's pop fanbase, but the studious narration and historical weight must have also seemed pretty staid in the context of 1960s counterculture.

If 'The Seventh Seal' is a grotesque patchwork of styles and a mess of philosophical contradictions, that's the key to its richness, and of *Scott 4* as a whole. This album is haunted by a teeming cast of characters and avatars, from the Knight and Death to heroes and duchesses. Emotions swing wildly; in 'On Your Own Again' Walker declares independence with *'You're on your own again/You're at your best again'*, before on the next track, 'The World's Strongest Man', admitting, *'I need your love/You know I can't pretend anymore'*. Ideologically it is hard to pin down, condemning dictators on one track ('The Old Man's Back Again') and then eulogising angels on another ('Angels Of Ashes'). The lyrics can be densely overwritten (as on 'The Seventh Seal'), but elsewhere there's a kind of meta-writing, where Walker retreats into repetition or word-play. It is considered one of Walker's most profound albums, but Walker himself has described his work of that time as indulgent, and hinted at his heavy drinking of the time. Perhaps all of this is true at once.

The Camus quote and 'The Seventh Seal' both outline a search for meaning, and that's the best way to approach the album. *Scott 4* carries a profusion of perspectives, and even – on 'Boy Child' – unstable identities. These contradictions are all part of the struggle. The reference to Camus is appropriate, as the Frenchman never seemed to care too much about consistency; he produced a stylistically brilliantly and restlessly thoughtful body of work that, nonetheless, in *The Rebel* (1951), a book-length essay that attempted to marshall his ideas, began to wrestle itself apart. It's worth reconsidering Bergman's film at this point. The story of *The Seventh Seal* is often described, wrongly, as portraying the grim and ultimately fruitless struggle of man against mortality, and the film itself has been parodied for what's seen as the worst excesses of pretentious/art-house/European film making. But it is not a downbeat film. The Knight of the film ultimately dies so that the other characters may live, and much of the film is set in the spring, and filled with bawdy comedy and sensuous excess. *The Seventh Seal* is a search for existential meaning, eventually (if tentatively) grasped, and *Scott 4* treads the same path.

'Angels Of Ashes' echoes the structure of 'The Seventh Seal'. It begins with an innocuous plucked nylon guitar before moving sedately, formally, like a template to learn dancing, through grand undulating chords. Like 'The Seventh Seal', there's no chorus, just verse followed by short verse: *'The angels of ashes/Will give back your passions/Again, and again/Their light shafts/Will reach through the darkness/And touch you/My friend.'* The song contains some of Walker's most visionary lines, though it's a moot point just how sincere they are: *'I can recommend angels/I've watched as they've made a man strong'*; *'You've been following patterns and fleeting sensations too long'*; *'If your blind hands can't grope/Through these measureless waters/You fall'*. Proverb follows proverb. The repetitive structure hints that he was writing these lyrics in isolation from the songs; the CD inserts for *The Drift* nearly forty years later, with its short blocks of self-contained text – as Rob Young has noted, 'a general, assembling troops on the battlefield'[11] – share the same focus on the word, with the song at its service.

Vision follows vision, until at the end there's a self-portrait: *'you can say that he laughed, and he walked like Saint Francis with love'*. Such faith seems absurdly idealistic for a one-time disciple of Brel, yet the evocations of desolation are so eloquent that they hit with the full force of the real: *'If you're down to an echo, they might just remember your name'*; *'In the unbroken darkness, where emptiness empties along'*; *'the fullness that fills up the pulse of duration is gone'*. If the angels are the hallucinations of a desperate soul, then it makes it that much more affecting.

'Boy Child' is *Scott 4* at its lyrically most abstract and fluid, with a headspinning arrangement by Wally Stott that sends an acoustic guitar (or a kora? A mandolin?) echoing across a huge soundspace. *'You lose your way/A boy child rides upon your back/Take him away/Through mirrors dark/And blessed with cracks/Through forgotten courtyards/Where you used to search for youth.'* The arrangement spins through space and time with the same grace as much of

Scott 3, and the lyrics describe motion through dreamlike spaces, *'extensions through dimensions'*. The real search, though, is inward. The 'boy child' is a mute companion to the story, suggesting a split personality: *'Old gets a new life/Reach out you can touch it's true/ He's not a shadow/of shadows like you see.'*

Moving from these Gnostic visions to the second and third songs on the album gives a measure of *Scott 4*'s breadth. 'On Your Own Again' and 'The World's Strongest Man' are songs of love, and so affecting that it's odd they didn't find a wider audience. But each lasts just a couple of minutes or so, offering little more than a fleeting parade of impressions. 'The World's Strongest Man' submits to all-consuming desire – *'I need your love/You know I can't pretend anymore'*. But the wordplay is so fluid it throws up ambiguities, mishearings and slippages of meaning, with lines that are either nonsensical or can be heard any number of ways: *'see birds flying through this hazy face'*; *'Can't you see the towers of mine they could shine like a dime.'* 'On Your Own Again' seems wholeheartedly romantic right up to its lonely conclusion: *'Except, when it began/I was so happy/I didn't feel like me.'*

In contrast, 'Hero Of The War' and 'The Old Man's Back Again' carry explicit political content for the first time in his work. The first is bitterly ironic, a welcome home with gallows humour for a maimed war veteran. 'The Old Man's Back Again' is 'dedicated to the neo-Stalinist regime' (the only track on the album with this kind of subtitle), inspired, presumably, by the Soviet invasion of Czechoslovakia following the Prague Spring of 1968, just a year before the song was recorded. There is anger in the pathologically driven and perpetually funky bassline, likely to have been played by Walker, a former session man: a display of force that's a rare concession to rock music on the album. The narrative is a gut-churning mini-epic, with old women watching stoically as the tanks and soldiers roll in, but the tone is set by the first verse, which channels nightmare visions torn straight from the unconscious: *'a shadow crossed the sky/and it crushed into the ground/just like a beast.'* There's a pre-echo here of 'The Electrician' and *The Drift*, where Walker bypasses context and explanation and plugs politics directly into psychological and physical violence – the true face of state power.

Throughout *Scott 4* you can sense Walker's voice struggling like a butterfly to emerge from a cocoon. Literary allusions and livid visions are crowbarred into dense, awkwardly scanning lines that need to be unpacked by the listener. The songs burst at the seams as they try to structure all these levels of meaning within the constraints of music which, however loosely, still fits the pop blueprint – with a balladeer delivery not always so far from Vegas, and none of the wildstyle studio tricks that rock was exploring at the same time. Several times across the album he bursts into scat singing, as if trying to find another way to use the voice. Occasionally he returns to, or toys with, a single word, as if stepping back from the song to play with its meaning: *'a shadow of shadows'*; *'finds beauty in loving love'*; *'where emptiness empties'*; *'longing for belongings'*. *Scott 4* is an unrepeatable masterpiece because it is in such a vivid state of flux.

Nevertheless, at the end, 'Rhymes Of Goodbye' hints at a resolution, and that the journey from pop automaton to autonomous writer begun on *Scott 3* is finally complete: *'I've come far from chains/ From metal and stone/From makeshift designs/And seeking a star.'* He is singing in the first person in what seems like autobiography, *'to grab for the truth'*, and ballet-steps precisely across notes and octaves, the fluctuations in voice suddenly floating up and down on the waves of emotions.

But the truth was fleeting: *'I turn and it's gone'*. Scott Walker's time of independence ended with commercial disaster, and *Scott 4* disappeared into a void of public indifference. For the next album, *'Til The Band Comes In*, he would be reined back into the fold with a contractually required sprinkling of pop covers. The luminous visions of *Scott 3* and *Scott 4*, disowned even by their creator as the work of an indulgent recluse, dissipated into the cold, rational light of day.

1. *New Musical Express* (13 December 1969).
2. Coxhill, Gordon, 'Scott Is Not Struggling For Recognition' in *New Musical Express* (26 April 1969).
3. Walker interview in *Radio Times* (6 March 1969).
4. Walker interview in *Melody Maker* (8 March 1969).
5. Walker interview in *Melody Maker* (5 April 1969).
6. Altham, Keith, 'Scott Walker Hides Away In A Gloom World' in *New Musical Express* (30 September 1967).
7. Coxhill, Gordon, 'A Secret Changes Scott's Life' in *New Musical Express* (18 January 1969).
8. Coxhill, Gordon, *NME* (18 January 1969).
9. Coxhill, Gordon, 'Scott Talks About *Scott 3*' in *New Musical Express* (22 March 1969).
10. Coxhill, Gordon, *NME* (26 April 1969).
11. Young, Rob, 'Knocking 'Em Dead' in *The Wire* 267 (May 2006).

A Dandy In Aspic

Ian Penman

Scott Sings Songs From His TV Series (1969)
'Til The Band Comes In (1970)
The Moviegoer (1972)

> *In my years alone here the formula has been unvarying: a*
> *small room, sepulchral lighting, a drink with a kick like a*
> *dromedary, plus music, including the cheap, thin, popu-*
> *lar songs I spent years trying to deny had ever floated on*
> *my breath.*
>
> **Gordon Burn,** *Alma Cogan* (1991)

Memories: Sunday morning sunlight through lace curtains, curled on the sitting room carpet, one ear to the speaker, a worshipper before the radiogram. Smell of furniture polish, and the pale grey box my dad's records were kept in. At the age I was, these albums seemed huge, in all sorts of ways: not merely as physical objects, but as audiophile markers of some sort of distant adult life. Even a wan balladeer like Matt Monro seemed striking; he wasn't wild like Jimi Hendrix or even Tom Jones, but neither was he palpably naff like Bill Haley or Val Doonican or The New Seekers – confusingly, he was the definite possessor of some kind of minor-key cool. Here was this everyday guy like my dad and his workmates, who now roamed the spotlight, was photographed, gazed out half-smiling on to the waiting scene. Later, I found out he used to be a bus conductor, which may have been one of the reasons people like my dad and his workmates liked him. He combined two worlds – the workaday one of sweat and dirty hands and nine-to-five obligation; and the dreamier one of pop and light entertainment, a get-out clause of fame, song, drift, ease. Concupiscence figured somewhere in this equation too, of course, not that I had really grasped that bit yet. But I did get that song was an alternative space and time: all the time in the world to look casual, sparkle at the ladies, lazily dream; the joy of opening your mouth and having something softly surprising emerge – smooth, harmonious, cloudily seductive.

This was the sound of victory.

Matt had a hit with one of the first big James Bond songs – 'From Russia With Love'. This in itself was a thing of some small fascination at the time: a song coupling Russia *and* Love in its title. Matt's reading of the song was characteristically low key, especially compared to how the franchise subsequently developed. As though he were singing a torch song and Russia were his unobtainable other.

This was who Matt was: not James Bond or Tom Jones or some improbably swarthy puppet on razzle-dazzle strings, but an ordinary guy who'd managed to smuggle himself into a real-life fantasy world. Portrait of the pop singer as an exile on Money Street: a place of cool abundance and discreet excess most of us would never know: long, tall drinks correctly sipped, socks made of air inside Jermyn Street shoes, deference shown, orders taken, all the codes that are a prompt, not an inheritance. *'Hello Mr Big Shot/Say, you're looking smart...'*

Matt had left behind alarm-clock starts to the day, every day, for ever. His audience loved it, that he was no longer under the hammer, now living a life gloriously and indefinably hung between the factory floor and the stars. But it was not just a matter of being vaguely between this class and that; more that showbusiness itself – as realm and image – was one way to show up the whole business of class for the pantomime it was: a world of illusion, strings pulled, who you know, not what you know. Tatty trunk of hand-me-downs or handmade suit and shoes – these are only our outermost skin, they are not being itself. We are what we are in the process of moving towards, where we are headed and what persona we may assume when we finally get there. Someone like Matt, in these early sixties days, gestured toward a space that figures like Bryan Ferry would later make their own.

I guess 'in-between' was where we found ourselves back then, too, in the mid-sixties. Halfway round the world, here we were: an RAF working-class family that got to fly round the world, stay in improbable places, live by the Mediterranean, harvest a different air. But one day it ends, and you are back on the estate, back to holidays in Blackpool and Yarmouth, back to where you once belonged. Who said anything about belonging? I have no idea where I am now supposed to belong: there is no old home town waiting. And music is one of the ways I find to digest this, enter it inside myself as fact and perplexity. Music becomes my own permanent floating home town. Belonging becomes something of an impossible dream. You get to escape – but you also have to return. All identity is fixed around this reserve of what returns, whether you want it to or not. I never really wanted to sing; but I often found myself, down the years, wanting to be song.

I was going to say I remember this one Matt Monro sleeve particularly vividly, but that's not exactly true. What I frequently conjured down the years, I now realise, was less a precise image, more the implied mood. These days, of course, the obligatory Google search produces the precise thing within minutes, and I have to say it's pretty much as I recall it, an odd combination of slick and naff: sci-fi silvers and gunmetal greys and Matt's Brylcreem-rich high-street hair. It is only now I realise that what I have been half-remembering all this time is Matt leaning on a recording console: the artist in his studio.

*

In the aftermath of war things can change disturbingly quickly. The difference between two years – 1949 and 1950, or 1950 and 1959, 1964 and 1966 or 1966 and 1970 – can be both dizzying and illuminating.

The Walker Brothers dissolved in 1967, and solo Scott came to term at a time when all things pop and style and culture and class were moving at a frantic and vertiginous pace. Within months, deep social disturbance could be boiled down into plastic 'hippy' wigs on sale in Woolworths. In retrospect, we can see the mid-to-late sixties as not just a time of ferment and creativity, but as the beginning of something far less noble: the co-option of a creatively fertile and risky Underground by global Capital. One way of seeing things: that Che poster on the wall is the beginning of the end of various hopeful beginnings. Unruly social forces siphoned off, stilled, and sublimated into safe consumer shells. A moment when things changed – fell, smashed, broke up on re-entry or contact with the real, both in society at large, and for many individuals. Falling on hard times. ODed in a bed sit. Drunk at the ball. Installed in the bin or 'resting'. Unable to take the pressure. Uneasy in the starlight and uneasy outside it. All at sea, sinking, sunk. Bloated, forgotten, gone. Some lives burn up like old betting slips. Sometimes it's easier to navigate the shadows and the shades.

Everything in those days was about appearances.

Look at this itinerary from the first year of Scott's solo career. Just take this all in –

6 August 1967: an appearance on *The Billy Cotton Band Show*, where (quite unbelievably now, and probably just as unbelievably then) he did a live version of Jacques Brel's 'My Death'. 'This song deals with death and aspects of it – I hope you like it …'

The rest of the summer meant appearances at various end-of -the world end-of-pier shows in Blackpool and Bournemouth and Skegness and Yarmouth. Tea and sunburn. KISS ME QUICK bowler hats.

Glamorous shoreline donkeys. Greasy potatoes inside newsprint. Weird English shit like that.

The year ended with a Christmas appearance on – where else? – ATV's *Down At The Old Bull And Bush*. You try to push your mind to visualise such an event, and it simply blanks. But this was the strange new given – this was light entertainment, this was MOR, in the telly age. Everything was up in the air and brightly, blindingly ill-defined; this was a moment in time when the ultra-savvy Nik Cohn, under the heading 'After The Beatles', could legitimately group together the following names: 'There was a lot of talent around, whole battalions of new names: Donovan, Tom Jones, Sandie Shaw, Dusty Springfield, Lulu, Georgie Fame, The Walker Brothers, The Small Faces, The Hollies, Marianne Faithfull, Dave Berry, Petula Clark.'[1] You would have a hard time (now or then) defining some of these acts – not radical, but not banal; not exactly hip, but not exactly terminally un-hip either.

In May 1968 he not only sang 'Jackie' on Frankie Howerd's *Howerd's Hour* but appeared as 'Jack' (not Jackie), wearing a huge white frilly shirt, in a Cyrano de Bergerac-based sketch. Frankie says: 'Oooh! He needs some aggravation. He's been a bit uppity of late. Some aggro may make him tour!' Frankie says! Frankie's more on the money than he maybe knows.

If it's September: *It Must Be Dusty*! (Like Scott, a Philips recording artiste, as it happens.) More TV, everywhere, all the time, plug plug plugging the latest 45, duets with lady singers in improbable wigs, with improbable teeth and improbable knees. Bits and pieces of groovy chit-chat.

We like to believe there were always huge chasms separating pop and MOR, but in truth it was never that clear. Nik Cohn liked the Walker Brothers – but he adored PJ Proby. In America, Jack Nitzsche worked on kitschy surf 45s, and Randy Newman wrote ballads for bucks. In London, the likes of a pre-Zeppelin Jimmy Page and John Paul Jones were worked off their young feet as session men – working on everything from The Who and The Kinks to Donovan, to Dusty, to Library Music, soundtracks, and so on down: Cliff Richard, Eurovision, Harry Secombe, what Jones called 'the bow tie brigade'. When Scott first went solo, his touring band was run by Ronnie Scott; help with live arrangements came from Stan Tracey, among others. Apparent divisions were, in a day-to-day, notes on a page, folding-money sense, permeable to the point of meaning-lessness. A strange meld of what would once have been end-of-the-pier, working men's club, light entertainment, pop, cabaret, all these little overlapping scenes. The hip session musician circle. The old-school Tin Pan Alley world of pro songwriters and agents and managers. And what's interesting about Scott at this time is that he found a way to work something of his own out, in the midst of several of these little worlds. When The Walker Brothers split, the crucial thing that made the difference between Scott and John was that John fell into something of a vacuum, where Scott was savvy enough to take along a very plugged-in support system: Johnny Franz for music, various arrangers, agents and managers, all of them either distinctly old-school and hard-nosed (the business half), or semi-hip (the arrangers).

Pop, sure, as in FILE UNDER POPULAR, but also ... something else.

The world of Scott's mid-sixties song has something in common with another unlikely habitué of so-called Swinging London.

'The landscape of Orton's London is bleak: a soiled world of loss, isolation, ignorance, and bright decline,' as John Lahr put it.[2] As it was for Scott, 1967 was also a great year for Joe Orton. Neither man was to enjoy their dazzling success for much longer, we now know. Both had falls coming, up ahead, that year. Doldrums for Scott, death for Joe. Looking back, what strikes you about both is that although they subsequently became symbols of 'the time', they were never fully part of it, not in a fully Beatles and Stones kind of way.

Always on the margins, looking on, slightly apart, not aloof exactly but not completely engaged. Circa 1967/68 it's easy to imagine Scott sharing Orton's stance; wry amusement, that is, rather than pervasive gloom.

For some people, this was the best it would ever get. For some music, too. The best of both worlds: the sudden illumination of serious art, mixed in with the cheap and heady cocktail rush of popular idiom. Cocktails and … cock tales. The acute, value-added perspective of the Outsider – not by a huge margin, but just enough. Orton's the length of a soiled cock in a public toilet; Scott's a gutter as big as the Atlantic.

1969. Scott has just signed off on the final instalment of what many will consider his greatest achievement: *Scott 1–4*. Actually, the timeline isn't quite so clear cut: in 1969 the album of his BBC TV series (called, what else, *Scott Sings Songs From His TV Series*) was slipped out between *Scott 3* and *Scott 4*.

For *Scott 4*, Walker had changed the name on the label to Scott Engel – which his advisers will later belabour as the main reason it didn't do so well commercially. Perhaps it could also be seen as an indicator of more personal problems. You could say that *Scott*s *1–3* bore an explicit signature or trademark: 'Here he is – Scott'. Whereas by the time we get to 1970's *'Til The Band Comes In* (and to an extent 1972's *The Moviegoer*), the tone can feel like a bit of an afterthought, like a sideline, merchandise: 'You liked that? Well – you'll like THIS too!' There no longer seemed to be as many guest spots, interviews, PR flashes: not such a hectic itinerary. The chart positions slipped and stayed slipped. The signature began to feel confused. *Sings Songs*, *'Til The Band* and *The Moviegoer* could almost be aimed at three entirely different audiences. (All three albums still feature big pictures of Scott, naturally. Let's not forget: this was one good-looking kid.) Although the dream – the whole point of Scott you might say, from a management POV – is that he is one of the few figures in the crazy world of pop that might appeal to so many discrete markets. Parents, kids, squares, hepcats: all.

And all the time, in the back of the minds of these managers, the distant Babylonic outline of Las Vegas looms, like a promised land. And so they let him do a little of what kept him moderately happy; let him drift and dip a little. There's always big opportunities up ahead ...

You have to remember, it was an entirely different world back then. Interviews tended to divide between *Down Beat*-style 'just-the-notes, man' stuff and *Teenbeat* 'what colour is his sweater today?' Q&As. There was no 'celebrity culture' (as we now must say) of rehab-prompted confessionals. Young kids didn't give interviews saying things like 'basically, a lifetime [sic] of doing drugs and being undiagnosed as having post-traumatic stress disorder and border-line personality disorder finally caught up with me ...'. They just drew the curtains and drank.

You don't even have to suspect the motives of his management at that time.

Valium and vodka as a 24/7 diet – really? But this is how things were done in those days. Even someone like me, given to delusional romanticism of the worst kind, can see this isn't a great way to run a life or heal its wounds. And not just in the obvious ways. For one thing – there's a certain sort of over-intellectual depressive who just *loves* working out all the logarithmic combinations of pills and drinks and other pills and other pill-drink combos.

I'm not necessarily saying Scott ... but, well, you know.

When still in The Walker Brothers Scott may have toured and hung out with the likes of Jimi Hendrix, but in terms of his song, he was far nearer the MOR realm of Matt Monro, when all is said and sung.

On *Scott*s *1–4*, there was already a lot more MOR ballast than has sometimes been suggested. Superior MOR, but MOR all the same. And if it's ballast, it's sublime ballast. Songs which pull off the most difficult pop trick in the book – managing to be both unassuming and utterly unforgettable. ('Windows Of The World' on *Scott 2* is one of my all-time Scott favourites.) The music pulls off the trick of looking in two directions at once, without feeling like it's pulling in two different directions at all. The surface may feel initially slight and bland, all quivering strings – but you're hooked, can't turn away, keep returning. Songs which subtly shape everyday language into something oddly memorable. Some detail or undertow. You listen till things go dark.

Post-1969, Scott increasingly hid his mordant world view behind the gauziest and gaudiest of light-entertainment exteriors – just as Orton sharpened his phallic steel on a stage of thin cocktail chatter. Orton needed the resistance of British reserve and vulgarity to pull against, and Scott based himself in light-entertainment calm. For both it brought out their cunning; softened what might have been sour cleverness into joyful stratagem. Can we call it native cunning? The main difference is that Orton was lowlife British, born and bred – whereas Walker was an American abroad, in some kind of elective exile. Anger cut and moulded to fit the enemy's idioms. But anger can become routine become apathy become depression: a bad cycle establishes itself.

'He thought, planned, waited, and, waiting, plunged into dreams,' wrote Orton in his diary.[3]

> On paper it was hard to explain, this congealment. He was now in his late twenties, with money, prestige and great talent, adored and protected at every turn, and he lived exactly as he chose. His future was full of new plans and projects; his freedoms, within the limits of human capacity, were absolute. He had a family, he was healthy, he was safe. So he might have been expansive. Instead, he was catatonic.
> **Nik Cohn, on Phil Spector**[4]

Scott 1969–72. A few crucial years of artistic and personal ... decline?

The received picture of the Scott of this time – Middle Scott – is a man adrift, suspended, inert. A ghost in his own life, floating on booze and pills. A divided man, absent from his own work, a hack actor playing the part of affable Scott, the dependable pro. A limp, half-hearted Scott. Still, he didn't stop working. Not that there are cellars full of shelved albums, full of great lost songs, as far as we know. But he certainly carried on, didn't drop out. The real disappearance didn't take place until after the supposed breakthrough of 'The Electrician' and the other three tracks on 1978's *Nite Flights*: this was the beginning of the real blank years, of which we know little or nothing. The myth of no fingerprints on anything at all – just sitting in a pub watching people play darts. (I love that detail – not even playing darts himself, nothing so active or gregarious as joining in a soothing round of arrows: even here he sits on the sidelines and observes, off to one side.)

This is the low-life myth of Middle Scott: the depressed recluse, fleeing from the limelight, girl mob torture, the awful relentless Q&A trivia of it all. There may be some truth in this caricature, but let's not overlook the fact that during this supposedly bleak and wiped-out time, he was unerringly productive, taking care of business. Even disaffected, he ploughed on: his own TV series on BBC1 (March through April 1969); guest spots on other performers' shows; a scoot into the producer's seat for this and that polite-jazz colleague; buying and selling two or three houses: Amsterdam, Copenhagen, Regent's Park. In sum, he carried on living and working. Whatever your opinion of Middle Scott, he was a pro. He huddles with the session guys and arrangers and gets the albums done. He doesn't sink or slip away into drunk afternoon decrepitude. He kept up something of a professional front, even if there were hairline cracks showing here and there. Slowing things down, while simultaneously speeding them up.

Such productivity may seem astonishing today, but was not so remarkable then. Rather, it was the expected thing. Managers came first, not singers or groups. Scott was still only in his mid-to-late twenties, but had a top-flight management team, and consequently all the apparatus in place to facilitate a round of steady recording dates. Even when his record sales declined he continued to get the opportunities to work. Your own TV series a phone call away. With Johnny Franz taking care of the musical side (hiring arrangers, session men, picking and shaping material) and the hard-nosed Maurice King on the business side. Maybe the security of this set-up was the corollary of Scott's own insecurity. Maybe, despite all the previous few years' mega-success, Scott in his mid-twenties was very insecure indeed. Even when he moved on a little for *'Til The Band Comes In*, he still leant to a surprising degree on the 'behind the scenes' guys. It has never quite been clarified why all the original songs on *'Til The Band* carry a co-writing credit for his new manager Ady Semel – not previously or subsequently known for his songwriting smarts. Or why another client of Semel, Abi Ofarim, sings one of the songs on this Scott Walker album. It's assumed to be some kind of business deal. But it would also appear to be a case of taking being a 'yes man' to a near pathological degree.

There may have been more pragmatic considerations at work here too – the Walker boys were something of a hot novelty in mid-sixties Britain, whereas tall good-looking Beach Boy surrogates were ten a penny back home in LA. (This was the opinion of such US music biz mavens as Kim Fowley and Jack Nitzsche, who were surprised at the huge success of the Walkers, and even more perplexed at the respect subsequently accorded Scott. Just more boy meat, they thought, disparagingly.) And then too, of course, there was Vietnam and being drafted to consider. Maybe it also has a bit of the flavour of sixties existentialism – the idea that you no longer *had* to be this or that person, conform to this or that role, definition: brother, son, husband, citizen, worker, lead singer, American...

In Scott's American youth, the Engel family had moved all over the place, according to the dictates of the father's job as a geologist with the Superior Oil Company. Always moving, never at home – never one real home or home town. The idea of 'home' recedes into a disjointed and hazy dream. Years later, in an interview, when asked how his unsettled childhood affected the yen for home and home life, settling down, Scott said: 'I gave up on this desire years ago. It's impossible.' The desire for home? An impossible yen, an impossible image – an improbable dream. The difficulty of feeling anywhere at home, even inside your own name. So you smooth away at everything over the years until –

Where does the singer of these songs belong? He seems, a lot of the time, to be quite simply stranded. Not just in the sense of being physically alone, but figuratively: in between affairs, in between jobs, in between beliefs, in between reasons, in between seasons. Where does life itself happen in among all this distracting movement and flare and dispossession?

> *If I could BE: for just one little hour!*
> *If I could BE: for an hour every day . . .*

There is such a thing as internal exile. You take the unloved part of yourself and force it down into a Siberia of the soul: a crypt full of abandoned voices or tones of voice. Whispered secrets, overheard sighs. Orpheus wearing one mask underground, something else entirely when out in the needlepoint light . . .

This is how the pros play the game; this is how you disappear, while appearing to remain in the spotlight. Two or three albums a year, whole sides recorded in an afternoon. Old-school agents and arrangers and managers. No new songs, Scotty boy? Pas de problem! The music biz professionals around him – Johnny Franz, Reg Guest, Peter Knight, Wally Stott – are the link between what might be thought the compromised world of light entertainment, and the fathomless depth of Scott's best arrangements; the latter of which didn't just slip away post-*Scott 4*, but rather mutated to suit a new set of circumstances.

It may seem odd to us now, the speed these records were put together and pushed out, but at the time this was how things were done. This was the craft. Session men, arrangers, orchestras. Soundtrack music, library music, radio pop, torch experiments, musical theatre – and then, odd alchemical experiments melting all of these together. A lighter-than-light musical vapour. Lift music for bungalows. Site-specific musical cushions, patterns, decoration. Conventions obeyed – to the point where they turn in on themselves like mad Baroque curls. Unreal music for real spaces. The algebra or mathematics of charts, arrangements, session ploys. Music stripped of the pretence of burning passion: Radio 2 as ontology. Oneiric radio drift, dead zones, memory mist. The thin line between arrangement and dishevelment.

Live work may be a penance, a Klieg-lit circle of purgatory, but the studio – in the studio, you can be alone, permanently in hiding. When you're in the recording studio it's like you're between checkpoints, a sonic no-man's land. This is how you disappear, while appearing not to, right inside song itself.

Today, with ProTools and laptop, you don't have to leave your own self-fashioned virtual space, and pop music has become a somewhat flattened-out zone. Back then things were still in the hinterlands of mono. Not a huge amount of tracks available for use in the live recording so all this orchestral swoon and session weave had to be sieved and compressed and recorded in live time. The way records such as these were made – all this layer and echo and wave, which dies on contact with light and camera and applause. A tiny circumscribed world of professionals, a strange little sodality or magic circle of experts, arrangers, hands. MOR, but an MOR that takes real musicians to assemble: pindrop nuance, sight-reading, ineffable expertise and near-inaudible spin. An MOR that is post-Brecht, post-Berg, post-Sinatra, post-Spector, post-soundtrack album. This is a set-up you could happily disappear inside for ever.

For many original fans, this period, which critical consensus marks his lowest, represents Scott at his highest. For them, Middle Scott is maybe even the heart of it all.

Received wisdom says: he was adrift, putting off all decisions about what he should do with himself next. Just filling in time, going along with the management. Just taking the money and shrugging. Image: a weak maybe-man drifting through determinedly tipsy afternoons. Critical consensus: outside a handful of sort-of-OK original songs on *'Til The Band Comes In* (good, but not as good as *Scotts 1–4*), Middle Scott is way below par. One of the problems with *'Til The Band* may have been that for a long time it was hard to get to hear any of it, and people relied on the general hand-me-down verdict that it was one half OK originals and one half dreadful sleepwalk standards. Where a more accurate assessment might be: three-quarters brilliant, and one-quarter just OK. (This picture of one side original and one side schmaltz was never accurate: there are ten originals split over both sides, and five standards bunched up at the end – almost like 'extras' tacked on at the end of a new album.)

But critical consensus is an odd thing. Whose consensus: who decides such things? Taste is a subjective and mutable affair. The more recent Scott-approved line goes: real Scott is more recent Scott (*Tilt, The Drift*), far worthier of attention and analysis because the artist is finally in control. He is far more himself now that he has full control. And if that means work that is darker than we are accustomed to, then so be it, for he is finally being true to himself, putting his art first, and now has the freedom to let us see and hear who he really is, the real Scott, no longer sheltering in the middle of everywhere. Whereas the Scott of Middle Scott is lost Scott: a shame (in both senses) because mere MOR, the merest, the MOR-est. Pulse-free Muzak: like a version of Sartre's *Huis Clos* set in an endless false-start take-fifteen session music afternoon ...

Avant-garde noise is seldom the background or soundtrack to anything – which is supposed to be part of its valour. But sometimes it can feel a bit 'preaching to the converted', music for an audience of people who all think the same. Sometimes a hint of something like old-time Protestant denial – the idea that if it's louder, difficult, more of an endurance trial, it is already more virtuous.

The dark, the real, the naked: no longer sheltering in the middle.

But the middle of the road – isn't that a rather dangerous place to stand?

Maybe we already suspect something is wrong with the inherited picture. It rests on one of those binary oppositions that seem to crumble with the slightest graze. For instance: isn't it odd that when he was at his sickest – heart sick, mind sick, soul hurt, swimming through booze and prescription drugs, denuded of hope – this was when he produced his softest, sweetest song?

Scott's late artistic redemption is all about regaining control. The marriage of unforgiving noise and unflinching textual exploration may see itself as the night-town side of popular song; but in Scott's hands the one thing it is never about is a meltdown of logic. It is, if anything, the near opposite: being allowed to record exactly how he visualises everything, down to the last squeak or rumble or scream. The paradox of a control freak who gambles all on the studio moment. HIS method, HIS pace, HIS sound. All in the studio, never live. In which sense, Late Scott and Middle Scott have far more in common than we might at first think: it is all about precise arrangements set in the studio, everything precisely calibrated and spun and spaced. Dark use of strings. Melancholy moods. Is the distance, in essence, really so far?

At this time in rock circles, mid-to-late sixties, the paradigm of authentic expression was interminable electric blues rock, played by callow young college kids. Scott, singing swimmy MOR with his great big hall-filling voice is considered provocatively and unforgivably inauthentic. But why exactly is Scott, on his own, singing a handful of prettily or sublimely arranged standards, more unbelievable than inexperienced boy-men pretending the primal alienation of the blues? (There was a great *National Lampoon* album sketch, parodying the ersatz musicology of the time: 'How did this indigenous black roots music come to be best played by white long-haired English homosexuals …?')

Rock distrusts MOR because it is both too banal and too smart. MOR is way too careful, too implacably adult; it luxuriates in its stylised lack of passion; in the argot of the times, thoroughly 'square'. No edge, no soul, no ache. A post-prandial dinner jacket snooze. Music to sip cheap wine and warm scampi to. A honeymoon bouquet made of music. It is too thin – there's nothing here to interest the turned-on listener. Or, maybe, there is way too much: too much arrangement, too many folds, veils, sweeps, curtains, airs. As opposed to the simple phallic guitar obeisance of rock, MOR represents a feminine abundance-of-absence. It is all surface – and the more surface, the more that might be hiding there. Behind all the fuss – all the slips and clips and buckles, stays and seductions, whims and wiles of arrangement – there is an unnerving absence. It is too nakedly sentimental – but also too multi-hued a seduction. It is both too artificial and too honest; too simple and simply too veiled.

MOR is unease-making because it is simultaneously too banal and too genuinely seductive. MOR and teenybop pop are what sixties women and girls go for. Rock projects its sex blast out to an audience of fellow boy-men. As seductions go, rock can be all noise and hot air and special effects and over in two minutes, where MOR/torch is a long lingering polymorphic mood. MOR involved different notions of the sexual – not homogenous, and far from straightforward. MOR singers exude unruffled savoir faire: calm, dependable, unaffected – but hiding these little sparks of shared memory-pull. The singer is an older guy who doesn't need to try. Just being who he is, is his seduction. The singer takes the stage alone, just him and his voice, a model of self presence: my voice alone is triumph enough, I have no need of sleight or trick, whizz or bang.

On stage, the singer does nothing but sing, has nothing else to fall back on. He isn't especially dressed up or down. Most of all, the singer has to convey a mood of ease and naturalness. Whereas rock – supposedly more natural, primal – has to beef up its stage act with all sorts of heightened huff and glare. The guitar, as phallus, should be the very definition of self-sufficient presence, the thing which defines everything around it. But it proves so dramatically *un*-self-sufficient, you must disguise or transmute its dramatic lack. Play with it in odd and gimmicky ways. Play it behind your back. Set it alight. Smash it to bits. Throw it up in the air. Catch it. Throttle it. Push and pedal its honest ejaculation through numerous on/off effects and detours. Render its outline fuzzy. Have your bass player get down on his knees and pay due (and faux) ambisexual obeisance. (Deeper paradox here: having an actual girl come on stage at this point to perform the act would somehow threaten to collapse the whole thing.)

Musical seduction is such an amorphous thing. It would take a whole other book to separate out all the boundary lines. Where, for instance, to draw the line between cabaret as such and the glorious soul of a certain time and place, a certain mood and inclination. Gladys Knight And The Pips, The Chi-Lites, live Marvin Gaye and the weird deep MOR of Isaac Hayes. Matching tuxes, elaborate arrangements and choreography. Vamped-up versions of old 'standards'. What used to be called a proper show. James Brown extemporises showbusiness as hard work, man's work. But never dirty: 'Ain't I clean?' was always the joyous Saturday night boast. An audience that had worked hard all week expected a real show for their money.

They'd worked damn hard for this momentary respite, this spangled breathing space, and were not about to feel guilty for wanting a big show. You get tired of hearing police sirens and bottles smash, and you don't want it on Saturday night from an aisle seat too. On-stage poise and grace – yes, grace – makes up for weeks spent in manual toil. Frilled cuffs and deep velvet lapels, not blue collar. At the end of the week you want the opposite of sweat. Someone who makes their living from just being themselves, Mister Natural: the impossible dream.

Let's return to that Matt Monro sleeve and its dark greens and icy greys and metallic blues. A forgotten seam of adult suburban cool. Cool, in the particular sense of not being hot. Not the gospel/soul-influenced shouter pop of Tom Jones, Lulu, Dusty. Not filling a big space, but retreating into smaller intimacies. A different lineage: Bing Crosby, Billie Holiday, Frank Sinatra.

Scott was in showbiz from age ten on, knew about putting on a show, an act – being someone else entirely out on stage, which is what rock culture snootily considers the original sin. Putting on an 'act' equals not being 'yourself'. (Do we need to rehash the old arguments about 'authenticity', haul out all the old examples? All those old blues singers taken out of their sharp Saturday night suits, and put back in dungarees for the Newport Folk Festival stage, because that was the 'authentic' touch the young white collegiate audience expected? And then electric Dylan ...)

The interesting stuff occurs in all the in-between places. Most of all a matter of sustained tone, mood, control. Up there on stage, a performance of effortless poise and restraint: the appearance of supreme ease, lack of effort. Definitely – and defiantly – not work. Never a labour, except of love. Who's to say who is a 'natural' singer and who isn't? Think about this: approved singers like – top of my head – Otis Redding or Robert Plant are far easier to copy or caricature than the almost abstract smoothness of a Matt Monro or Tim Hardin. Texture is the thing, mood and texture: the singer almost become a blank, occupied entirely by the song. Almost like an abstract proposition, an esoteric form of sung rhetoric, a lost discipline.

So where exactly do you draw the line separating passion from fakery? Showbiz crooning is a tangled web woven of equal parts technique, predisposition, smarm and (yes) sincerity. The rock snob's idea of MOR is that sincerity is something the singer puts on with the wig and make-up, which is perfectly ridiculous and contemptible. Well – for one thing, nine tenths of live rock involves practised routines and inflated performance. And for another, it's anyway no easy thing – the appearance of ease, the avoidance of any sense of weariness or repetition or contempt.

Look at Dean Martin – a man whose live act was mostly a send-up of the very idea he could take this dross he was singing seriously. But it's no easy thing to do this, and do it consistently, without pissing off your paying audience. In fact, his audience seemed to love him all the more for it – that he was so confident in his talent he could play it for laughs. Isn't this in fact approaching the impossible dream? That here is this ordinary Joe, not just getting paid wheelbarrows of folding to air his God-given windfall of a talent, but getting paid *even more* to lark around with it! It takes rare comedic talent, an acrobat's sense of timing, and innate self-knowledge to pull something like this off – and not have the audience baying for your blood and their money back. Maybe Martin was even smarter than we imagine – maybe he realised that the *idea* of 'Dino' was the real pull; that having fun with the idea of this tipsy but always in-control persona was far more fun than just staying within the nimbus of a rather limited and one-dimensional song. He realised that the strange in-between play of selves involved in the live show was the thing, not Dean Martin as just one more OK singer you sit at home and listen to. Light entertainment as the transubstantiation of weak flesh into abstract cool.

*Nothing can match the loneliness of a pianist in a large
hotel ...*
Jean Baudrillard[5]

Scott's contemporaries in stylistic terms were singers like Jack
Jones, Andy Williams and Matt Monro. The sort of singers who used
to be known, and not disapprovingly, as right smoothies. These guys
don't get parachute widths of panties thrown at them, but later, in
audience fantasies of transcendental class and smooth touch and
slow vibrato ... who knows what the shadows contain?

The way Scott sings elides questions of sincerity. An odd voice:
is it American or is it English? Or some kind of new Euro-blue
torch song (der blaue Engel)? Because he's an American blow-in
– no inconvenient class traces. Verging on neuter, in fact, isolated
between the poles of hip and arch, Scott seems at times near her-
maphroditic: so withdrawn into a hinterland of edgeless and glassy
introspection and landscaped musical anonymity he almost doesn't
seem sexually human. Almost, at times, an angel. Or some other
creature not of this carnal world. A creature wished into life out of
the void of the recording studio.

A creature that wouldn't have lasted long, in short, in the bear-pit
atmosphere of British working men's clubs. Which might have been
his purgatorial destiny, had his solo rise not happened to coincide
with the rise to living-room dominance of TV, and the influx on
to TV of a large part of the light entertainment catalogue. All this
strange variety that erupted when what used to be the strict preserve
of beery working men's clubs and the literal end of the pier suddenly
found this new home-from-not-really-at-home in the hygienic any-
thing-goes TV studio. A smaller screen to unravel behind.

But TV appearances can be hellish just like other live performance – you have so little control over the backing, the sound
quality, the context. You can't weave together some sound to
wrap around yourself like a luxurious stole, the way you can in the

hermetic tomb of the studio. All the mixing-desk props it takes to sound this natural: singing that melts so far inside itself it comes out the other end, vapour.

It feels like Chet Baker is the obvious comparison here; but Baker's neutered blankness is of a different order altogether. You always feel that Chet is keeping in place some squirm or swarm of emotion: rage, regret, frailty, need. The voice is barely there, but traces of naked emotion shine through. With Scott, the voice is *all there*, a full presence, technically flawless – but there's an opacity where emotion is concerned. It's not that he's wearing a mask – it's more like he is already his own mask. Some of the songs of Middle Scott may be all the more genuinely haunting for being so opaque, a perfect mask. Which is also what's so perplexing about some of this stuff. Such a huge weight of technique brought to bear on something with the gravity of a soufflé.

The deal is done: warm handshakes, big pens, big cigars. In spring 1969, Scott gets his own BBC TV series, a pretty big deal for the time. Nothing more mainstream than this in light entertainment. This is the dotted line all the other dotted lines lead to – especially for someone who comes from outside the usual channels. Scott may not be Brian Jones – but he's not exactly Val Doonican either. Which is the thing about Middle Scott: where *do* you place him? The look is vaguely – not hippy exactly, but certainly Beat-ish, bohemian. Clean, not scruffy. This is ideal, think the managers – not too young-seeming, not too old-seeming, not too Yank-brash and not too Brit-grey. Not too anything. Perfectly intermediate. The middle of the middle.

The album of the TV show of the solo act, then. The sleeve: Scott, gazing off into space like he wishes he were anywhere but here. It's actually got a slightly odd layout, this sleeve. Right at the top is a big curlicued SCOTT with red and white whorls and whirls, just the tasteful Vegas side of psychedelia oozing into the frame – almost like they're hoping it might be mistaken for *Scott 4* and a half. It's the trademark name that gets the big push over the top – the TV series right at the bottom like an afterthought, where it might even be missed in among the album racks:

SCOTT
Scott
Walker
sings songs
from his
TV series

In the cover shot (perfect corduroy drainpipes; cool black US collegiate loafers; hair not too long; skinny-rib cardigan that's quite indie circa The Libertines' first flush), Scott projects just the faintest air of oblique moodiness, the pose echoing Paul Newman in some revisionist Western like *Hud* or *Hombre* or *The Left Handed Gun*. Hands in pockets, and around his neck a big key. Big, but no big deal – you could easily miss it. The key to inner Scott? It's almost too good to be true, isn't it? Somewhere between Proust and hippy commune symbol. (We've thrown away all keys, man.) Not a fake key, not hepcat jewellery à la Sammy Davis – just a big clunky front door key. What's that all about, then? (Much later, we find out it's the key to a monastery he ran to, when it all got too much. One report says he went to study Gregorian chant. One to get away from the fan mobs, avoid fledgling thoughts of self-harm, suicide. Always something there to remind you.)

He's not looking out at you with slowburn sincerity the way Matt or Sacha or Andy would – his look isn't an invitation further in. He's looking off, up, above the horizon, lost in the night time line of his own thoughts. Light above, dark below. Light entertainment surface, darkness under the cardie.

Inside is an even moodier black-and-white head-and-shoulders shot. Neither pic especially references the TV series – they feel far more *Scott 1–4*. (The big monochrome shot for the teenage walls – I hadn't noticed before, but Scott's artfully arranged pose bears a more than passing resemblance to Bowie on the front cover of *Heroes*.) As a 1967 album sleeve, aimed at the mainstream, it feels odd – only by a couple degrees, but odd all the same. It doesn't come out of the Tom Jones swinger mode – Jones the Cock – all chest hair and chunky jewellery. It leans more in the direction of Matt Monro and understated poise. But where Matt wears a shiny suit, Scott is – not scruffy exactly, but definitely playing a game with how understated he can get away with. This is a Scott who is young but not gauche or callow. Older in tone and grasp than the Superpop generation but not – you know, *old* old. American but not too shiny. British but not too obviously wilted. European but not too bum-pinchy.

Matt probably makes his female audience think of holiday romances in pale tablecloth Europe, waiters with aspirations to class, old-fashioned courtliness, moving your chair out for you before you eat, a single rose on the tablecloth. Whereas Scott ... Scott's sex deal feels almost post-coital – except maybe there's no coitus to begin with. (Does that mean he's *pre*-coital then? That the promise of the final act is always to come?) You go back to the hotel for an afternoon 'nap' or to see his 'etchings' – and that's exactly what you get. 'Do you want to take a peek at my Cocteau?' Then he falls asleep with a book in his hands ... or, a lot of sensitive talk and confessional and he leaves you to drift into sleep while he sits staring out the window, moody sod. Mussed hair, pout, voluptuous lethargy, absent-minded disappearances during the night. (If he echoes anyone from that time it's maybe a sort of a male version of Brigitte Bardot.) Cigarette smoke and stale leftover drinks. Antonioni stick figure people in unfurnished rooms. Trendily bare of decoration. High ceilings. *'And sleeping late afternoons.'*

Now, run your eyes down the list of songs. Look at these credits.

Look at all these names. Rodgers/Hammerstein II. Bacharach/ David. Aznavour/Kretzmer. Anderson/Weill. Old-style polished piano key guys. Professionals in the business of song. Princes of the mainstream. Songs for theatre, TV, hit parade, you name it, we got it. This is the kind of song where the singer has to do his behind-the-scenes homework, appear completely natural, completely at ease, a guy comfortable in his own skin. Like Sinatra, Mel Tormé, Matt Monro, Jack Jones, Sacha Distel, Aznavour himself. This is the milieu he's identifying with – a milieu which, even back then, was on the cusp of becoming something of a lost world. Under the main title it says, in slightly smaller letters: 'With accompaniment directed by Peter Knight.' Accompaniment? Soon we'll need pass notes to understand this stuff when it gets reissued. Here, verbatim, is how one of the songs is transcribed on the sleeve: '5. If She Walked Into My Life, from the musical production *Mame.*' The musical *what*? (I'd prefer it if she walked into my life from the musical production *Cabaret*, but hey, you know, whatever.)

And here, verbatim, is how Scott started one of the shows from his TV series: 'Thank you! Hello again and welcome to another show. Tonight we've got quite a variety of music and people for you to meet, and of course … MY good friend … Mr Johnny Franz!'

You've got to hand it to him: he's got the patter down, like a real pro – this wasn't some angular rocker who switched horses in midstream, he'd been doing this stuff since he was ten: it's what he knows. Even in his teens his favourite singers were Bobby Darin and Jack Jones. So, to not honour this legacy would in a way have been the more dishonest choice. And he takes it completely straight – which in the end is what hobbles the collection.

If the sleeve carries a vague promise of Scott launching his own oblique beatnik take on these standards, then it fails to materialise. I like MOR, and I like Scott doing MOR, and it's not a *bad* record by any means – but it does feel undeniably rushed, half-awake, ticking the boxes; given the breadth of material he tackled in the series, there are three or four inexplicable choices of song. Not that they're bad songs in themselves – they just don't suit Scott, his voice, persona, mood. Unlike *Scott 1–4*, that's what's missing here: a sustained mood. The songs hop about all over the place – uptempo, downtempo, relaxed, cornball, old timey, groovy; show tunes, standards, torch shivers, saloon songs, big band grabbers. Which may work on a punchy upbeat TV show, but as something you might want to listen to, over and over again – no. Compared with *Scott 1–4* the sound seems distinctly thin – which may be true to how BBC light entertainment of the sixties and seventies came across on TV, but misses the specific opportunity of the LP format as somewhere a mood might be floated and sustained.

In fact, you could say that *Sings Songs* isn't MOR *enough* – it's far too light entertainment to sustain a proper MOR mood. The golden age of torch song coincided with crucial shifts in recording technology and the advent of the long player, with more sophisticated recording techniques and the forty-minute format allowing more of a stress on mood, space, timbre, songs right at the edge of silence. (If you want a prime example of this, try side one of Sinatra's magisterial *No One Cares*.) Singer and listener become ghosts of one another – alone at two in the morning, three drinks down, blurring the edges. Singer as sonic ghost, gregarious star now playing the loneliest guy on earth. The ambiguous 'you' of each midnight-striking somnolent song.

By comparison, TV presentation of song and sound left a lot to be desired: thin, squashed sound, hack 'light pops' orchestras, under-rehearsed and thrown together. So an album like this is neither one thing or the other – not genuinely acoustically 'live', and not an intelligently crafted mock-up of early-hours solitaire – can consequently feel a bit out of sorts. It's the kind of collection you might find in the foyer of the London Palladium after a performance: a souvenir of the show, to play at the weekend. One for the new fans who can't remember which name he's using this month.

It opens with the ill-advised breakneck dash of 'Will You Still Be Mine' – and while you can see why a bit of a heart-starter to get things going was thought a good way to go, Scott never feels a natural fit inside such 'Hey folks, c'mon in!' fare. There's nothing else in the Scott songbook that goes at such a clip – except the handful of Brel numbers where the relentless tempo had a different logic and power all its own, where there was a good reason it was going so fast, like a boorish finger jabbing you in the chest. Here it just makes you think of some cheesy accompanying film of a groovy young gel in pink Chanel, running around acting MAD! In the autumn leaves of London or Paris or New York.

But hold on a minute – this music was being made by a man who (according to his own testament) was not just 'acting mad' at the time, but probably going through something of a protracted nervous breakdown. In a weird way, the upbeat backing makes it somewhat unsettling to hear sentiments like: *'When Julie Christie doesn't make me tingle/When I can't sing in tune or/Make a single!'* (He sings the latter with classic hokey exaggerated stops: *'Sing. In. Tune. Or. Make. A. Single.'* All in bits.) Or this: *'When glamour girls have lost their charms/Sirens they just mean false alarms/When lovers heed no call to arms ...'* You kinda wish he'd done it as a genuine blues.

And while it would be stretching it to hear the *'Will you/Still be mine?'* refrain as a scarifying line addressed to his own sanity, at song's end he repeats this title phrase once, twice, three then four times with something like – not exactly desperation but it certainly teeters on the edge of something unsuitably unstable for such a piece of fluff. And it sure secures itself inside your head – half of me regards it with distaste; the other half can't stop humming along.

Things calm down a bit with 'I Have Dreamed', which doesn't really distinguish itself, and dips unconvincingly close to Matt Monro territory (Monrovia?). The strings cross the line into plain sugary. It's there, then gone. 'When The World Was Young' is classic cabaret, its lyric contrasting the world of parties, girls, drinks, with a softly utopian memory of hay, hammocks and blossom – without Scott sounding like he's truly inhabiting either. You can believe the melancholy inherent in lines like *'Often my eyes/See a different shine'* and *'Only last July/When the world was young'*, but Scott seems way too prissily urban a creature for us to really accept this supposed longing for a country stile to plonk his ass down on.

The ease of 'Someone To Light Up My Life' (co-written by Antonio Carlos Jobim and Vinicius de Moraes) and the saloon glide of 'If She Walked Into My life' raise the stakes nearer the quality of the MOR standards on *Scott 1–4* – the latter has some nicely discreet semi-blues semi-jazz piano, presumably from Johnny Franz. Again, you can't help but notice that under the light is a lurking emptiness. We're not talking the full-on darkness of 'In My Room' or 'Free Again', but time and again, consciously or not, these songs point to what is missing, rather than any cause for celebration. *'Searching for something or someone/To light up my life ...'*

Side two opens with 'The Song Is You', taken, like 'Will You Still Be Mine', at way too brisk a clip – Scott's voice too big and deep to balance on such a slender and tricksy pivot. Likewise, no one seems to have decided on a suitable Scott-sympathetic tempo or arrangement for 'The Look Of Love' – it comes across as a very good song made over into an egregiously bad choice. 'Country Girl' works better. It's of a piece with the MOR of *Scott 1–4*, with nicely melancholy woodwind and lyrics that once again evince an ability to find the saddest mood or moment in any given scene. *'No hope for rainbows in the sky/In solitude cried the country girl ... Sadness befell me/A sorrow filled my heart/A longing to never depart/And memories.'* And memories – of course memories. It sometimes seems as if the singer is absolutely preoccupied by memory.

The Aznavour/Kretzmer 'Who (Will Take My Place)' is one of the best things here – not exactly hard-edged, but its gorgeous arrangement exists on a different level. The ache of recent memory is swapped for a lover's glum meditation on the near future: *'Who, when my life is through ... will take my place?'* It's gloomy as maybe only a French love song could be, starting with the simple, poisonously idle thought of your lover sleeping with someone new and slowly rolling and tumbling into a whole glum metaphysics of the afterlife: *'Who, when my life is through/Who will know the joys I have known with you .../Who will take my place, when I sleep alone?'* It takes a few listens before you realise 'when I sleep alone' is Aznavour-speak for death. It develops into what's almost a toned-down tilt at the world of Brel:

> *Why do the gods above me*
> *Play this cynical game?*
> *Life – isn't what it seems*
> *Fickle as the wind, fragile as a dream*
> *When I end my years, who will ease your pain?*
> *Kiss away your tears ... and bury me again.*

It's spoiled only by an over-dramatic Big Finale, which obeys the formal conventions for TV big ballads. It's a pity they didn't programme things to lead straight into Scott's icily diverting take on Anderson/Weill's great 'Lost In The Stars' – their separate but similar takes on love and death and being left alone in infinite space-time would make a cool pairing. (The perfectly nice but far slighter 'Only The Young' is lodged between them.) 'Lost In The Stars' has a notable intro: this strange eddying woodwind that sounds almost synthesizer-like, keening strings in eerie descent, space noise. It's subtly inventive and inventively subtle and Scott starts to glide and soar as he sings, and it makes you reckon what just a little more effort might have made of the rest of *Sings Songs*. Scott sounds like he's living both these songs, not just giving them a dust-off and run-through before the red light on the camera pops on.

'Sometimes it seems God's gone away ... And we're lost out here in the stars. Little stars. Big stars. Blowing through the night ...' Great line to end an album.

Song was a glorious space he inhabited for a year or two, before it all became mere strategy, time-filling, a career on hold for a few 'lost' years of steady work. Song like a cross between a maze and a motorway. Long drowsy-sharp afternoons in tomb-like recording bunkers, switching between the couch and the microphone, zone-out and the endlessly malleable soft torture of familiar melody. It was charts and arrangements, friends and colleagues, session humour (jazz men are cynical sods). Song was what just happened, what he just happened to be good at. They all said it, of course: he could have been Las Vegas big with a voice like that. A face for the daughters, a voice for the mums. Hip enough for the boyfriends, solid enough for the dads. A singer out of time. An impossible dream.

Song was a moment out of the sun. His own songs, other people's, nights spent in the classiest kind of coma. Well, hey, whatever, wheel it out. Pedal steel? Sure. More strings? Ladle 'em on. Dusty backroads, sunny porches, favourite dogs, Cadillac fins, haystack trysts, rye mash … sure, hey, whatever. What are we doing today? The format is chanson, the feel is backroads Americana, the studio is in Bayswater, Marble Arch. Tomorrow I'll be back in Copenhagen. I wonder what I look like on my passport – it's been a while since I looked.

Song is voices in air. Then it becomes tape, vinyl, TV series, tour: up and down and up and down we go. Up and down the country, up and down the charts. What must it be like, miming words you didn't write, pretending the ecstasy of a perfect guitar solo you didn't ever play? But all that's in the future; right now it's the kiss of life for another standard. Pencil marks on a chart. Professional decorum. None of them what you would call *bad* songs, they just acquire this reputation of being a bit beside the point, a bit peripheral to the main business. But what *is* the main business if not song? Maybe there are no bad songs, only bad versions. In fact, 'The Impossible Dream', which closes side one of a distinctly sideless collection, is one weird bloody lyric when you get down to it. One of those songs like 'My Way' that everyone in the world (Donna Summer, Susan Boyle, Bryn Terfel, Lesley Garrett, The Mormon Tabernacle Choir,

Maria Bethania) has sung, but hardly ever subtly or well. One of those songs that everybody thinks they know but actually only half knows, because it's mostly always been background. One of those songs whose opening fanfare makes you wince; but one of those songs, the more you look at it the odder it gets. What is the impossible, why is it your dream? Who is your own unfightable foe?

Lines like *'To bear with unbearable sorrow/To reach the unreachable star'* can be touching, can take you by surprise if you're in the wrong mood. The song you think you know, the lines you don't remember. *'To love/Pure and chaste from afar ...'*

'Heavenly cause' and *'glorious quest'* and righting *'unrightable wrongs'*: this is the sort of guff a Kennedy and Reagan, a Blair and Obama might quote, with a great big straight face. Disillusion, drama, lost dreams, nostalgia, need. 'To be willing to die so that honour and justice may live ...' Politics as the business of making people believe an impossible dream, all the while knowing it's pure hokum; whereas pop/MOR at its unlikely best is the art of making people *think* they're listening to hokum, while slipping them a taste of some impossible thought or forbidden desire. A music where the secret payoff is 'hidden' right out in the open ...

Scott was an exile. A happy exile, presumably, but an exile all the same. Exile – a ghost in your own life while still alive; a spectre with an assumed name. Procrastination as survival tactic: putting off any identity that is too solid or showy, drawing attention to itself. Merging into the crowd, the mainstream. What you risk is that this reliance on the nowhere-in-particular becomes your terminus. You grow so used to being in-between – enjoying its wave-like lull – and end up scraping by as Citizen X for so long that you wake up one morning and find this is what life has become. Indefinite exile, ghost talk. (The flâneur as angel: Walker *and* Engel.) Exile becomes revenance becomes dematerialisation. You can reappear any time, rematerialise anywhere, under any name. Everywhere begins to look like one more stage set. A TV studio in Oslo. A dressing room in Liverpool. A hotel in – where are we tonight? I don't know where backstage is, any more. A Californian from Ohio. An Englishman in Copenhagen. A German in Batley. A Berliner in Berlin.

Remember that much repeated quote from Wenders's *Kings Of The Road*? 'The Americans have colonised our subconscious.' With Scott it goes the other way: Europe colonises his subconscious. Art-house movies, Penguin Modern Classics, World War Two ruins, the post-*Rite Of Spring* classical repertoire, all in all the ghosts of a certain history. A nineteenth-century man and his twentieth-century songbook.

Something worth noting: the only performances that really don't work in this period are the ones where he tries to sound American. Any songs that mention backroads and tailfins and Kentucky country miles make for a truly awkward fit. (Even odder: he will later claim that the only albums he likes from these fabled lost years are the Country and Western ones, from later on in 1973–74.) It's like he's acting a part he's only just got the script for. It's not that they lack 'heat' – a lot of his songs from this period do, and are none the worse for that, because he's better suited to glacial than hot. It's more an off note inside. He brings an engaging plausibility to certain European clichés he just can't seem to muster for American ones.

So what must it be like some night you're up there singing 'Impossible Dream' or 'Look Of Love' for the nineteenth nervous breakdown time this month and the Valium kicks in and you suddenly have no idea where you are, you know this is the STAGE, but as to what club what street what town or city the club might be in – and all these people here tonight to see and hear you and – who is it they think you are? Who is it you think YOU are right now? You draw an impossible blank. You are now – Colchester? Watford? Wigan? Henley on where? Is this what spies feel like when they lose the thread of who they are, one night or day? No more context, no more plot –

this isn't a mask any longer, this what being me comes down to now. Here I am right out in the open, a picture of whoever it is they think I am. What's my name this month? When we were young we were 'Scotty Engel – the Baritone from Ohio'. Then a Walker Brother: an ersatz twin to a goof-off and a bittersweet golden boy. Then the *Scott* years. And finally reverting back to … Noel Scott Engel. Full circle, Scotty boy, full circle.

The natural-feeling poise of performance – maybe that's what draws them in, the audience, at the end of a long sweaty week: prices going up, kids freaking out, the country gone to the dogs, all the subtractions from already paltry wages. Maybe they like affect-free. Maybe they like neutral, smooth, everything in place and a sense of effortless control, glow and purr and promise. 'Didn't time sound sweet, yesterday?' On this neutral sign-less shore.

Somewhere to hide, out in the open, between stations. Airport bars and cocktail lounges, at home in the middle of nowhere, one more intermediate stage. There is an advanced state of retreat where emotions become almost abstract. Not quite cohering, and never belonging. Time mist, hotel Muzak, the moon on the wrong horizon. Smoke in the morning air.

The middle of the road can be a pretty dangerous place to be.

The virtue of not quite belonging (neither hippy nor establishment, Vegas nor UFO) can shade over into indecision, procrastination, an endlessly suspended vocation. The virtue of not signing up can shade over into failure of nerve. To do what you know it's time to do: a problem with time and ethics. Refuse to join up one too many times and you can wake up all not joined up. And no one can understand what you're saying when you move your thin blue lips. To do what you know you should do in time. Once that slips away – you could be doomed, kid.

So: can we link this up with all his lyrics about the wasted and stunted lives of others? His own songs, and the covers, often seem to circle back to this pervasive mood: '*When I look back on all I've seen/What I've become and might have been …'* At a certain point you can't help but see some of these songs as warnings he's writing out to himself like speeding tickets. Except it's something like the opposite of speeding – being too slow on the uptake, allowing himself to be steered this way and that, too much passive acceptance. Just going where he's pointed. Doing just enough to get by.

Spend some time on YouTube, and read what old fans have to say about songs from the Middle Scott period. Far from being the nadir of critical consensus, for them it's the height of his work. People love this stuff – always did, still do, unapologetically, totally.

These are songs that people associate with the onset of adulthood – falling in and out of love, marriage, family, first nights, life decisions. The real fabric of life – its big disappointments and small rewards. Not so much 'let's spend the night together' as 'let's spend the rest of our lives together'. Popular music is democratic. Elites have no real power. People love or venerate what they will, no matter what the critical consensus says. The history of a certain 'hip' sixties is often written around the lives of a few dozen swinging people in London; but this isn't the whole story. No surprise that more than forty years on, these supposedly banal songs still burn bright for many people, with real grace and mnemonic pull.

There's the idea of Middle Scott as musically largely worthless, or mixed at best. And there's the matter of mythic Scott: the original template for what Peter York once called pop's Neurotic Boy Outsiders. Gloomy solipsism and self-indulgence: self, self, self. The irony being that it is far hipper figures who fit the mould of being genuinely selfish, terminally solipsistic (not to mention casually sexist). Plus, rock was always far more reliant on image than Scott's gently subversive MOR. Under a lot of rock's glamour-as-spell was emptiness, where Scott is oddly anti-glamour. In photos from that time, Scott looks worried rather than smug: a face of distracted circumspection.

No Regrets

As for the supposed solipsism of Scott, it's an interesting exercise to review his songs (from *Scott 1* through *'Til The Band Comes In*) and see how many are sung as, or about, other characters. A wide spectrum of the dispossessed, overlooked, looked down on: old soldiers, single mothers, lonely drag queens, ridiculed eccentrics and loners. Life at a lower volume; a quiet murmur of disappointment, like rain falling on a river. Alone in your room looking out through smeared windows, or isolated in the passing crowd. A sense of listening to voices on the margins, the sadness of other lives, that is glancingly political. Scott's prostitutes, hustlers, transvestites are not lumped together, but dealt with in individually tender portraits, emerging as if from discreet eavesdropping, in and out of time: Duchess, Big Louise, Jean the Machine, Joe, Two Ragged Soldiers.

Not only does he not share the casual sexism of his rock/pop contemporaries, but some of Scott's best songs are sung from a woman's point of view. Put it like this: if there is existentialism and if there are existentialist heroes, then why do they so often appear as spies and assassins and war heroes, and not, say, a single mother or unhappy working girl? Why is the figure of the exile likewise likely to be a writer or politician and not a 'guest worker'? MOR (especially American MOR of a certain era) is often given to a valorisation of the 'good life'. Whereas what Scott's songs ask is something more along the lines of: what is a good life? Scott peoples his songs with a cast of marginal souls out on the 'outskirts of life', dwellers on the threshold of caste, hierarchy, you've never had it so good. The unswinging in pursuit of the ungettable: the unemployed and discarded, the perplexed and pole-axed, old ladies, young strippers, ageing prostitutes, the neglected wives of piggish businessmen. The refuse and refusees of both capitol and capital.

Everything hidden right out in the open.

On *'Til The Band Comes In*, lyrically speaking, he goes further into what's almost an odd little personal code, elliptical, at times hard to fathom. There are moments, indeed whole songs, that are definite pointers to future 'fragmented' lyrics. The joltingly brief 'Cowbells Shakin'', with its impressionistic interior monologue of an exile dreaming of home, could easily slip on to *Climate Of Hunter*. In the middle of the brash and upbeat title song he slips in lines like: 'With my sub-human sound to the ground!' and on 'Little Things (That Keep Us Together)': *I can't wait to see just how high/His eagle on colour screens is gonna fly!*' The more you let them seep into you, the more you realise just how odd some of these songs really are. They weave together child's-eye views of the city, TV news about an unnamed (but Vietnam-echoing) war, gossip and paranoia, in a seamlessly light lyric voice. This is not song as singing telegram, where the lyrics add up to something that could be scribbled down as a cheap motto ('Let's spend the night together'/'All you need is love'/'Imagine no possessions'). If there's a vaguely unifying theme it's not love and the holy couple, but the prison of time, looking back, nostalgia ...

For all that it may have been a gloomy time for him personally, *'Til The Band Comes In* is, if anything, his lightest work: light because adult, and adult because confident enough to be light. (Maybe he just thought he had little to lose: maybe the pills and booze made him light-headedly 'fuck you' about what might conceivably have been his last album for quite a while.) *'Til The Band* has suffered down the years, partly from its reputation as a botch job; and partly from the fact of cowering in the shadow of *Scott 1–4*. But far from falling away from the standard of the *Scott*s, it represents a discreet step sideways, and contains a handful of songs as good as any he ever did, including two or three of my own absolute favourite Scott tracks: 'The War Is Over (Sleepers)', 'Little Things (That Keep Us Together)', 'Joe'.

'The War Is Over (Sleepers)' is simply one of the most beautiful things he ever did, and it's a mystery why it isn't rated higher in the Scott canon. It's one of those songs where everything meshes utterly – lyrics, voice, instruments; an arrangement subtle as breath, full of space and texture – the strings so subtle at times they seem to imply rather than fully intrude; a sublimely evocative guitar line like moisture on window panes in a sleeping city.

> *Everything still, everything silent*
> *As after the rain. We lie here listening*
> *To night close down ...*

This mood is so cloudily sublime, I listened to it for years before I noticed the far stranger second stanza, which may be the closest Scott ever came to some sort of obliquely confessional line concerning his nomadic childhood:

> *Stare like a child*
> *Wait for the signs*
> *To decide once again*
> *Just when they looked here to stay*
> *We're to leave our world, our air.*
> *It really isn't fair ...*

It's so smartly and unfussily written, it could refer to any one of the glazed and weary exiles on the *'Til The Band* suite. Jean from Hungary. The anonymous correspondent from Sun City. The tired and rueful exile in 'Cowbells Shakin'', dreaming of his village thousands of miles away. All the others exiled inside their own memories.

'Til The Band is a kitchen-sink pop opera – each song registering different inhabitants in a London block of flats. It never feels like a sterile 'concept' being bowed to or borne, but has real humanity and pulse. Humour, pathos, sexiness, arrangements that swing from cleverly minimal to audaciously MASSIVE – you can imagine it making a pretty convincing musical. *'Til The Band Comes In*: this is already a great title for a musical, no? Listen to 'Little Things (That Keep Us Together)' and tell me this isn't a potentially great musical number. Such a perfect arrangement! Such a rousing chorus! And

under the beautiful ascending and descending melody lines, you don't initially notice that this sunrise list of 'reasons to be cheerful' turns out to be more like 'reasons to commit suicide'. Once again, you wonder if Scott isn't drifting nearer to his own life than ever before: *'It's on nights like this/That your neighbour dies/He was so alone/He had nothing left/Little things that/Call for a drink...'*

All the time, the unnamed 'war' trundles on, and the young protest and old sicken and a postcard from 'Sun City' arrives, and to cap it all, these weird random lines that shoot out like CS gas canisters: *'We forgive you Spiro Agnew!'*

'While the war's going on ... while the war's going on ...'

This may be the apex of Middle Scott. Everything right out in the open but hardly anyone seems to have noticed. Why? Because it was set not to a twelve-bar blues but to a gorgeous caroming Broadway melody?

Think of the narrator as – well, a washed-up light entertainer, a singer whose 'day job' is nightclub standards; an insomniac who makes international phone calls and slides into gin, a Mister Lonely still pretending he's Mister Cool, but reduced now to trying his chat-up lines on the Speaking Clock lady. A kind of MOR everyman – semi-hip, semi-anaesthetised – fallen on bad times, his last connection with life is projecting biographies on to the other dwellers in his block of flats. He thinks that by empathising with his neighbours he is retrieving some of his humanity, in one last feeble existentialist gesture. Maybe he is really only framing them, in the only way he knows how: in song. Life has *become* song. He can't live, really, outside the sentiments of the songs he sings. Later – *when the band's gone home* – we might get this uneasy feeling that we only have his word for it: we only have his fever-dream version of these lives. So why does he need to make a musical drama out of an everyday crisis?

In the uproariously brash 'Jean The Machine', he's a drummer for a stripper exiled from Hungary, and small-mindedness becomes full-

blown Cold War paranoia when he's lectured by his gossipy landlady
... *'My landlady said: Jean's a Commie spy!/My landlady said: it's a
front/She bumps and grinds codes/To an audience of immigrants!'*
Light entertainment hegemony as a Cold War front – perfect!

Tales from this slightly seedy showbiz world continue in 'Joe' and
'Thank You For Chicago Mr James'. The latter is the familiar one of a
rich promoter and his ingénue, except the ingénue here is a boy not
a girl. The *'young country boy'* is trade, basically, but not dumb trade.
He thanks his older sophisticated patron for *'All the shiny suits/All
the shiny names'*, but has to move on. *'You're an empty place/I'm a
moving frame ...'* It's sung straight (so to speak), with no distancing
quotation marks of any kind. In 'Joe', the elliptical shorthand of the
lyrics is matched by this misty parlour jazz, full of delicate blue echoes. A distinct lightness of touch: the strings so soft, evanescent, you
barely notice they're there, hovering in the background, one more
twilight shade. The piano is almost a definition of savvy lounge playing – just enough colour and twist not to be banal, but never flashy
or clichéd. It's the little things that make all the difference.

'Joe' is an elegy to a lost footsoldier from the trenches of
light entertainment, who seems to have died alone. *'A postcard
from Sun City/Was found laying by your side/A kind of desert
place/Where old folks dry away ...'* What was this – 1970? Was
this the first such mention of Sun City (outside of indigenous circles)
in popular song? A lightness of touch, so airily seductive, indeed,
that – in the web of this gauzy lounge music – you may not notice
how distinctly odd the lyrical shorthand Scott has slipped into is:

> *You've been beyond the boundaries*
> *Understood it all and thought of nothing*
> *The ultimate in simple to your eyes*

The singing is devastatingly subtle. He sings the line *'No one left
alive ...'* (which sets up an echo with other mentions of the war
going on outside the windows) and then inserts a micro-pause,

before continuing the old ghost's story: 'No one left alive/—/To call you Joe.' He contrasts the *'madness and cries'* of youth in the streets with the more detached wisdom of the old guy; which is quite an odd position for a young singer to take at the end of the sixties. (Is this the first protest song of its time to likewise mention meals on wheels?) If 'Joe' is posthumous, gone, a ghost, then the singer is – who, or what? Maybe someone anticipating his own future decline, a kind of errant or angelic double:

> *They say towards the end*
> *You hardly left your shabby room*
> *Where once you loved to go a-walkin'*
> *Through the day ...*

The same mood continues in 'Little Things (That Keep Us Together)'. At first the title seems to be a straight declaration, a classic Broadway-style song – a celebration of the bits of life that make it all worthwhile when all around you is murder and starvation and mayhem. But as it piles misery on misery – all in an upbeat manner – you begin to wonder if this isn't actually a kind of critique. The singer of the song seems to have stepped over the line from seeing jumbo jet crashes and starving children on the news, to seeing everything around him as if through an alienating screen. 'On days like these when your brother dies ...' What IS the point of song if this is all it can do – merely tick things off as if it were a shopping list? Which makes you wonder, once again, about that odd phrase in the title song:

> *Here on the outskirts of life*
> *You know where to find me*
> *Still alive, with my*
> *sub human sound*

Is this how he saw himself in 1970? Not thriving but merely 'still alive'? And not working on perfecting the delicate art of song but mired in 'sub human sound'? Think about that choice of word again: SUB HUMAN. And then back again to 'Little Things':

He put a gun to his head
He was so alone
He had nothing left
Little things that
Call for a drink …

And then to the superficially jokiest track here, 'Time Operator', which has the bored sex symbol, the man famous for his golden looks, this bedroom poster idol, alone at 3:18 in the morning, drunk, flirting with a woman at the end of his phone line. *'But I'm not alone, no/Like all my neighbours say.'* But he *is* alone – so alone he's chatting up the prerecorded Speaking Clock lady. It's kind of a superstar blues, in a way, but done so subtle and self-deprecating and witty that you don't mind; and don't even notice just how bad a hole this guy is in:

The man come to shut off my water
And the man come to shut down
My lights, yesterday.

Has he run out of money – or is he just a helpless baby who can't operate the levers of everyday life, lost inside his star-life narcissism? *'You just picture Paul Newman – and girl, he looks/A lot like me.'* Musically there's far more going on here than you first notice. Icy strings, mixed-in sound effects, a subtly bluesy trumpet rather than the expected guitar, and even a round of smartly deployed percussion. It's like an IDEA of blues or bluesiness – spacey, near abstract, not needing to work up any kind of hairy sweat to prove its blue bona fides, and all the more convincing for that. At 3'21" it ends as it began, randomly, falling into a slow fade like its subject, just one more inconclusive link in the chain of wasted lives …

How was all this missed? Did people just look at the grinning

Scott on the cover and take in the standards tacked on the end of side two and take other people's word for it that this was just Scott singing on the meter, so to speak? An awkward fit, maybe – it didn't really fit any particular milieu or scene of the time. It wasn't rock. It wasn't straight MOR. It wasn't earnest folk protest or softly sensitive singer/songwriter or overtly maudlin balladeer. It has the sheer ease and economy and space of jazz. It has the balls of classic show tunes. It has the anger of protest. It has the unassuming cleverness of a Sondheim. Maybe that's the problem – how much it jumps around. Even this makes a kind of sense: each song is set up to reflect a different person, a different life, a different nationality, even a different era. As if each character had their own signature sound or riff or melody. Thus 'Jean' gets an outrageously upfront honky-tonk vamp, shading into sheer bump 'n' grind – like her life itself, starting out arty and young and vivid and hopeful and then settling for ground-down cliché. 'Joe' gets an old-guy saloon song treatment. 'Little Things' is arranged precisely how a show tune about celebrating life against the odds would be.

There's a danger of over-quoting lyrics and making *'Til The Band* sound like a sterile conceptual diagram; for one thing, all the evidence suggests it was pretty hurriedly bundled together. Which makes it all the more remarkable, both for the breadth of its concerns and for how composed and in control Scott seems – again, note, for a man who by his own account was less than fully engaged with his work at this point; or permanently drunk; or suicidally depressed; or all three.

Take 'Time Operator': on one level it's a kind of send-up of the Scott persona, but you have to hear how Walker sings it – half send-up, but so finely judged there are traces of immanent heartbreak inside the laughter. Like: this could be the prelude to terminal self-delusion, flirting to stop from screaming, and all this dead-hours goofing-off or half-cut seduction is because he can't do anything else, has lost the ability to connect to real people, has become a cliché and despises the cliché and fears the real loneliness behind it; finds no release or relief in his song any more, doesn't believe in his art any more, and knows full well that situations like this only get darker. What is really being flirted with here? (Who is the ultimate Time Operator if not death?) You started out thinking it was killingly ironic fun flirting with this image of yourself as some kind of Howard Hughes figure … but you forgot the punchline: even Howard Hughes can't buy off time. Take away the intravenous codeine and hotel tombs and zombie helpers and Swiss account gazillions and *'girl, he looks a lot like me …'* Until eventually the phone call won't be to the Speaking Clock but the Samaritans when he's swallowed a few too many Valium, how many, hell, who knows, I lost count a ways back, lady … My name? I think my name is Joe … or it was once upon a time … yeah, just call me Joe …

When people say *'Til The Band* is let down by its 'other side', they're often just repeating received wisdom. Such criticism reveals once again the old rock snobbery that only self-penned tracks qualify for the real prizes. Why, it's almost like he were a CHICK singer or something! Well, for those of us who have no problem with 'chick' singers and Bacharach/David and light entertainment, this isn't such a big deal-breaker. And if MOR is the 'weepie' of contemporary music – a condescended-to idiom, a melodramatic sob too far – it treats many of the same themes. I think of how McKenzie Wark puts it in a book about the Situationists: 'On the subject of love, bourgeois novels are variations on two themes. The first is the couple in love getting together despite all obstacles; the second is how unhappily they live ever after.'[6]

Take 'What Are You Doing (The Rest Of Your Life)' – one of the scorned tracks from the supposed 'bad half' of *'Til The Band.* The song sets out, following the convention of such things, full of hope: *'I have only one request of your life: that you spend it all with me …'* Piano acts as breath-trace punctuation, there's a feeling of suspension and weightlessness, strings that feel both glacial and comforting. And then things slowly go blue and anxious and querulous with the thought of all *'those tomorrows waiting deep in your eyes ...'* Superficially the lyric appears to be just another string of lazy Tin Pan Alley clichés; but this romance feels too needful, almost a hallucination:

> *I want to see your face in every kind of light*
> *In fields of dawn, and forests of the night ...*

Like all the best torch songs, it navigates the tricky line between living warmth and deathly chill. Contra rock's cultish stress on 'meaningful' statement, this is all about temperature, tone, mood. Chilly distance may be preferred to immanent warmth. The lush musical swoon makes emotional distance incarnate, seductive, and the string arrangement leaves us completely up in the air: left waiting for a resolution which looks unlikely to arrive. Which reminds me of something Fassbinder said he learned from Douglas Sirk (the German film maker exiled in Hollywood, who crafted the fifties/sixties 'weepie' into a form of transcendentally classy auto-critique): 'You don't believe the happy ending – and you're not meant to.'

Am I projecting too much on to mere makeweight songs? Or isn't that the whole point and glory of such songs? That being slight or fluffy is no barrier to smuggling themselves illegally into places within our listening hearts? You could argue that the rock cult of 'hidden meaning' sets up its own occlusion. Whether it's classic Dylan or Prog rock or even, let's face it, *The Drift* and large parts of *Tilt* – once you've worked out the crossword clues ... that's that. Message received. The thrill of exposing something for yourself, finding something surprising in the sonic shadows you had no reason to suspect would be there, is barred for the listener. The supposed liberation of 'doing it exactly your way' in the avant-ish route Scott has lately taken – is it really a liberation for us all, or just for him? It certainly liberates Scott from being a slave to the prerogatives and demands of anyone else whatsoever. I'm not arguing outright for MOR froth over murky Lieder. But, as a proper listen to *'Til The Band* proves, this other MOR-ish tradition can open on to a dizzyingly odd space, where the simplest word or phrase or clichéd declaration can end up freighted with impossible richness and ambiguity.

For God's sake: what are you DOING with the rest of your life?

A lot of his own songs on *Scott 1–4* and *'Til The Band* are London-birthed and shaped, and a London that was already halfway disappeared or supplanted – a London out of Patrick Hamilton and Betjeman, with TS Eliot's 'yellow fog' and stiff little bowler-hatted men returning home to paltry meals and too much sherry and port and gin. Graham Greene captures the feeling very well: 'There seemed to be a seediness about the place you couldn't get to the same extent elsewhere, and seediness has a very deep appeal: even the seediness of civilisation. Of the sky-signs in Leicester Square, the "tarts" in Bond Street, the smell of cooking greens of Tottenham Court Road [...] It seems to satisfy, temporarily, the sense of nostalgia for something lost.'[7]

London, and parts of Europe, seemed to satisfy a yearning in Scott for something with a solid past – seedy, sad, faded, but a past all the same – where America maybe represented butle, change, impermanence. Instead of a big twenty-four-hour buffet breakfast with twenty different items to choose from, one sad lonely fried egg on your chipped plate at seven on a Friday morning. It's an odd tone, and quite an unsettling one – as though the singer has a deep and unhappy nostalgia but doesn't know precisely what for. Knowing you had a home, once, but no longer having any idea where (or when) it might have been.

Something about England called to him – at times, bizarrely so. Scott always seems far more at home in songs about English streets or fields than he does trying to be a cowpoke or midnight cowboy in songs set back home in the USA. And this doesn't just mean London-set songs. In 1971, between *'Til The Band* and *The Moviegoer*, there was his one attempt at something vaguely like a hit 45 – 'I Still See You', a version of the theme song from *The Go-Between*, the 1970 film adapted by Harold Pinter (for another US exile, Joseph Losey) from the LP Hartley novel which bequeathed us that much mis-applied line, 'the past is a different country'. More English than this you could not get.

The problem with the film is that it makes too concrete (in place and time) what is best viewed and experienced as a far more figurative landscape – precisely that 'different country' which is memory, whether common and worth celebrating or more deeply individual and untrustworthy. The paradox of the film is that, in needing to serve up an actual image of that lost England – of tea and croquet on the lawn, ladies with parasols, happy peasants in the fields – it loses the deeper charge or twist it should have brought to the tale. It feels inert, half-thought-through, over-reliant on the very mechanisms it ought to be undermining. You can see why Scott might be drawn here, though: this deeply melancholy piece about lost time, regret, looking back, being stuck in time, lost youth.

> *When I look back on all I've seen*
> *What I've become, and might have been ...*

You can see why he might be drawn – but also, you could say it's an odd thing for a happening young pop star to be putting out as a single in 1971. It's a far older man's song to sing. It's also something of a lost gem: Scott takes it straight, doesn't give in to any temptation to over-emote, and it emerges as genuinely heartbreaking – in a way that the film just isn't. (You can't help but wonder if the cerebral Pinter just couldn't see it through to the end, whereas at this moment in his life, interestingly, Scott could.) The opening strings are like lonely ghosts in sunlight. The contrast is almost literal between the light of life and the shades of memory.

*

Exile can be awakening illumination, or psychic sleepwalk through a stalled and frozen time. There are some holding manoeuvres it can be a real pleasure to lose yourself inside – and almost without your noticing, exile becomes your fallback style. A certain way of doing things, making connections, avoiding things you don't want to know. Everything you do begins to have the taint of a delaying tactic. You engage, but never fully. You don't quite belong anywhere any more – to this or that genre, this or that community or country. Except the community of exiles, obviously: the set without a set of homeless citizens.

Exile: I will sort the deep stuff out later, somewhere down the line. My true vocation, my true style? Later for that shit, there's plenty of time, I'm still in my twenties, after all. In the meantime, I will do whatever is asked of me. Merrily roll along. Tick off the projects. Roll with the punches. Merge with the scenery. Be a good employee and citizen. Do things the way they do here. Dot my I, and eat my 'tea'. Wait for the signature on the document. Confound by complying.

'Here on the outskirts of life ... you know where to find me.'

It took me for ever to see, but that line could be key. Think about it. Your marginality becomes who you are. What should be beyond the pale becomes your role, your persona. Like an existentialist joke: you know where to find me – out among the lost. It is actually another way of obeying convention. People know where to find you: you will be out there on the perimeter, doodling, delaying, playing at being an important influence. The studied neutrality of ticking over – recording sessions, charts, bottles of scotch – becomes what everyone expects. Songs where you don't have to worry – most of the real work has already been done. The words so polished, you can see your hangover in them. Every sickness has a routine. Even procrastination. Studio, photo session, tour bus, appearance, escapes to Europe: delaying tactics.

A missed-out-on childhood means an implied future you've never come to terms with. Because you never had a real home, you never had a sense of somewhere to return to, start counting down from – to measure the approach of death against. Is that far-fetched? For a moment you seemed to fully occupy time – you and your name were everywhere. And then you unveil the *full name* in all its awkward glory and what happens? CRASH. What sort of deep-down hurt does that occasion? So you recede again, 'til … the band comes in. Even the part that's you, your songs, you get someone else to co-sign. The new manager, the latest one. Like a guarantor: look I'm a serious guy, I'm playing by the rules!

'Til the black band comes in: until time comes up with something that really can't be ignored. One day you're told you have to go back into operation and wonder if you know how any longer. Another anonymous dressing room, another backstage at another club, another town or city or country. I think we're … somewhere, uh, North tonight. Singing live, all those eyes seem to detach themselves and float up and crawl all over your arms and legs. Who am I today? When I open my mouth to sing, who appears? Who disappears? And which of the two are the pills and booze for? And all these different names, flickering off and on … which passport did you use this month? What does it say on your passport, anyway? Let me guess. Singer of other people's words? Fixer? Profession: reporter?

RETIRED. That's what you want it should say.

His extended crack-up produces the smoothest music in the world. Easy-on-the-ear melodies that feel distinctly icy, with a weight of compacted absence, sadness, wasted time. Flawless like cheap glassware – pretty songs with no real prettiness. Light entertainment that lets no light escape.

The irony here being that the lost years of Middle Scott – when he had the nervous breakdown, maybe thought each and every morning about suicide; when he was yo-yo-ing ups and downs and taking two bottles of vodka into the recording studio – all this produced his stillest and sanest-sounding music. Later, sanity restored, and fully reconciled to who he is and exactly what kind of audience he wants or doesn't want, he will produce music that teeters on the edge of complete and almost caricatural horror. The only question being: which do you find more believable? Which more true to life? There are dozens of avant pop acts, who strive, with ever more self-defeatingly clever conceits, to produce half the weirdness Scott managed here, without a thought in his head. Weary, sozzled, at a loose end, thinking no further ahead than the next bank statement, the next standard, the next bottle. This plastic-flower entombed affect. Vodka blue and voluptuity.

Which just confirms that you can't *intend* a 'haunted' work, can't sit down and pick and choose and shape and fashion something cleverly 'haunted'. You can only hope to be surprised, years later, by something you didn't even suspect was there at the time. (In your own work or that of others.) What you thought was a winning and winsome smile now appears a horrifying mask. Cocktail piano, dotted Is and crossed Ts, the right material, shirt pressed: and it turns out to have been a death rattle all along.

Bearing all that in mind, isn't it possible to see the previously maligned Middle Scott as something like the MOR equivalent of side two of Bowie's *Low*? Doesn't this make more sense, the more carefully one inspects the context? The sound of a nervous breakdown isn't always going to be flailing and screaming and dark poetry – which is a real misconception. The sound of true depression is not deep dark intensity and shiver, it is four-in-the-morning TV static. True depression is blankness, complete loss of energy and libido, inertia, going through the motions, inch by inch. With real depression, not only do you not feel extremes, you worry about feeling anything whatsoever. That's the killer – the fact that you seem to have lost the ability to feel even the basic plot lines of life.

This was what first drew me to the idea of the torch song years ago: the idea that the softest song in the world might also harbour the harshest truths. The rock culture idea of noise, leather jackets, shouting, boys making a big noise, and the equation of this rather staid convention as the more 'authentic' and 'risky' and subculturally wild option was ridiculous, something we should all have grown out of long ago. The 'last gang in town', indeed! And yet here we are thirty years on, and there is still the idea abroad that certain types of music (drone, noise, horrorcore rap, whatever) are somehow riskier than others.

How can something jar us, that is nothing but jar? Doesn't unrelieved darkness become as easy as any other unrelieved diet? A darker Muzak that ultimately creeps too far into a tidy corner, with a large element of control freakery at work, every last detail ticked off, taken care of … sealed. No hope of some slow unfolding illuminating shock. Can much of the avant-garde really shock us any longer? Especially now, when most avant-garde performers have a diary full of global institutional commissions? Don't we know exactly what to expect of the aesthetic of a great percentage of the avant-garde? After a certain point don't we get exactly what we came for? Old bruises from a century ago, like so many Penny Blacks and upside down airplanes. The shock all upfront in the concept, the programme note, the nostalgia for a time when it really MEANT something, when the politics of it put the performer in real peril.

If someone produced a lot of Scott's middle-period music now (like one of those conceptual art events at which 'classic' or infamous gigs are recreated), people would be falling over themselves to laud its 'haunted' quality. This is now a permissible – maybe even an obligatory – reading. But originally, Scott was maybe recreating something that didn't exist in the first place. Improvising an absence. Hold it up to the light. See?

Who is this, you think, actually singing? Who sings when your real 'I' isn't singing? With Middle Scott, you think: this is the sound of someone impersonating a quieter self in order to disguise something he doesn't want us all to know. In a way, Middle Scott is far harder to know than Late Scott. Which makes one wonder about the relative values we think we have invested in this stuff. Cheap sentiment versus grand project. The supposed emptiness or emotional absence at the heart of a lot of MOR can be shocking in ways you just don't expect. It carries odd messages you weren't expecting, and it reaches right down and tears your heart out. And this is one reason why such songs become prized mnemonics for people, markers of times past, little capsules of concentrated essence. They were already deeply compressed, these songs, almost a form of dispossession: eerie, precise, low on flourishes. A kind of erasure or exorcism of all traces of self-identity and self-expression. Realm of pure song. There is no identity here, only a voice. The expected quality of yearning taken and abstracted, frozen into a song like a maze where the way out is all too clear; this kind of half-slovenly inertia that produces a undeniably erotic effect. The sound of sinking so far inside your own mood you come out the other side: Muzak through the stained looking-glass. Standards which are usually posed like the sonic equivalent of a lover's rose, instead arranged like a hyper-realist portrait of a plastic flower arrangement: light entertainment as Pop Art.

Of course Middle Scott is all surface; but as we well know, surface can become quite fugue-like with the right degree of concentration. This is the entire basis of the secrets of spell-casting and invocation.

Why the moviegoer? One answer might be: what do you do when you're young and alone and at a loose end in a foreign city? Scott said at this time he was going to the cinema up to four times a day. It becomes a form of waking fugue. Round and round. Double bill. Interval. Bar. Double bill. A face in the faceless crowd. Flâneur, barhopper, anti-cineaste: the moviegoer has no principles of taste or selection or prejudice. Melodrama, comic strip, porno, thriller, Spaghetti Western, whatever. Alain Delon in *Borsalino*? Perfect! As it happens, at this point in the early seventies, great actors like Scott's on/off doppelgänger Paul Newman were, as the story goes with Scott, losing themselves in slick and compromised work. Maybe Scott felt attracted to it for this reason. Or maybe it was just one more mental anaesthetic.

Let's face it – nobody needs to see something like *Le Mans* ever again, do they? Hang on, that's not Paul Newman, that's Steve McQueen. Didn't Paul Newman do one too, though? A big four-hour film where he's racing cars? Yeah, well, whatever. They all merge after a while. The strange thing is, although this may be the dodgiest film in a pretty ropey selection, it turns out to make for one of the best songs. 'A Face In The Crowd' (theme song from *Le Mans*), which opens side two of *The Moviegoer*, is one of the best things here. Another little minor-key gem.

It opens in this odd semi-ambient space – the distant sound of cars, going round in circles, which fades imperceptibly into a surprising and notably dissonant orchestration, this big slow verging-on-Penderecki off-note. This glacial intro lingers for a full thirty-five seconds before ebbing into the lush and more conventional orchestral swell you would expect. If it all seems way too elaborately ominous for the lyric up ahead, the song itself is odd in its own way, too. It starts out regular enough, but then you realise that far from going for the expected route of the rugged existentialist hero out on his own, daring and resolute on the tracks, it takes the watching spectators (and waiting girlfriend) for its central figure(s). *'We're each of us a face in the crowd ...'*

But if there is undertow or subtext here it's mainly provided by that schizo arrangement, which is the really interesting aspect. And as it began so it ends: Scott signs off with this would-be upbeat line – *'Together we can try ...'* – but as he repeats it, in comes that creepy off-note again with its off-putting dissonance. We've come round in a circle like the drivers. And the off-note has the pronounced effect of making you doubt the lyric's sentimental conclusion. Like Fassbinder said: you don't believe the happy ending and you're not meant to. The song invites thoughts of marriage and settling down, but the dissonant note signals: *only bad things up ahead*. An awful car crash perhaps – or, what's maybe worse, no dramatic turns at all, just the drip drip drip of life as it is lived off the heroic track: more routine, more routine failure, more loneliness up ahead, down in the pits rather than up in flames. 'Moving along through the miles and miles of yesterday.' And the long boring Autobahn of tomorrow.

The first three songs on side one – even I can't find much to scare up here, I'm afraid. But the Lalo Schifrin/Norman Gimbel 'That Night' (from *The Fox* – no, me neither, but apparently it was based on DH Lawrence) uses the same formal device as 'Face In The Crowd'. It opens with a long-drawn-out, near-dissonant intro, like a Mantovani version of Penderecki or Boulez. Pastoral setting, lounge piano; and as Scott sings the comforting closing line *'on that hill, on that night ...'* the music slips back into the same creepy anxious-making tone that it kicked off with. Very odd, and truly unsettling – as if any promise prompted by the boggy lyrics and pastoral strings and smooth piano is being put inside clammy quotation marks; again, it feels like you're not meant to believe the happy ending.

'Come Saturday Morning' (from the 1969 Liza Minnelli vehicle *Pookie*) is borderline cornball, but it's a finely judged (border) line. If you listen just a few times, I swear you will end up humming the main theme: *'Saturday morning, I'm going away with my friend ...'* There's something about this that is – I don't know, again you don't quite buy it. There's something troubling about the use of that word 'friend' ... or maybe I'm just a sick individual who likes to see looming fall where there's only harmless American pastoral. Something to note here is that Scott is far more convincing singing as a neurotic girl than he ever manages to be as a macho roustabout.

A lot of these films are middle of the middle of the mainstream

– the selection seems to have been done with a 1972 young married couple's night-out in mind. 'The Summer Knows' (from yuck-fest *The Summer Of 42*) again kicks off with a lovely orchestration – no unexpected dissonance this time, but not mere schmaltz either, and it repeats the intro-outro loop; no off-note but just melancholy enough to suggest something not altogether comforting about the imminent *'last embrace'*. At a stretch you could say it's all about youth running out, the transience of happy times. We'll probably never know if it was a deliberate choice, but many of these songs are sung from this jaded, backwards-looking, regretful perspective. Scott was still relatively young and golden, yet the predominant tone tends towards: here we are, autumn is curling to its frail end again, and I don't think there's much to look forward to up ahead, do you? There's this settling of accounts thing going on, over and over. Some of this can be put down to the characters in the films and the song-writers themselves being middle-aged; but it still seems notably odd for such a young singer, at the start of a long career. On *'Til The Band Comes In* he'd already leaned in this direction with 'Hills Of Yesterday' (from Sean Connery vehicle *The Molly Maguires*):

> *Once we strolled the hills of yesterday*
> *We were young in those hills far away*
> *You and I once shared a dream*
> *So long ago ...*

Scott – what *'so long ago'*? You were still only twenty-eight! Even songs about starting out on life's long road seem to be tinged with this fatalism, this jumpy, unsettled, melancholy cast of mind. *'The miles and miles of yesterday ...'* You think of a character like Paul Newman's eponymous anti-hero in *Hud*: outwardly young and sexy, but, in his soul, one step from the grave. What was once the open range is now the end of the line. A certain confused, elegiac masculinity figures here – which would soon be the predominant post-Vietnam/Watergate tone of a lot of the best American films of the

1970s: *The Conversation, Junior Bonner, The Parallax View, Night Moves, The Long Goodbye. The Moviegoer* is right on the cusp of this time. All the old tough-guy roles – cowboy, spy, reporter, soldier, private eye – are seen not as paragons of spunky autonomy, but forms of deluded self-reliance; would-be tough guys who identify with their role to the point of obsessive aridity, lockstep, even death. Nothing so slender as a best gal's love will be enough to redeem these damaged, myopic wraiths. The melody in the air is one of lost time – and that lost time can never be redeemed. You can't stay 'Junior' your whole life through.

You could even say: the mythic figure who once might have been cowboy, spy, reporter, soldier, private eye, etc, is now pop singer, moviegoer, critic. (On the original cover of *The Moviegoer*, Scott sports a singularly ill-judged choice of soft white cowboy hat. Make of this what you will.) It's a point John Lahr made elsewhere, about America's shift from knockabout physical comedy, to the jousting verbal neurosis of Lenny Bruce, Woody Allen and others.[8] The end of the line for the American frontier ego – not just the big guy on his big horse, but everybody around him. Vietnam was a failure that couldn't be admitted upfront and in plain terms – only in codified ways inside the culture. If Scott had stuck to songs that reflected this – even in very coy or opaque terms, then *The Moviegoer* might be held in higher critical esteem. As it is – even someone who loves some of it (as I do) has to admit it doesn't really hang together as a whole. Unless you want to argue that a collection spanning songs from both a Mary Queen of Scots biopic and a Le Mans semi-documentary accurately reflects the state of mainstream cinema at the start of the 1970s. Which, actually, it does. To call some of these films forgettable is being kind. I have a huge capacity for this sort of rubbish – but even the ones I remember, I don't remember that well. (Without looking them up I couldn't remember the Steve McQueen ones from the Paul Newman ones. And I get paid to remember stuff like that.)

Besides the strain of melancholy and retrospection and failure of will, the other thematic strain on *The Moviegoer* is what could loosely be called a political one. This is an aspect of *The Moviegoer* that's been overlooked. There's 'Joe Hill' (from *The Ballad Of Joe Hill*), about the US Labour organiser and member of the Wobblies who was controversially executed in 1915; there's 'Ballad Of Sacco And Vanzetti' (from Italian docudrama *Sacco E Vanzetti*) about the two Italian-American anarchists who were also executed in 1927; and, though this might be stretching things in the general direction of special pleading, there's also 'Easy Come Easy Go' from Depression-era drama *They Shoot Horses, Don't They?* OK, it's not explicitly political, but it's not exactly the ultimate feelgood date movie, either. We might at a further stretch include 'Loss Of Love' from the Vittorio de Sica film *Sunflower* – which is set in the Russian front during World War Two, and was apparently the first Western film to be shot in Russia. This leaves a pair of adaptations of great authors into rather humdrum films: 'Glory Road' comes from *W.U.S.A.* – a wan, Paul Newman-starring version of Robert Stone's brilliant novel *A Hall Of Mirrors*; and 'All His Children' is from the adaptation of Ken Kesey's *Sometimes A Great Notion* (retitled *Never Give An Inch*), directed by and (again) starring Paul Newman.

The best of these putatively 'political' nods is 'Ballad Of Sacco And Vanzetti' (written by Joan Baez & Ennio Morricone), which joins the growing ranks of lost gems. Musically, it's really rather splendid. Church bells peal and a revolutionary band starts up and it commences with forty-five seconds of gorgeous strings. If the spirit of Greene-land circa *The Power And The Glory* could be reconjured as South American pop, it might sound like this. It kept reminding me of something and then I got it – 'The Old Man's Back Again' off *Scott 4*, already one of my favourite Scott songs. It has an equally finely judged vocal, rather than the radical kitsch one might have feared.

Musically, 'Joe Hill' isn't in the same league, unfortunately; and you have to wonder why he even thought about attempting Neil

Diamond's 'Glory Road'. Diamond's imprint feels all over the song – at times you imagine you can hear how Diamond would have sung it, under Scott's half-hearted recitation. It's a misfire – one of those quasi-Country songs Scott seems to have a fatal liking for, all this stuff about backroads and pickups and Kentucky dawns that suits Scott like, oh, I dunno, Chet Baker singing The Archies' 'Sugar Sugar'.[9] The other big mistake here is 'Speak Softly Love' (otherwise known as the theme from *The Godfather*, and far more haunting without its yucky lyric), complete with ersatz Italian stylings. What strikes you about these misfires is how it's only when Scott tries to anchor his singing 'I' in real nationality that it falls truly flat. He's far more at home in some abstract or figurative locale. It's a mystery why a certain sort of pastoral English melancholy suits him so well, where anything explicitly American feels so empty and fake. (Other offenders include 'My Way Home', the B-side to 'I Still See You'; and 'Reuben James' on *'Til The Band*. Both feel forced, but the latter is more cringe-making, the moment when Scott actually gets all the way through the line about *a no-count coloured man* a particular low point.)

One thing about Middle Scott is that any time a pedal steel rears its head you should head for the nearest door. Country and Western is the one idiom he sounds utterly wrong in, and not in some interesting or uncanny way. OK – it's only interesting inasmuch as the one musical idiom he sounds plain wrong in is the True Bluest American one. On the one hand it seems an odd choice for the Nixon era; on the other, you have to admit there was a lot of interesting stuff happening in Country at that time (Mickey Newbury, Gram Parsons, Willie Nelson, et al). But as for any comment on the State of the Union, things worked out far better when approached obliquely.

> *He was stalling his plans, for he had none...*
> *The Wall seemed a perfect symbol for his state of mind.*
> Derek Marlowe, *A Dandy In Aspic* (1966)

What was going on here, then? We'll probably never know. Scott never was big on biography, on confession, on 'feelings'. (The one thing that Middle Scott and Late Scott have in common: the singer-songwriter's 'I' scoured from the text. All horizon, no core.) Is there any point in trying to fill in the psychological details of his lost time? Instead, imagine an entirely different story. Imagine another world – in which, say, these three Middle Scott records were all there was. This impossibly handsome boy child, who arrives, records a TV series (now wiped) and this handful of odd records, and then disappears like a Cambridge spy, wind whistling through the trees by the Thames or Unter den Linden ...

Imagine hints and rumours: he was a spy posing as a cocktail lounge pianist and then a minor pop star. International receptions, the diplomacy crowd, the embassy circuit. He was a pianist and a spy. Couldn't make up his mind. Blew his cover. Was never meant to go hit-parade popular like that. THE SPY WHO WENT INTO THE CHARTS. Had to back out, wind back down into anonymity. So deep undercover he could no longer tell the difference. The songs only seem to be meaning-free, in an MOR limbo. Look, listen closer. It's all about the Cold War, espionage, realpolitik. The impossible dream. The war going on. Missing bodies, ruined lives – like some casualty who's stumbled out of Robert Stone, Thomas McGuane, Rudy Wurlitzer. Or Derek Marlowe's odd, ultra-hip, Nabokov-lite masterpiece *A Dandy In Aspic*. Played by Donald Sutherland or Elliott Gould – or Paul Newman. Imagine him as a character out of mid-period DeLillo or Didion. A lounge singer who becomes caught up in some murky geopolitical web. One minute he's behind his piano in a posh New York or Miami hotel, starting to give off a sour vibe of washed-up, directionless, here for ever more (think Jeff Bridges in *The Fabulous Baker Boys*). The next he's standing by unable to intervene as someone is tortured – an illustration of a certain human capacity or failing you might sum up in the phrase: 'I would describe myself as neutral'. And all the trouble this can maybe bring to you over the course of a life. And the amends you eventually make. Watching as trains go by at the wrong time of night. Shutting your ears to the bad news, getting worse by the day.

I repeat: I have nothing to tell you: I've told you all I know. I just do show tunes, theme songs. I don't know why, but I think maybe you think I'm somebody else. I'm more and more convinced of this.

Hop, skip and jump to 1973.

Strictly speaking, this is outside the remit of this essay, but let's allow ourselves some leeway. It's still under the legend of his supposed lost years. The track, from 1973's *Any Day Now*, is a cover of Caetano Veloso's 'Maria Bethania'. And the first time you hear it you can't quite believe that he's actually doing what he appears to be doing. The first few times you reel back in horror and confusion, not quite believing he's singing this lovely song in – what? This weird cod-Caribbean/South American accent? Really? And then towards the end he takes it a stage further, does this bizarre – would you call it scat singing? It sounds like Peter Sellers doing South American Chinese. But then, I have to admit that after a while I found myself humming along with it and going back to play it again and again. Against impossible odds of bad taste and fudge and shame, it somehow works. The arrangement, it has to be said, is rather nice. As to how much this has to do with the inherent qualities of Caetano Veloso's song, or something specific to Scott's very personal take on it – who knows. Anyway, the song itself is a fascinating choice.

'Everybody knows that our cities/Were built to be destroyed!'

The song was contemporaneous – from Veloso's self-titled 1971 album, written and recorded during his own exile in London. I was going to say 'self imposed', but that's not really accurate. He may finally have made the choice to go abroad and live somewhere else than Brazil, but it wasn't exactly something he just decided to do one day, on a whim. I wonder if they met? Veloso's Wikipedia entry says: 'Two of his favourite philosophers were Heidegger and Jean-Paul Sartre'. Maria Bethania was his sister, and also a popular Brazilian singer.

'Maria Bethania, please send me a letter/I wish to know things are getting better.' Migration and homesickness. Dictatorships, hegemony, repression. I don't want to tarry here too long, but who can resist a quick meditation on twentieth-century exile?

The Chilean film maker (and political exile) Raúl Ruiz said that exile makes you feel like 'a stranger everywhere'. You can see how this could be sapping, wearying – having to start each day fresh again. But also how it might be attractive, as a way to live, for some people, when still young. An impossible dream. A certain way of dealing with uncertain times, both offhand and studied. Oblique, like a telegram between friends or lovers. The way in which ordinary language falls out of the mouth of an exile.

Ruiz: 'But sooner or later you have to accept this situation where you will never be back in your home ... so to react you have to invent fictions ... where in fact you don't have a home – the idea of home doesn't exist.'

Hop, skip and jump-cut thirty-odd years – to a scene from another movie. Here's Caetano Veloso sitting poolside, poised nicely between nature and culture, between a fascist past and a neo-liberal for ever more. A song like breeze through leaves, barely there. A song that comes as close to my perfect song as any ever recorded. Another soundtrack, another moviegoer song: 'Cucurrucucu Paloma', stuck in the middle of Pedro Almodóvar's *Talk To Her*. Like wind through leaves, barely there.

Somewhere among all these scattered interstices and map refs and code words is a song I always dreamed of: softer than fleece, harder than granite. Both utterly open, the easiest purr or curlicue in the world, but also tectonic, world-shifting. (Scott, yes, but also Tim Hardin, Chet Baker, Nilsson, Tropicalismo, 'The Girl From Ipanema', Arto Lindsay, Stevie Wonder, Serge Gainsbourg, Lee

Hazlewood, Mickey Newbury, Jim Webb, Dr Buzzard's ... Let's stop there before we find we can't.)

Almodóvar himself knows more than a little about the masks and role playing – the putting on and taking off – of identity and sexuality, and how to smuggle radical otherness into debased and denigrated idioms. The weepie. The woman's pic. The melodrama. Can you keep the past as a form of treasure while living entirely for the now? Can you mourn and love at the same time? Love someone in a coma? Love yourself in a form of coma?

Regardless of economic climate or cultural jump, one business never seems to stop booming: nostalgia. More and more people want to travel back to the music of their youth. The lines demarcating fake from real are increasingly hard to fathom.

Nostalgia may be the second oldest business in history. Once it was golden, once we were halcyon. Once the days were, the nights too. Nostalgia: a constant looking back, a vague feeling that once there was a home, it felt safe, it felt good. No opposing viewpoints, no COMMENTS box. Nostalgia for a once golden time. A knowing again what we once knew, but lazily or rapturously forgot. The non-addictive soma, the ever-sparkling dew. The tree without poison or season. The air yet to be named, or missed.

From 'nostos': concerning a return home and/or survival. Homesick. HOME-sick. A wistful or excessively sentimental, sometimes abnormal, yearning for some past period or irrecoverable condition.

The home you finally return to may be the place of safety – but here is its double edge, both its lure and its disappointment. You are safe there, but may lose your edge. What's so bad about sentimental anyhow? Why the big proscription against sentiment? 'Marked or governed by feeling rather than reason or thought.' By which definition you could say that fascist supporters and mad loners and extreme right nut-jobs throughout history have been 'sentimental'. A politics of poisonous reaction rather than reasoning things out, with actual facts, and logic, and clarity; mist of wish and make believe rather than facing up to adult reality.

On the other hand, what's wrong with a wash of sentiment now and then? Don't you ever get tipsy and play records from long ago, perhaps your own youth? If you don't, you're very much the exception that proves the rule. If we were reason and thought all the time how would that be? How would we feel, in the morning?

Maybe we're all homesick to some degree. Maybe that's it.

A lovely YouTube clip from 1972: Scott tastefully low key on some edgelessly international pop slot. Could be any one of a dozen countries.

The song is 'Loss Of Love (Theme From Sunflower)' from *The Moviegoer*.

The set is full of groovy people, jet-set movers and swingers. Hip but not hippy: tasteful, tomorrow's people today. Scott sports a cool suit, not buttoned right up like older crooners. No cravat like some younger swingers. Classic crisp white shirt. Could still just about wear the same entire ensemble today and not look out of time. Scott croons desolate words without sounding or looking at all desolate. His voice is like a warm autumn breeze – warm, rather than icy or broken. He looks neither young nor old, happy nor haunted. *'I see only shattered skies/Not a ray of light to find ...'* You can watch it a dozen times and not really register those words. This odd MOR poetry – like the set, like the audience, like Scott himself: no stress, no edges, no real identifying marks. The song ends with a minimal but telling movement from Scott: he raises his arms skyward then slowly down. He could be acknowledging a Pope or drunkenly drawing down a blind. He is compellingly un-animated. A still point. He could be the unhappiest, drunkest man in Europe – but he looks like a perfectly Scandinavian picture of health.

'Sunlight blinds my mind ...' Afterwards, you remember the song, if at all, as a ripple, a rustle, light falling through trees on a

happy afternoon. General mood, rather than specific detail: love, loss, sunflower, bump, log, who knows. *'Sunlight blinds my mind …'* Shrug. Forgotten. Who knows. The words a kind of light entertainment Esperanto. *'Sunlight blinds my mind …'* Song and lyrics merge and lose definition and become pure sign. Nature. Love. Weather. The banality of code. I believe today should turn out bright again. The specialist you want is just round the corner. Do you smoke this brand? Sunflower. Shirt. Love. A mood or tone which leans toward neutrality like a beckoning anaesthetic. Not full knockout, just softened edges, taking the static away. *'A chill blew out the flame …'* No undue emphases, at times verging on one long sexless purr. Songs for a certain type of confident traveller through the long grey migraine night of international airspace. Confidence or privilege verging on blankness, anonymity, absence. How long is it since I was home this time? *'Sunlight blinds my mind …'*

Where am I tonight? What city, what club? Oh, fuck no: complete blank.

Is this what double agents feel like when they lose the thread of who they are, one day or night, chatting away to someone and then suddenly the uninvited thought: who is it whoever I am talking to expects me to reply as? The one who speaks, the one who sings, and the one who simply is: are they all necessarily identical? Is this even Being, any longer, strictly speaking? Because this isn't a mask: this is me. This is me singing. This is you, now: here I am right out in the open for all to see. And is this who they all came to see? To look into these blank and lessening eyes? What do they do afterwards? What do they WANT? To devour me? Like those Bacchae chicks?

Tonight – ladies and gentlemen! Please! Give it up! For –

Direct from a railway line in Mittel Europa, on the wrong track altogether … Here I am, even if I've completely forgotten who it is I'm trying to remember to be. I think my timing is maybe on the

verge of being lost for ever, you know, and then – false flags for ever.
Into the spotlight – this is the spotlight now, isn't it? Am I shaky or
is it the air in here tonight? Booze rhymes with wooze rhymes with
schmooze rhymes with whose rhymes with lose rhymes with loser.
In the spotlight all these shivers like skeleton winds on little yellow
pills and –

With worries please
Come down from there –

I have to say something now – I think it's actually in the contract. I should fucking Miles them, that's what I should do. Turn
the back, face the future past. Give them the big glorious golden ass
for a spotlight. Would that work for a singer? Say something, anything. Let's not talk about, let's not think about last things, now.
Ladies and gentlemen, this next song was written by one mean
motherfucker –

'Little things/That call for a drink –'

You said a mouthful right there, boy!

I like it most of all when the strings go impossibly high or
implausibly low but you can't ever get that live. Maybe that's why
Brian Wilson never tours too. On stage it's all about being seen, not
being heard. Just another dummy in a hired tuxedo, you big micro
… phoney. They all want me to go to Las Vegas next next next but
that's the last thing. The real last thing. The least interesting. I want
the SOUND. I want SOUND to devour me. Put an end to it all like
that.

And you know the real sadness? They'll hate me for this and won't
get it at all and how could they? How could they know it's not *them*
I feel contempt for and it's not the band and it's not even the songs –
which I love beyond logic, some of them. What I feel overwhelming
and soul-sickening contempt for is plain and simple love minus zero
ME. Noel Scott no longer Engel fucking WALKER. Fuck ME. The
contempt is all in this spot here. Step right into it, Scotty boy. Makes

you feel cold makes you feel old an antique to be SOLD. Ladies and
gentlemen ...

Hit it, boys, hit it!

1. Cohn, Nik, *Awopbopaloobop Alopbamboom* (London: Paladin, 1973).
2. Lahr, John, 'Introduction' in Orton, Joe, *The Orton Diaries* (London: Minerva, 1989).
3. Orton, Joe, *The Orton Diaries*.
4. Cohn, Nik, 'I'd Rather Be In Philadelphia' in *Ball The Wall: Nik Cohn In The Age Of Rock* (London: Picador, 1989).
5. Baudrillard, Jean (trans Turner, Chris), *Cool Memories: 1980–1985* (London: Verso, 1990).
6. Wark, McKenzie, *The Beach Beneath The Street: The Everyday Life And Glorious Times Of The Situationist International* (London: Verso, 2011).
7. Greene, Graham, *Journey Without Maps* (London: Vintage, 1936/2010).
8. Lahr, John, *Woody Allen In Automatic Vaudeville* (London: Methuen, 1985).
9. I shit you not, hepcats. Check it out on *Blood, Chet And Tears* (Verve, 1970).

Rootless Countrypolitan

Amanda Petrusich

Any Day Now (1973)
Stretch (1973)
We Had It All (1974)

Few decade-plus discographies are without a single dud. For every *Blonde On Blonde* there's an *Empire Burlesque*, and whether these comparably deflated moments are the product of malevolent commercial interests – or an expression of artistic fatigue, or some combination thereof – is ultimately irrelevant. Whatever the source, each misstep is proof that art is fickle, artists are fallible, and transcendence is fleeting. Even the most practised auteur can falter. The well is never bottomless. We all get lost.

In the early 1970s, Scott Walker was drifting – which can be a remarkable position for an artist. Except when it isn't.

At the start of the decade, Walker was living in Amsterdam with his girlfriend, Mette, and a big, drooling St Bernard. He has since admitted this was a particularly barren stretch, creatively speaking – his so-called 'wilderness years' – and following the commercial non-achievement of *Scott 4*, Walker was considering ditching the music business altogether. According to his biographers, he was dejected and removed, and scuttling off to the cinema up to four times each day. It's a telling little detail: Walker was already a fervent cinephile, and movies, maybe more than drugs or booze, provide a cheap, convenient haven for an aspiring escapist. In the cool, quiet blackness, a kind of nothingness becomes possible. Shrugging off a long day – or a regret, or a failure, or some unspecified ennui – by buying a movie ticket and exchanging one complex life for another, less realised one is a clean and easy out; for plenty of people, the relationship between time spent in a theatre chair and general disaffection is exponential. If nothing else, it speaks of Walker's disengagement – of a desire, maybe, to temporarily disappear.

In the spring of 1970 Walker applied for British citizenship, and the following autumn he acquired an apartment in London and released his sixth solo record. *'Til The Band Comes In* is an uneven, schmaltzy collection of originals and standards that hints, however briefly, at a potential new style: high, lonesome Country music. Throughout the first half of the 1970s, Walker (fulfilling, first, a contract for Philips, then one for CBS) would repeatedly toy with twang, applying his cavernous baritone to smooth, Nashville Sound-aping ballads. That the American-born Walker was trying on a country voice in the midst of becoming a naturalised Brit is so palpably ironic, it's tempting to wonder if Walker wasn't imbuing his otherwise-staid performances with lingering questions of identity – simultaneously surrendering and embracing an American self.

In a parallel life, after all, Walker would still be living in California. It's not so difficult, really, to picture him loping through Joshua Tree in a fringed leather jacket, passing a guitar to Gram Parsons (who, at two-and-a-half years his junior, was ostensibly a peer), scuttling over rocks, burying bits of song lyrics in the rough, gravelly sand.

Instead, I think of Walker in a dark Amsterdam theatre, slugging from a warm bottle of Old Grand-Dad. Paused. Tired of music, tired of himself.

In the early 1970s, country music – at least in America – was in a state of aesthetic flux. The genre had proven its commercial viability, and by 1975, country was mainstream, ubiquitous: Loretta Lynn had been on the cover of *Newsweek* (beaming below the headline 'The Country Music Craze'); Robert Altman had properly skewered Nashville in a film of the same name; and then-President Richard Nixon had attended the dedication of the new Grand Ole Opry house (he played 'Happy Birthday' for his wife Pat on the Opry's piano before handing Roy Acuff a yo-yo).

This kind of broad appeal wasn't possible without a bit of glossing over. As Bill Malone writes in *Country Music USA*, 'the country music industry had discovered that its best interests lie in the distribution of a package with clouded identity, possessing no regional traits.' Country had been gentrified for mass consumption, a process that started in the 1950s when Chet Atkins and his compatriots began injecting Country singles with mild, maudlin strings and sweeping choruses, while simultaneously cutting back on the less anonymous bits (like, say, fiddle). It's this particular strain of Country – countrypolitan, as it eventually came to be called – that Walker was trying on in London, but elsewhere in the US, mutinous sects had calcified. In Bakersfield, California, a raucous, rock-infused retort led by Merle Haggard and Buck Owens – designed with discordance, not palatability, in mind – offered up an initial antidote, and that seditious mission was at least partially maintained by the so-called Outlaws throughout the late 1960s, and picked up again in the 1970s as Country-rock pioneers like Parsons proffered an ambitious, psych-leaning version of Country (famously dubbed 'cosmic American music'). That Walker initially ignored – or that his handlers overlooked – these ambitious, modern iterations of Country music feels both incongruous and tragic. Walker's Country (as evidenced by his earliest experiments, at least) was flat, sexless, and maudlin, devoid of any suggestion of boldness, or of the discursive ingenuity that would fuel his later work.

In 1973, Walker released *Any Day Now*, his final record for Philips. In the cover shot, an eerily lit profile, he sports a pained expression that unfortunately (if accurately) presages its content. His features look pinched – a series of squiggly, worried lines. Of all Walker's lost records – none of his pre-*Climate Of Hunter*, post-*Scott 4* solo records have been fully reissued, and some are still tough to hunt down in their entirety – *Any Day Now* is both the hardest to find and the trickiest to advocate for. Walker reportedly recorded his vocals in one day (half before lunch, half after) and his voice, while objectively faultless, is limp and apathetic here. He occasionally trots out his newfound 'Country' accent, imbuing these tracks with a little bit of lilt, but mostly Walker just sounds broken. He wanted to write, but Philips, with only one record left under contract, refused to indulge that particular desire; the tracks collected here (Randy Newman's 'Cowboy', Jimmy Webb's 'All My Love's Laughter' and 'If Ships Were Made To Sail', Bill Withers's 'Ain't No Sunshine' and more) are smarmy and flaccid, rendered almost entirely without feeling. When Walker's vocals do manage to transcend blankness, there's something ominous about his performance – listen long enough, and these tracks start to seem custom-built for gruesomeness, for montages of bursting bodies, rotting flesh. The juxtaposition – Walker's cheerless delivery of otherwise pleasant narratives – is foreboding, verging on sinister.

Walker was released from his contract soon after the record's release. He hit the club circuit, playing short, self-effacing sets for quick cash. Things got grim. According to various reports, Walker opened these shows with, 'I hope you're well-loaded tonight. You've got to be to watch this show!'

Shortly thereafter, Walker and his management negotiated a new deal with CBS Records. Although it wasn't specifically stipulated in his contract, Walker again believed he would be allowed to write his own material; he was not. His next record, 1973's *Stretch*, is a slick and mesmerizing collection of Country songs composed by and mostly for other people. It was recorded in London with an able session band (including the famed BJ Cole on steel guitar), but Walker's backing musicians never approach the impermeable perfection of

Nashville's famed A-Team. At best, they offer up an odd, detached approximation.

Still, *Stretch* feels deeper, better. *'As far as you're concerned, don't be concerned with me,'* Walker intones on Mickey Newbury's dark, countrified 'Sunshine', and whether it's fuelled by resignation or genuine engagement, Walker's delivery is nuanced, heartbreaking. Likewise, his low, grainy rendition of 'No Easy Way Down', a track already immortalised by Dusty Springfield, Carole King and Jackie DeShannon, is unreasonably good: Walker's voice is airier than normal, fading, at times, into a slow, misty drawl that hovers for a moment before dissipating entirely.

Walker's next record for CBS, 1974's *We Had It All*, unceremoniously closed his Country period, an anticlimactic end to a mostly failed experiment. In a move that still seems inexplicable, the record consisted of five tracks that had been recorded and released, in 1973, by Waylon Jennings for his landmark LP *Honky Tonk Heroes*. The seventies were a curious time for pop music (hit songs were recycled mercilessly), but the thought of Walker and CBS plucking five cuts from an already-successful, one-year-old genre record and then re-recording them in England would seem hubristic if it weren't so bizarre.

On *Any Day Now* and parts of *Stretch*, Walker's deep, bone-shaking voice – all drama and portent – felt inherently out of step with countrypolitan's sweet, jangly schema; that kind of blatant mismatch could have been compelling (and plenty of Country singers, from Johnny Cash on out, have toyed with that exact tension) if it didn't also sound so pained. Walker's voice is better suited for outlaw Country's Texas-born expansiveness, but BJ Shaver's blustery songs demand a certain swagger, and Walker couldn't (or didn't) adopt it with anything resembling ease (and ease, of course, is paramount for aspiring outlaws). His vocal performances are strong on *We Had It All*, but still hollow. Hearing Walker refer to himself as *'a simple-headed man'* in 'Black Rose' is a little like watching a toddler with a broken teapot in one hand repeatedly insisting that he didn't do it: it's a sad little lie that nobody believes.

We Had It All ends with 'Delta Dawn' – a hit for Tanya Tucker in 1972 and then again for Helen Reddy in 1973. Walker is trying his best – *'Delta Dawn, what's that flower you have on?'* he bellows earnestly, while a choir sings backup – but he also sounds vaguely absurd, all aw-shucks affect and misplaced pomp. Consequently, listening to 'Delta Dawn' feels like being hit in the face with a bowling ball. There is little delicacy. There are no surprises. It is nothing at all, except exactly what it is.

There's something deeply heartbreaking – if understandable, even sympathetic – about Walker's longstanding disavowal of these records. He has tried his best to keep them buried, a body decomposing, year after year, under the swing-set in the backyard. It's likely that Walker felt manipulated and powerless in 1974, stripped of his hard-won autonomy, positioned on a stool in front of a microphone and animated on cue, like a handsome, fluffy-haired marionette. It's a challenge to contextualise these releases in the grander narrative of Country music because they exist almost entirely independent of it; they're inconsequential to the genre, and inconsequential within Walker's oeuvre. For an artist intent on achieving a kind of maniacal perfection, the experience of listening to these songs now must be humiliating.

I am drawn to these records in the same way I am drawn to the memory of my own bad decisions, creative or otherwise – reliving them silently, projecting different outcomes, wondering why I didn't dig deeper, change course, say no, say yes. It's easy – satisfying, even – to get caught up in a kind of anguished nostalgia in which I separate myself from the choices I made; I bury them in the backyard and pray for absolution. When I am feeling particularly indulgent, I even find cold solace in the futility of Walker's mid-career slump. A writer who couldn't write, or wasn't allowed to write, or failed at writing is its own tiny, privileged tragedy, but it's also one I re-cognise. Writing is so often a reaction to terror, a way of imposing authority (and meaning, and order) on a universe that's inherently anarchic. It's a desperate compulsion, and to deny it is to gum up your psychic pathways, to get yourself in trouble. Walker couldn't write, so he sank. He darkened.

It's easy to sentimentalise the notion of creation – to assume that inspiration is sparingly doled out by some celestial hand to a tiny scrum of conduits, who then carry on with the divine work. Walker, especially, seems to believe this: songs come when they come. No cheating, just wait. The process of making something, then, becomes more about following a metaphysical prompt than, say, working hard; this is a precious and dangerous way of thinking about any-thing, but it is also sometimes true. How else do skilled, practised artists become so stuck? Why isn't creativity self-sustaining? Why isn't it a thing you can't unlearn, a thing you can't stop? Scott Walker was waiting, maybe, but why couldn't he make these records better than they are?

In the end, he didn't believe, and they are bloodless.

Walker couldn't write his way out of the early 1970s, so he sang instead; I like to believe that he chose Country music because of its promise of salvation, of homecoming. But even four decades later, it's still difficult to determine exactly how much authority Walker may have had in the selection of these particular tracks – was his temporary embrace of Nashville smarm commercially or artistically driven, or just a curious by-product of exhaustion? Was it really a grand personal statement, a way of having America and England and everything all at once? Despite its more gruesome, pop-aping iterations, Country music has always been a refuge for the lost, and I can't help but hear Walker's sudden acceptance (it's his face on the cover, after all – his body swathed in a cut-off denim vest) of Coun-try as a distinctly expat gesture. I waffle, of course, on whether his support of this music was based in longing or in self-disgust.

No Regrets

These songs, with their bravado, their narration, their wild, sentimental promises, are easy to find solace in because they're engineered to offer it; Country music is escapist and confessional by nature. In performing these tracks, could Walker have been imagining an alternative existence for himself, a life where he never left home, never felt the crush of unbridled adulation, never collapsed? Maybe his embrace of Country feels so strange and false because it was built on an impossible hope – that by going back he could somehow go forward.

Extraordinary Renditions

Biba Kopf

The Walker Brothers: *No Regrets* (1975)
Lines (1976)
Nite Flights (1978)

Taking off under cover of night, the song barely registers on the
event horizon before disappearing into the blackness beyond, where
nobody cares how loud you scream. Moulded from its introductory
synth-string part, the song's fusillade wasn't designed with the comfort of its human cargo in mind. Once its passengers are securely
belted inside its thin-walled cabin, the only in-flight entertainment
offered them is being drowned out by the turbine roar of the song's
rock-disco engine; it's powered by the remorseless machine rhythm
ratcheted together from its finely turned bass, kick drum and hi-hat
components.

But we're getting carried away; backpedal to the moment the
song reaches cruising speed and Scott Walker's voice cuts in with a
report from Hell:

> *There's no hold*
> *The moving has come through*
> *The danger brushing you*
> *Turns its face into the heat and runs the tunnels*
>
> *It's so cold*
> *The dark dug up by dogs*
> *The stitches torn and broke*

> *The raw meat fist you choke*
> *Has hit the bloodlite...*

Then a tiny curvature of guitar trips the song up and topples it else-where:

> *Glass traps open and close on nite flights*
> *Broken necks, feather weights press the walls*
> *Be my love, we will be gods on nite flights*
> *Only one promise, only one way to fall ...*

Departing from airports unknown for destinations undisclosed, 'Nite Flights' welcomes you on board. It's the astonishing title track of the third and last album released in 1978 by the re-formed Walker Brothers. Following a brace of mostly AOR covers sets, it was the first to be entirely composed by the trio, with Scott and John each contributing four apiece, and another two coming from Gary. More significantly, Scott's songs broke the writing silence he'd sustained since his 1971 LP *'Til The Band Comes In*.

'I went into some kind of despair mode at that point and started drinking very heavily, more than I did normally, and that went on for a long time, and it didn't stop until [The Walker Brothers] did *Nite Flights*,' Scott told an interviewer in 2006.[1] 'That was the end of the contract record really because the record company was going to close. So we got together and made the album we wanted to make because it was all folding anyway. And that reignited everything for me. Then I thought I wasn't ever going back, I was going to keep going forward.'

Indeed, after he'd heard that the re-formed Walker Brothers' bankrolling label GTO was virtually bankrupt, Scott seized the moment and proposed to John and Gary that they should demo-cratically record the album they had always wanted to make as their third and (most likely) final release for their paymasters. Democracy is a fine thing, for sure, but in truth, of *Nite Flights*' ten songs, Scott's four spinechillers are the only tracks you keep coming back to. Two precede 'Nite Flights': 'Shutout' and 'Fat Mama Kick', which describe some unnamable science fiction sorrow. Both are somewhat unusually written by Scott in a Ballard/Burroughs-style language, complete with newly minted neologisms such as *'ratmosphere'* (on 'Shutout'), which he never returned to after the songs were over. But with 'Nite Flights' and his closing contribution 'The Electrician', Scott was already moving towards his later work's profoundly humanist responses to long-buried or forgotten moments of recent history, revealed only obliquely, through painstaking juxtapositions of pared-back images, shorn of all directly emotional content. But he hadn't quite disappeared his music from the real world on *Nite Flights*, and indeed the enduring value of hearing 'Nite Flights' and 'The Electrician' together as a pair is how they eerily anticipate, by twenty-three years or more, the acts of extraordinary rendition carried out after 11 September 2001, when George W Bush's administration stepped up the US War on Terror. Extraordinary rendition was the CIA's sinister euphemism for the clandestine flights they organised to transport often illegally abducted terrorist suspects across the world to undisclosed detention centres beyond US jurisdiction, to be tortured by proxy, with any useful information handed over to the CIA. Between the mysterious journeys to nowhere described by 'Nite Flights' and the TE Lawrence-like transports of terror and transcendence projected in 'The Electrician', you have to wonder where Scott's all-seeing eye was looking when he was writing them.

Before Bush's New World Order annexed it, however, 'extraordinary rendition' used to be the kind of high praise connoisseurs of the vocalist's art would bestow on rare showstopping performances, where the singer goes deep inside an evergreen standard or popular song of the moment, and through a combination of pace, phrasing or plain old chutzpah, makes it entirely new again. Both solo or with The Walker Brothers, be they the Mk1 trio who jetted over to the UK in 1965 or the more 'mature' mid-seventies version, Scott has sung any number of extraordinary renditions, including most of his Brel songs, Tim Hardin's 'Black Sheep Boy' and Henry Mancini's 'Wait Until Dark', as well as some sixties Walkers covers and UK TV performances for, among other shows, his own short-lived BBC programme as well as those hosted by Dusty Springfield and Frankie Howerd (Scott hamming up Brel's 'Jackie' on Howerd's set is a YouTube must-see).

Fantastic as they are, Scott's 1960s performances had everything and nothing to do with the Swinging London that let The Walker Brothers move in. His voice might have run deep and dark, but his face was always so young; and recorded with old-school orchestras of light entertainment, The Walker Brothers' early mini-opera pop hits could have come out anytime in the 1950s, sixties or seventies. Between 1965–67 The Walker Brothers released three albums, and the light entertainment industry had them working all the circuits to sell them before their moment was over. After they scored a massive hit with 'Make It Easy On Yourself', they were sucked right into sixties pop insanity, much to Scott's rising horror, as hysterical fans did their utmost to rip their idols apart. John and Scott occasionally contributed songs, mostly as B-sides or album fillers, but The Walker Brothers weren't really like The Beatles, The Rolling Stones or The Kinks, who wrote and played much of their own material. The Walker Brothers' repertoire had more in common with early sixties girl groups, or big girl vocalists like Dusty Springfield, Lulu or Cilla Black. The few observation-type songs Scott smuggled into The Walker Brothers' playlist and his early solo albums were kinda Kinksy, just about, but beat pop they weren't – their lyrics and arrangements had more in common with the 1960s vogue for black and white kitchen-sink films.

John and Gary always took Swinging London in their stride but Scott, now solo, just wasn't made for these times. The emerging counterculture and hippy underground made him shudder. He felt closer to cabaret vocalist Jack Jones than the likes of Syd Barrett. On his first four solo albums (discounting the 1969 *Sings Songs From His TV Series* LP), he worked with BBC light entertainment types like Wally Stott (later Angela Morley). The failure of his first, entirely self-penned album *Scott 4* must have hit hard; *'Til The Band Comes In* did no better, even though ten of its tracks were co-written with his current manager Ady Semel, brought in to curb *Scott 4*'s more wayward European existentialism. Demoralised by their failure, Scott simply stopped writing, spending the next seven years releasing indifferent covers albums, first solo and then with the re-formed Walker Brothers, through which Scott the singer slowly gravitated towards mature American Country going on Country rock, written mainly by grizzled, avowedly non-Nashville songwriters and performed by UK session players. He couldn't have moved further away from the safe European home of his great 1960s releases.

However, it was hearing a Scott original that prompted John to call his ex-Brother about re-forming the trio. 'During the summer of 1974,' John reports in his 2009 memoir, 'I was watching television, and on came the film *Deadlier Than The Male* – the movie for which The Walker Brothers sung the title song. As I heard it again it struck me that we sounded really good ...'[2] And so they did, in that oddly anachronistic way The Walker Brothers played it in the 1960s. Over co-writer, record producer and close ally Johnny Franz's appropriately Baroque-Bond spy movie quatsch arrangement, Scott's lead vocal folk-spins wisdom from the banal verses he'd contrived to lend truth to the chorus, which was parsed from Rudyard Kipling's 1911 poem 'The Female Of The Species'. The song starts up along with the delayed film credits the moment a jet explodes, just after the glamour-girl assassin who blew it out of the sky serenely parachutes into the sea, where her bikini-clad partner picks her up and spirits her away to set up their next killing. So The Walker Brothers' reunion was seeded in a picture of a disintegrating plane as their 1960s selves played on, and it ended three years later with them embarking on *Nite Flights* to God knows where.

Could The Walker Brothers' second coming have followed a more inappropriate trajectory, especially given Scott's reported fear of flying? Yet it feels exactly right that The Walker Brothers' reawakening is rooted in their first-run selves rendering such an effective track from the ostensibly throwaway song composed for a failed international jet-set spy movie, one of many such attempts to cut a share from the James Bond franchise. For a start, it landed them back in the same jet-set dream version of the 1960s they used to glide through as imported American pop stars, hobnobbing with actors and young wealthy sun-seekers at elite clubs beyond the reach of the screaming teens who put them up there in the first place. From here, a conflicted Scott could resolve the inevitable contradictions posed in realising his utterly unique vision of a new kind of Anglo-European popular song through old-school light entertainment means, way after the burgeoning hippy counterculture had broken with the mainstream and established rock as the noblest form of self-expression. When *Scott 4* sold next to nothing, he could only look on appalled as the untidy rock rabble around him thrived. 'I hated myself so much for all the years of bad faith,' Scott told a British newspaper in 2006, recalling the lost years before he started writing again on *Nite Flights*. 'I still do. I'm very wary of it. It bothers me that I wasted all that time, you know? I was making records to pay off bills. I'd bought a big flat and all this kind of stuff. I get so annoyed, because I should have figured out another way, but I was just very vulnerable after the fourth album. The place was crawling with … hippies and there was no way around that, if you weren't in their uniform. It was tough.'[3]

Scott was as lost as his two ex-Brothers when he answered the phone that summer of 1974. 'I decided to call Scott and talk about re-forming,' continues John, in *No Regrets*. 'I reached him at his home in Amsterdam and he too thought it was a good idea, so we planned to meet up in London within a few weeks ...'[4]

Borrowing money against his next Walkers royalty cheque, John flew back to the UK; Scott, meanwhile, commuted between business dealings in London and his family home in Amsterdam, occasionally going out drinking with John to talk up their future possibilities. Once Scott proposed the idea to Gary, the reunion was a done deal. John and Gary might have been more worldly than Scott when the trio originally split, but their individual takes on the 1960s' shifts and changes left them none the wiser. In fact, they come over a whole lot dumber in *No Regrets*'s litany of what-if encounters with that decade's good and great. (The dumbest being John hanging loose and recording an unreleased album for the one Rolling Stone nobody except him gave a shit about, Bill Wyman.) By the time The Walker Brothers reformed, he'd released two albums and a dozen singles. For his part, Gary was big in Japan for three minutes, releasing a so-so international psych album as Gary Walker And The Rain. Other than that, one of his half-dozen singles was a hit in Italy. One way or another it's no surprise to hear that in the beginning, according to both John and Gary in *No Regrets*, the three of them were positively euphoric, all the personal and artistic tensions that broke them up in 1967 temporarily forgotten, as they excitedly talked about The Walker Brothers working as a collective endeavour again for the first time since they finished their 1965 debut *Take It Easy*. With advance money from their deal with GTO, the trio moved into an apartment in London's Kings Road, where they began searching out songs to record for their comeback album *No Regrets* (1975) and its successor *Lines* (1976). 'I just picked up tons of albums, it was the only way of doing it,' Scott commented at the time. 'I suspected that publishers wouldn't be hot-footing it to be getting Walker Brothers material because I knew all the cynicism that was going around. I thought fuck it. I'll get it myself. The album had to be done quickly and it had to be done in a certain way, I didn't want to take the group into such an old sound because that would have been embarrassing.'⁵

For both albums, Scott and co-producer Geoff Calver pretty much continued with The Walker Brothers what he had already been doing on his early 1970s solo covers LPs, here recording American outlaw Country and AOR songs by the likes of Tom Rush ('No Regrets'), Emmylou Harris ('Boulder To Birmingham'), Kris Kristofferson ('I've Got To Have You'), Jerry Fuller ('Lines'), Jesse Winchester ('Brand New Tennessee Waltz') and Boz Scaggs ('We're All Alone') with London session musicians. The democratic nature of The Brothers' reunion determined that Scott and John would share the lead vocals between them, but the playlists thankfully broke in Scott's favour across the four sides of vinyl making up *No Regrets* and *Lines*, as John's voice had coarsened into hoarse-grained West Coast rock anonymity – the kind Scott would have most likely abhorred if it came from anyone else. John's leads couldn't be further removed from Scott's vocal-led songs over the two albums. Scott's voice had dropped down and deepened, his delivery far more poised and less prone to the emotional button-pushing he and the 1960s Walker Brothers used to indulge in, much to the hysterical sobbing delight of their fans. In effect, his *No Regrets* and *Lines* performances registered both his and The Walker Brothers' 'maturing' – from a pop phenomenon living on borrowed time in the last days of pop as state-controlled light entertainment, into adult-orientated music, albeit one without portfolio. That is to say, the mature, adult Walker Brothers had no real fanbase left to target. In the post-hippy age of rock and confessional singer-songwriterdom, the best such adult-orientated covers albums could hope for was to somehow reach those aforementioned connoisseurs of the vocalist's art, for whom rock and pop modes of expression are cheap and vulgar, and for whom the singer will always be more important than the song or its creator. The light entertainment industry hadn't entirely disappeared from the UK by the mid-1970s, and there were enough old-guard media types in positions of power ready to give the re-formed

Walker Brothers' adult reorientations a chance. Released ahead of the album as a single, 'No Regrets' climbed to number seven in the UK pop charts, landing the group various TV appearances, Vera Lynn's 1975 Christmas show amongst them. The available YouTube clips from the period reveal The Walker Brothers to be happy and relaxed, John and Scott cracking smiles as they watch each other's lips to keep their cues. But that delight in each other's company wouldn't last.

'No Regrets' turned out to be The Walker Brothers' final hit, and the good times the group shared at the start of their reunion fizzed for about as long as the shelf life of the single and subsequent *No Regrets* album. The internal antagonisms that ultimately destroyed The Walker Brothers in the 1960s reared up again during the recording and promotion of the following *Lines*. Frustrated by Scott's reluctance to play live, John began drinking more heavily. And GTO appeared to have already lost interest in the group, according to John and Gary in *No Regrets*, both of them citing the label's failure to promote their version of the Boz Scaggs song 'We're All Alone', in light of Rita Coolidge scoring a hit with her version. Of all The Walker Brothers' mid-1970s covers, 'We're All Alone' is the only one you could truly call an extraordinary rendition. Everything about it is perfectly poised, down to the simplicity of the drum part, contemptuously delivered in that supper club connoisseur's favoured mix of discipline and arrogant disdain, with Scott's voice rising agonisingly slowly over its duration to bring the song to a peak of emotion as the iced strings melt beneath him. In retrospect it's tempting to hear Scott's coolly delivered leads on *No Regrets* and *Lines* as early experiments to erase all emotional excess from the voice so as to leave the words and composition to do the work. But that would ascribe these performances far too much significance. For sure, 'We're All Alone' is a truly extraordinary rendition of an overfamiliar AOR hit, but nearly all the other Walker Brothers' 1975–76 covers only aspire to the status of extraordinary rendition in the CIA's post-11

September 2001 sense of the term: abducting songs from their original roots contexts and relocating them in the borderlands Scott seemed intent on establishing to separate himself from the critically dominant post-hippy rock world that so appalled him.

Indeed, after *Nite Flights*, he reconsidered his covers work throughout the whole decade as whoring, a time when he simply went along with his record companies' and managers' attempts to remould the failed 1960s pop visionary as a mature singer of adult songs, regardless of their point of origin.

In his 1976 *Melody Maker* interview with Colin Irwin, Scott had indicated that his desire to be left alone hadn't removed him from the political world. 'I worry about politics. I worry about the elections. It really depresses me, you know, that whole thing with Nixon, because I went through all that. My family all voted for him, you know. I called them and said "You cretins, you're wrong" ... If I see something on television like the Cambodian thing or something, I get terribly distressed about that. It's very distressing. I'm like every other little guy who sits and watches and wonders what exactly he can do. You can go and fight, sure, but you don't want to do that because that's exactly what you're pissed off about. And you don't have enough bread to do anything else. Unless you're Howard Hughes.'[6]

You'd have to read very closely between the covers on *Lines*, released later the same year as that interview, to find anything remotely political in their song selections. Their take of Jimmy Cliff's 'Many Rivers To Cross' falls in line with the film songs Scott covered on his *Moviegoer* album, but you have to wonder how hard The Brothers furrowed their brows about recasting Cliff's downer reggae-soul as godawful AOR gospel plough. It would also be interesting to know if Scott's own anti-war feelings, as obliquely expressed in *Scott 4*'s 'The Old Man's Back Again' (about the Soviet-led Warsaw Pact invasion of Czechoslovakia), had anything to do with his choice of 'Brand New Tennessee Waltz' by Jesse Winchester, a conscientious objector to the Vietnam war whose exile in Canada might have shaped his song's Heimat yearnings. In the event the politics had to wait until 1978, when The Walker Brothers' label was on the verge of going bankrupt, and it was already clear to Scott, John and Gary that they were right to split up when they did the first time round. Hardly anything they had done together in either decade proved any common intent beyond pragmatic business matters, nor did they really share any artistic goals or purposes. But the project at least bought them all a bit of time and, in Scott's case, enough confidence to begin writing his own songs again. Perhaps the 1976 punk attack on rock's hippy righteousness convinced this man, now in his mid-thirties, that he could do it his way, just like Johnny Rotten and co. Certainly, Scott's ideal of musicianly neutrality, where players are called in primarily to serve the song's needs rather than show off everything they can do in the time allotted, found more common ground with Berlin/Eno-era David Bowie, and emerging groups like Wire, Siouxsie & The Banshees, Warsaw/Joy Division and Buzzcocks. Even so, nothing other than the musical economy of Scott's co-production work on *No Regrets* or *Lines* gave any indication of where he found within himself, or the world beyond his locked front door, the four eerie songs he wrote out of the blue for *Nite Flights*. As stated earlier, 'Shutout' and 'Fat Mama Kick' essentially seemed to be a matter of getting himself in the right frame of mind for the title track and 'The Electrician' which follow. Every time I hear them, I have to keep reminding myself that he wrote them twenty-three years ahead of the stepped-up War on Terror. Perhaps such songs, challenging a world power's self-declared monopoly of terror and violence, could only have been written before the 9/11 attacks on New York City and Washington without incurring media wrath and damnation.

Regardless, it's not as though the USA hadn't been clandestinely involved in anti-communist struggles in Cuba, South America and farther afield in all the Cold War years before Scott wrote his *Nite Flights* tracks. Indeed, formerly classified US manuals released to the public in January 1997 document decades of the CIA's covert training of interrogation techniques to perceived 'allies' in their war against the domino spread of communism through South America, especially, and methods of electric torture are clearly listed in the curriculum. Despite America's heated denials, the CIA's part in General Pinochet's overthrow of Chile's democratically elected left-wing President Allende was a running news story in both the left and mainstream media through the first half of the 1970s. How much Scott knew about or took an interest in his former homeland's interference in developing nations considered likely to take a wrong left turn is unrecorded, as he has always been extremely reluctant to give away much about the origins of his songs. Rightly so: even such profoundly affecting tracks as 'Nite Flights' and 'The Electrician' are all the more queasily real for the way they're not directly protesting a particular cause. But Scott appears to have said a little bit more about 'The Electrician' than he'd normally give out in a 1984 radio interview: 'A political song ... having to do with ... the Americans sending in these people, trained torturers in South America ... I imagined these lovers in a conversation... If you listen to the words of "The Electrician" it really explains itself after I've started.'[7]

Well, he's dead right about the song hiding nothing from the listener. But the act of tracking the song's slowly turning cycles of pain defeats all attempts at understanding the piece as a whole, with its first-person switches between torturer and victim, as each jerk of the handle brings the lights down low, and every jolt sends the prisoner shuddering from excruciation to otherworldly ecstasy. The song's drifts between utter abjection and almost religious transcendence are musically realised through New Zealand musician and arranger Dave MacRae's mystifying blur of strings, which keeps the song and victim both delicately poised on the brink of consciousness until the cycle of pain starts all over again.

Scott's lyrics for 'The Electrician' are nowhere near so stripped down as his songs on *Tilt* and *The Drift*, but they display he had already advanced his writing process: slashing lines to base phrases whose meanings are constructed in the process of performance rather than from reading them off the page.

There have been other artists' renditions of 'The Electrician' and 'Nite Flights', most of them far from extraordinary. Longtime Scott Walker fan David Bowie completely over-emoted his way through 'Nite Flights' on his 1993 album *Black Tie White Noise*; but The Fatima Mansions showed Bowie what an outsider group could do with the song on their 1994 album *Lost In The Former West*. And New York City's Sightings, an often fabulous, blunt noise-driven guitar group seemingly well positioned to enact a post-9/11 take on a song abstractly rooted in the CIA's covert training of 'torture by proxy' interrogators, barely raise a glower in their take of 'The Electrician', on their 2007 album *Through The Panama*. Burroughs once claimed that noise kills pain and it only hurts when the noise stops. Sightings' guitar-noise take of 'The Electrician' certainly leaves you feeling nothing. But then, with its heartstopping moodswings between chill extinction and ecstatic release, Scott's original is political music like no other, and nigh impossible to render any other way but his. Just as 'The Old Man's Back Again' projects the listener inside the propagandised mind of a naive young soldier shocked by the hatred his invading presence causes, so 'The Electrician' reveals the deeply ambivalent and shockingly intimate relationship between the torturer and his helpless victim. And at the merciful moment when the song sounds like it's about to black out, as if in honour of the victim's drift into unconsciousness, the strings kick in and the little white dot of the lights going out spontaneously reverses into blinding bright light.

This, beautiful friend, is The End.

No Regrets

1. Reid, Graham, Scott Walker interview in *rocksbackpages.com* (May 2006).
2. Walker, Gary & Walker, John, *No Regrets: The Walker Brothers – Our Story* (London: John Blake, 2009).
3. Petridis, Alexis, 'A Tale Of Booze, Pills And Pork' in *The Guardian* (5 May 2006).
4. Walker, Gary & Walker, John, *No Regrets*.
5. Irwin, Colin, 'Scott Walker: No Regrets' in *Melody Maker* (14 February 1976).
6. Irwin, 'Scott Walker: No Regrets'.
7. Walker radio interview with Alan Bangs (British Forces Broadcasting Service (BFBS), 1984).

Isolation Row

Damon Krukowski

Climate Of Hunter (1984)

> *And now, what's going to happen to us without*
> *barbarians?*
> *They were, those people, a kind of solution.*
> From CP Cavafy, 'Waiting For The Barbarians' (1904)[1]

If the first four tracks on the final Walker Brothers album, *Nite Flights* (1978), announced the rebirth of Scott the songwriter, *Climate Of Hunter* was the even longer-awaited return of Scott the auteur. Only the second album containing all original songs in his career, it is the true follow-up to 1969's *Scott 4*. But what a difference those fifteen years make. In a retrospective interview filmed for the documentary *30 Century Man*, Walker speculates that had he not taken a detour after *Scott 4*, he would have arrived at the same place, just 'sooner – I would have been there a lot sooner'.[2] Could a much younger man have made *Climate Of Hunter*, however? Not because of its darkness, so present in Walker's youthful work as well. But there's an abstraction to *Climate Of Hunter* – and to all of Walker's subsequent albums – that is missing from his earlier records, or was perhaps inaccessible to the artist at that time. Walker's work from *Climate Of Hunter* onwards would seem to exemplify Edward Said's description of 'late style': 'There is an insistence in late style not on mere ageing, but on an increasing sense of apartness and exile and anachronism,' which leads not toward a greater 'harmony and resolution, but … intransigence, difficulty and contradiction'.[3] The 'difficulty' of these later works of Walker's, so often remarked on, is in this view not a resolute thumbing of the nose at the audience, or record company executives, or any other aspect of the pop music life. It is, on the contrary, art made of irresolution. If Scott Walker had alternately embraced and shunned the role of pop star from his UK debut through the second, definitive end of The Walker Brothers, in *Climate Of Hunter* he sidesteps that issue altogether. No longer waiting for the barbarians in the form of the dreaded, yet hoped-for, mass response, he embarks instead on a practice in which, as Said puts it, the artist treats his or her work 'as an occasion to stir up more anxiety, tamper irrevocably with the possibility of closure, leave the audience more perplexed and unsettled than before'. No wonder, then, that these late albums haven't followed one another quickly, or fallen into any kind of linear progression, à la *Scott 1, 2, 3* … On the contrary, in Said's words, this 'type of lateness … is a sort of deliberately unproductive productiveness, a going against'.[45]

Which is not to say that these albums are merely hermetic. The abstraction of *Climate Of Hunter* has at times led to its critical dismissal, and certainly contributed to its failure as a commodity for Virgin Records. But as a work of art, its openendedness would seem to undercut the simplified teleology of 'success' or 'failure' of communication with its listeners. *Climate Of Hunter* addresses us quite directly as an audience – even Walker's gaze on the cover, meeting our eye, with mouth open and one hand pointing at us as if in the middle of a remark, asks us to listen. And the album's first line – *'This is how you disappear'* – cannot but help be received, at least at first hearing, as a statement directly from Scott to those who had been waiting for something to emerge from his own disappearance since the end of The Walker Brothers. However, that seemingly direct address does not turn out to be from a knowing pop star, or even a former pop star, to his devoted fans. The song 'Rawhide', which opens the album, is hardly an attempt at a return to pop, nor is it a wry look back at the form. It is instead … well, what the heck is it?

There are echoes in this first lyric of the well-known song of the same title, theme to a Western TV show about cattle drovers from Scott Engel's teenage years – a kitsch classic the likes of which Scott Walker might have sung on one of his 'lost' albums of the 1970s. But the mysteries begin as soon as that first line draws us in:

This is how you disappear
out between midnight,

called up
under valleys
of torches
and stars.

Foot, knee,
shaggy belly, face,
famous hindlegs,

as one of their own
you graze with them.

Cro-magnon herders
will stand in the wind,
sweeping tails shining,
and scaled
to begin,

SHUTTING DOWN HERE

Where are we now? If we try to parse it, it would seem we are quite literally in the dark. But a more fruitful question might be: where is Scott?

Returning to Said's thoughts on late style, his comments on the great Greek-language poet CP Cavafy might equally have been written about the later lyrics of Scott Walker: 'His poems enact a form of minimal survival between the past and the present, and his aesthetic of non-production, expressed in a non-metaphorical, almost prosaic unrhymed verse, enforces the sense of enduring exile which is at the core of his work ... a form of exile that replicates his existential isolation.[5]'

This 'enduring exile' that Said identifies in Cavafy's poems resonates both with Scott Walker's career at the time of *Climate Of Hunter*, and with many details of the album. Walker was forty years old when he wrote these songs, in the late summer of 1983. And by forty, his layers of self-imposed exile had only multiplied: from a Californian in London, to an Anglo-American in Copenhagen, a TV personality at the cinemathèque, a pop star without an audience, a Walker without Brothers. This ever-increasing isolation is, to me, the fundamental sound of *Climate Of Hunter*. The music on the album emerges from a silence that is something more than the hush of a carpeted 1980s-era recording studio. When the gates close on its drum hits, the sounds don't just stop, they disappear – as had Scott before the album begins, and would soon again after its finish.

By his own account, Scott Walker had spent the years between *Nite Flights* and *Climate Of Hunter* 'working toward what I call a silence, where this could come to me rather than me force it', as he told a radio interviewer in 1984.[6] 'I was looking for the right atmosphere,' he explained to another journalist in the same year. That atmosphere he finally found in 'a cottage in the country. I looked in the paper and saw this workman's cottage near Tunbridge Wells, so I rented it for two months, on my own. I put all of *Climate Of Hunter* together down there.'[7] Those two months of isolation are carefully inscribed on the LP cover – 'composed by scott walker, aug–sept 83' – despite the artist's reluctance to place anything but the barest information alongside his music. As he told Muriel Gray on the British TV pop show *The Tube* in a rare appearance to promote *Climate Of Hunter*, he was concerned that even titles 'would lopside or overload' his songs which were already 'finished as they were' – a situation that would cause Virgin Records to try and promote a seven-inch single called 'Track Three'.

The soloists on the album were similarly placed in isolation, away even from the very tunes they had been asked to play – according to producer Peter Walsh in *30 Century Man*, Scott's melodies were 'a closely guarded secret' throughout the sessions. Without guide vocals, or any kind of lead chart, the studio players called in had to rely on something other than the usual, as they lay down their individual tracks. 'It keeps everything a little more disjointed, there's no chance of everyone swinging together too much – which is what I don't want,' Walker explains in the same documentary. Not that he didn't communicate what he wanted from everyone involved – he just refused to do so in standard terms. 'He was very graphic in describing what he was aiming for ... using colours, shapes, dimensions, landscapes,' recalls Walsh today. 'At one point I remember he made a quick sketch for me of how he wanted me to modify the monitor mix.'[8] Evan Parker remembers Walker explaining to him, over a bottle of Chablis, 'I'm thinking about clouds of saxophone. I'm thinking more about Ligeti than anything else.'[9] Parker – a consummate improvisor – was comfortable with this kind of direction, and performs beautifully, playing with an openness that potentially relates to everything gathered around it. But guitarist Ray Russell, a pop and rock music stalwart, fared worse – his lead lines on the record really do sound like they were put down blindfolded, and sit stiffly in the mix without reference to anything else in the arrangement.

This disjointedness was deliberate on Walker's part. Was it because it matched the atmosphere in which he had finally composed these songs? When he came back from his isolation in the country he immediately entered the most urban, and urbane, situation for a musician: an expensive recording studio with 'the busiest session team in London', as Peter Walsh describes the rhythm section he put together for the purpose. Parts had been scored, a full orchestra session booked, and yet, as arranger Brian Gascoigne recalled later, 'Scott was extremely reluctant to let anyone know what was going to happen.'[10] The harmonies themselves masked his intentions. 'What he's after is the boundary between chords and discords,' explains Gascoigne, sitting at a piano in a later video interview and demonstrating the type of ambiguity Walker would ask him not only to build into the arrangement, but then hold on to for sixteen bars at a time. 'The strategy is to get this great seesaw going back and forth, and the pivot for it is to get the musicians into the no-man's land between melody and harmony, conventionally [understood], and the squeaks and grunts of the avant-garde.'[11]

A logical comrade in this seesaw strategy might have been Brian Eno – indeed, Eno's enthusiasm for Scott's songs on *Nite Flights* is said to have had a hand in his new solo contract at Virgin,[12] and if any records from the period share a sound with this second arrival of Scott the auteur, it would be the Eno/Bowie 'Berlin' albums. Bowie and Eno are both said to have approached Scott Walker offering themselves as possible producers for what eventually became *Climate Of Hunter*,[13] a situation that in either case might have shaped and contextualised his efforts with an eye on a larger pop audience. But Walker rejected these overtures. 'His only reason was that he wanted to pursue his own ideas,' recalled a still exasperated-sounding Dick Leahy, head of The Walker Brothers' last label GTO, when asked in 1993 about the Bowie possibility.[14] As for Eno, Walker himself told the *NME* in 1984, maybe only half-joking: 'I thought rather than destroying his career too I had to do one on my own.'[15]

On his own, then, even while surrounded by colleagues in the studio, is how Walker went about constructing the album. This is especially palpable in the vocals, which Walker prefers to put down quickly, at the end of the sessions, with the minimum number of people present. That voice always seemed to rise above even the densest arrangements of The Walker Brothers and Scott's first round of solo work, through its sheer strength and charm. But Scott's own view is that his baritone 'tranquilises people ... so people stop listening to what they're hearing'. And what he wants instead on his late albums is for the voice to be 'pitched, as the lyrics, vertiginously'. All in the service of the lyric – and never comfortable. 'It's a genuine terror that I'm not going to get it right. And I only want to do it once or twice if I can. And I just have to absolutely get it. I fail lots of times but at least I'm trying.'

The result can send shivers down your spine, perhaps because the 'genuine terror' Walker creates for himself in the studio is communicated directly, or perhaps because he sounds so utterly alone as he faces it. 'Ultimately, it's just a man singing ... I just want to get to a man singing, and when it has to have emotion, hopefully it's real emotion.'

Which brings us back to those seemingly impenetrable lyrics. Eno, so engaged by this period of Scott Walker's, might well agree. In an extended interview included as a bonus on the *30 Century Man* DVD, Eno talks at length about Scott's strength as a lyricist: 'I don't find the lyrics at all problematic. In fact, I find them completely engaging ... Normally I think lyrics I could do without. For me lyrics in most songs are a way of just getting the voice to do something ... In Scott's songs, that's not true at all: lyrics actually draw you further and further into the music. And they're so rich and full of ambiguity that they actually withstand listening to again and again, like music does. They don't spell it out for you, so you haven't "solved the problem" in the first two listens. That's why I say he's a poet.'

*

No Regrets

At the risk of trying to 'solve the problem', it seems worth taking a closer look at some of these lyrics on *Climate Of Hunter*, as if they were in a book of poems rather than on a record album. Walker works hard to place his words at the centre of the music – speaking about his latest album, *The Drift*, he has said, 'Everything is very low end, very high end, and the voice right in the middle, where it should be.' So what did he place there, at the album's core?

Exile and isolation would seem to be a key into the difficult lyrics of *Climate Of Hunter*, just as they explain much about the music. 'Rawhide', that opening track with its disorienting hunter-gatherer vocabulary, leaves an impression of loneliness on a vast, geological timescale. It begins with a cowbell moving across the stereo picture from right to left (east to west?), like cattle passing on the horizon, reinforcing the brief sense of familiarity generated by the title. But the shaggy upright figure who grazes with the herd in the opening lines seems to be not on the American plains, but in some kind of prehistoric 'Cro-magnon' past – at one with nature in a manner far beyond a television Western. Nevertheless, this is no pastoral scene by the time the strings enter, in anxious quick slurs, midway through the arrangement:

> *Freezing in red,*
> *bent over*
> *his ice-skin*
>
> *The insomniac gnaws*
> *in the On-Offs;*
>
> *he is glazed*
> *in the hooves*
> *all round.*
>
> *It is losing*
> *its shape.*
> *Losing its shape,*

as the heat in your hands
carve the muscle
away.

'*The insomniac*' might be the hunter (and Walker has said that he himself suffers from nightmares), but I hear it more as the hunter's victim. Either way, '*in the On-Offs*' is like a line straight out of Beckett. On-Off suggests wake-sleep, or, given the images that follow, life-death, but as a plural it takes on the more disturbing idea of slipping repeatedly between the two states, back and forth, the jaw working all the while as it '*gnaws*': death throes. The carving of the body in the next verse dissolves a stiff shape just as horns enter the orchestration, playing long, sustained tones against the strings' tight runs, until eventually the strings, too, relax and join the horns in what feels like a peaceful coda. While Scott sings:

Motionless brands
burn into
a hipframe

As a saviour
loads sightlines
backlit by fires,

on the ridges
of the highest
breeder

The last word of the song is a final, unexpected turn – shifting us from the appearance of a saviour on the highest ridge, to what then seems instead to be the owner of the high ground, or perhaps the highest placed in the human herd, the '*highest breeder*' – and thus leaving us not in a state of salvation, but rather a kind of stable, permanent anxiety. Tomorrow will see the same death throes, the same victories and defeats of the *famous hindlegs'*, the same disappearances.

This epochal opening to the album, situating us together with the singer in mythic time, could be taken as a grand, even stadium-rock gesture toward commonality – we're all Cro-magnons here – but the details of the song ultimately work in an opposite direction. 'Rawhide', the television theme song made famous by Frankie Laine, similarly portrays a lonesome hero (played by Clint Eastwood, no less), driving his cattle *'Through rain and wind and weather/Hell-bent for leather'*, but that off-the-rack American fantasy depends on a direction – *'Rollin' rollin' rollin''* goes the refrain – and a goal: the big payday and party at the end of the road. Scott's 'Rawhide' finishes instead with a puzzling, static image. What might this *'motionless brand'* be?

Consider the end of the Frankie Laine tune:

> *Keep movin', movin', movin'*
> *Though they're disapprovin'*
> *Keep them doggies movin'*
> *Rawhide!*
> *Don't try to understand 'em*
> *Just rope, throw, and brand 'em*
> *Soon we'll be living high and wide*
> *My heart's calculatin'*
> *My true love will be waitin'*
> *Waitin' at the end of my ride*
> *Rawhide!*

If this idiotic lyric wasn't in Scott's mind as he wrote his own 'Rawhide', it had to be sitting there somewhere in his memory. In any case, placing one against the other would seem to elucidate some of that mysterious last phrase to Walker's song. *'Motionless brands/burn into/a hipframe'* is a frozen version of what was, in the Western ditty, a blur of activity (*'Just rope throw and brand 'em'*), but it also serves as a kind of empathetic riposte to the bizarre instruction, *'Don't try to understand 'em'*. These *'motionless'* brands – they hover, in our mind's eye, about to burn ... whom? Perhaps they are directed at the hunter, rather than the hunted. Or are the two one? The *'hipframe'* they mark might be cattle, as seen on TV – but I can't help but also hear an echo in that phrase of Swinging London. Wasn't Scott himself branded in the 'hip frame' – the pop frame of reference – and left motionless in that moment he spent at the top of the charts?

This biographical reading of the ending is likely going too far – a canard that matches the invitation to read the opening line, *'This is how you disappear'* as a personal statement from Scott, the former pop star. But behind it is a feeling, more likely intended by the singer, of identification with the branded. The motionless brand is a nightmare image, a permanent threat – an injury about to happen, as opposed to the action-figure GI Joes of *'Don't try to understand 'em/Just rope, throw, and brand 'em'* who inflict their harm on others, rather than themselves. So who is the hunter, who is the hunted? By the end of the song, that would seem to be an open question, as the lyric's ambiguities leave the two terms confused.

Regardless of the rhyme of these associations with the author's ideas, here we are for sure, in the climate (mood/spirit) of hunter, looking for sense in these difficult, open-ended lyrics of Scott Walker. As Said writes of Cavafy, Walker has deliberately placed us in 'an ambiguous but carefully specified poetic space in which to overhear and only partly to grasp what is actually taking place'. That carefully specified space – an exile's place, in Said's terms – is I think delineated throughout the album. As überfan Lewis Williams points out, the structure of *Climate Of Hunter* is symmetrical (something much more readily apparent on LP than on the later CD reissue): 'Side two ... mirrors side one too closely to be anything but intentional,' he writes.[16] Each side of the original LP has four tracks – the second

of which features Evan Parker on sax, the third of which features
Ray Russell on lead guitar, and the fourth of which omits the rhythm
section otherwise featured throughout. It is easy to find many such
parallels – the cowbell that opens side one, with the bass harmonics
that open side two, and so on – but what is more interesting to me
here is the idea that the LP feels constructed like a physical space. In
this regard, the tracks listed only by number may not be as blankly
titled as they seem – since the one thing that is made absolutely clear
about them is their place in the sequence. 'Track Three' was a rather
absurd title for a single, but what could not be missed even in isolation is that the song properly belongs to a carefully specified space:
the space of the album.

Images of this space – the place of exile – occur throughout the
album's lyrics, but are especially important to the last tracks on each
side: 'Sleepwalkers Woman', and the sole cover in the collection,
'Blanket Roll Blues'. If 'Rawhide' is a disorienting opening for the
long-time Scott Walker fan, 'Sleepwalkers Woman' would seem to be
their reward for making it to the end of side one. A flat-out gorgeous
orchestration, with familiar touches from Scott's earlier career, like
reverb-heavy plucked strings over long sustained bowed ones, here
Walker allows himself the same lush romanticism that the album's
first tracks avoid so assiduously. The harmonies have tension, but
the washes of chords make the song feel like one long cadence – it
resolves again, and again, as Scott reaches the end of each verse. The
lyric, too, resolves more than once: *For the first time/unwoken/I am
returned* is the conclusion to the first half of the song, a phrase sung
twice and then repeated melodically by the orchestra a third time
(an instrumental device in direct contrast to the preceding tracks,
which feature solos recorded without any reference to the melody).
The journey towards this emphatic resolution begins:

> *In the time*
> *of an exile,*

from the jails
of another,

where soundings
are taken
raw
to his
eyes.

Those images of exile and jail are echoed in the second half of the song, which similarly begins in a place of isolation:

He arrives
from a place

with a face
of fast sun.

Arrives
from a space,

his refuge
overrun.

This place, a blank space that had been a refuge but has since been lost, would seem to be as lonely a starting place as possible. But the second half of the song again works towards a resolution via an idea of 'return':

For the first time
forgetting
I am returned.

Her mind moved
on the silence
I am returned.

No Regrets

The development expressed here – from exile to return – would seem to be achieved not only in the lyric to this song, but also on this side of the album. 'Sleepwalkers Woman' – no apostrophe, so we might read it as two consecutive nouns, as well as with the implied possessive – is a destination as ambiguous as the starting point of 'Rawhide', but it is clearly an arrival. *'There are no voices here'*, Walker sings, about the place he finds himself at the end of side one. *'We have entered deserted.'* Where the singer has entered is as ambiguous as where he began, but as Eno says about Scott Walker's lyrics, 'It's not to do with meaning, it's to do with making something happen. It's not to do with telling someone something, it's making something happen to someone, which is what you do with music as well.'[17]

In other words, we may not be able to parse exactly what is meant by the arrival expressed in 'Sleepwalkers Woman', but we nonetheless feel something of what has happened to this singer who begins, *'This is how you disappear'*, and finally declares, *'I am returned'*.

This process of side one doesn't continue linearly on side two, so much as repeat in a cyclic variation. *'It's a starving reflection'*, is how 'Track Five' begins, with a meditative intro that is then interrupted by a series of almost frantic images of motion – some of them mirrors of phrases already encountered in 'Rawhide', such as 'gnaw' and 'On-Offs':

> *WE CHEW UP*
> *the blackness*
>
> *to some*
> *high sleep*
> *travel,*
>
> *a faster*
> *silence.*

One
to go long
again,

in the going-
-gone again.
Full stare passages
striking less face;
outside
on the move
a shattered heart
pace

This forward-moving lyric is set to a quick and simple backbeat, a kind of disco march, but in the latter part of the song the keyboard starts to push the harmony in surprising ways, building more slowly and dramatically toward a cadence that never quite arrives. Horns finally enter, as they do at the end of 'Rawhide', just as an image of melting is again introduced:

And the heat
from the shore,
melts down
to receive us;

floodlit foreheads
howled open,
and so nearly
blessed,

as they soften
round dog-joys
of unfinished
strangers,

rubbed out
on a point

afterburning

The body/animal images here rhyme with 'Rawhide' as well, but the point of view seems more resolutely from the hunted rather than hunter – marched down to a floodlit place, and *'rubbed out on a point'*. Is it a slaughter? Or perhaps another view of branding; this time not in anticipation of pain, but rather its *'afterburning'*.

Whether this reflection between songs and album sides was deliberate on Walker's part or not, the record continues through the end to toy with our expectations of direction. Just as the *'shattered heart pace'* of 'Track Five' gives way to a false cadence, an ending that's never quite reached, the entire sequence builds toward a conclusion, 'Blanket Roll Blues', that leaves the singer in the same isolated and dislocated space described by – that first line again – *'This is how you disappear'*.

When I crossed
the river,

with a heavy
blanket roll,

I took nobody with me,

not a soul.

I took
a few provisions

some for comfort
some for cold,

but I took
nobody with me,

not a soul.

This closing lyric is the only one on the album not written by Scott Walker. Marlon Brando sings it in the Sidney Lumet film *The Fugitive Kind* (1959) – Tennessee Williams's own adaptation of his play *Orpheus Descending* (1957), which reimagines the Orpheus story in a Gothic Southern town, with a guitar-carrying drifter as the archetypal poet-singer. Walker told a radio interviewer at the time of *Climate Of Hunter*'s release that this song had been 'in the back of my mind for years and years ... and it seemed like the perfect sort of period at the end of all this'.[18] That period marks an arrival, just like 'Sleepwalkers Woman' – the singer has already *'crossed the river'*, a phrase that matches the *'I am returned'* refrain closing side one. But this time the 'carefully specified poetic space' that Said finds in Cavafy is more clearly delineated (Tennessee Williams being a much more explicit writer than Scott Walker). It is a space occupied only by the singer, even as he addresses us from it – a place of loneliness, and exile. It is where we began.

1. In Cavafy, CP (trans Edmund Keeley & Philip Sherrard), *Collected Poems* (Princeton, NJ: Princeton University Press, 1992).
2. Scott Walker quoted in *Scott Walker – 30 Century Man* (dir Stephen Kijak, UK, 2006; Oscilloscope DVD, 2009). Except where stated, all Walker quotes in this chapter are taken from interview segments in this film.
3. Said, Edward, 'Thoughts On Late Style', *London Review Of Books* vol 26 no 15 (5 August 2004).
4. Said, 'Thoughts On Late Style'.
5. Said, 'Thoughts On Late Style'.
6. Walker radio interview with Alan Bangs (British Forces Broadcasting Service (BFBS), 1984), quoted in *30 Century Man*.

7. Cook, Richard, 'Scott Walker: The Original Godlike Genius' in *New Musical Express* (17 March 1984).
8. Email interview with the author, 10 September 2011.
9. Evan Parker interviewed in *30 Century Man*.
10. Brian Gascoigne quoted in Watkinson, Mike & Anderson, Pete, *Scott Walker: A Deep Shade Of Blue* (London: Virgin Books, 1994).
11. Brian Gascoigne interviewed in *30 Century Man*.
12. Watkinson & Anderson, *A Deep Shade Of Blue*.
13. Watkinson & Anderson, *A Deep Shade Of Blue*.
14. Watkinson & Anderson, *A Deep Shade Of Blue*.
15. Cook, 'The Original Godlike Genius'.
16. Williams, Lewis, *Scott Walker: The Rhymes Of Goodbye* (London: Plexus, 2006).
17. Brian Eno interviewed in *30 Century Man*.
18. BFBS radio interview, 1984, quoted in Williams, *The Rhymes Of Goodbye*.

The Significant Other
Brian Morton
Tilt (1995)

He who sleeps in continual noise is wakened by silence ...
William Dean Howells, *Pordenone* (1882)[1]

Scott Walker is that very rare phenomenon: a completely genuine charlatan. Lest this seems dismissive or capricious, the defining character of the charlatan is that he sings his wares, even if they have no therapeutic worth, no *virtue*, even if the singer knows that all the virtue is in the singing, not the snake-oil. The performance is the thing. Everything else is coloured water and pseudo-scientific labels.

So it is with Walker. Elaborate claims are made on behalf of his work and its efficacy. Its ingredients are obsessively analysed. But the labelling is often misleading, if not wilfully deceptive. Walker's reputation is now secure, yet outside the mainstream, but simple understanding of the great empiric, and particularly his mid-nineties masterwork *Tilt*, is still hampered, with footnotes getting in the way of the notes, cultural references drowning out the Song.

The most insidious of these was the suggestion that Scott Walker was pop music's Thomas Pynchon, if not its JD Salinger. Released in 1995, *Tilt* came out of a period of silence, not unprecedented but craftily turned to advantage. An early playback of the record for trusted reviewers was conducted in circumstances that resembled either a samizdat audition or a gathering of the Early Church. *Tilt*'s tablets-of-stone gravity has faded with the passage of time, but its aura persists, along with the notion of a 'reclusive' artist – such a packed and usually meaningless designation! – who had declared a plague on the houses of commerce and middlebrow entertainment and set off on his own solitary course. For a time, the only biographical datum ever adduced about Walker in his post-Walker Brothers life was that he hung around pubs in Vauxhall watching guys playing darts, a throwaway remark made to the late Richard Cook in a then-rare interview which somehow became enshrined (through no fault of Cook's) as a salient fact about Walker: the lonely observer, hugging peripheries, solemnly embracing a grim nostalgie de la boue.

Like Pynchon, like Salinger, Walker remained very much connected to the world, but on his particular terms. Salinger's obsessively defended privacy notwithstanding, all three simply opted out of the usual cultural forums – media interviews, personal appearances, book tours or performing tours – and their refusal was couched in the gently self-denying libertarian spirit of Herman Melville's *Bartleby The Scrivener*, who simply 'preferred not to'. And yet, while not a recluse in the conventionally understood sense, which implies perpetual withdrawal or innate withdrawnness, he did spend some time in 1966 at Quarr Abbey on the Isle of Wight, but was there to study Gregorian chant, not to take the tonsure. The word 'recluse' does apply to Walker in its other, more abstruse usages, substantive and adjectival: it can also refer to the contents of a store or hoard, or to describe recondite ideas; more obscurely still, 'recluse' can also mean an underground reservoir ... no quibbles here, surely, about its relevance to Scott Walker. As I hope to show, its root also leads back – with a little philological juggling – to a tradition of singing that precisely locates Walker's idiosyncratic lyricism and locates it at a period and cultural context that might seem remote from that of a twentieth/

twenty-first-century pop troubadour but which nonetheless offers intriguing parallels.

The other descriptive barnacle that attaches itself to Scott Walker's name is 'existentialist', a word that comes freighted with images of black berets, Gauloise smoke, anomie, enervation and dread, moral nullity and acte gratuit, jazz, and certain kinds of mournful minor-key singing; but only involves any of these strong signifiers in the most incidental way. If existentialism is a philosophy which insists that existence precedes essence, then Walker – as a musical artist rather than qua moral being – doesn't comfortably inhabit the term at all. As a composer, he might be described as an essentialist whose sense of form and trajectory is prior to and shaped without immediate reference to content. And yet Walker's lyrics evolve not so much associatively as experientially. To understand a line, one must move on to the next line, or to put it in the language of CK Ogden & IA Richards's *The Meaning Of Meaning*, what is required in order to understand a Walker lyric is that 'it form[s] a context with further experiences'.[2] The songs accumulate density as they progress, but in the process become more knotted and 'obscure' rather than more open. This discourse belongs to the science of 'significs', a branch of rhetoric and linguistics developed in the 1890s (and most fully explained in an entry to the mighty 1911 edition of the *Encyclopaedia Britannica,* written by its originator, Lady Welby). Significs might seem to have been superseded by its modern descendant or the relevant aspects of critical theory, but it retains a great deal of its intellectual authority in this case, not least because of the studiedly 'old-fashioned' aspects of Walker's music.

He is, of course, at some level a naturalist as well. The only other well-known resident of Walker's birthplace, Hamilton, Ohio, was the Gilded Age novelist William Dean Howells, who, like Scott Walker, left the Midwest and settled (for a time, at least) in England. He was the man who helped set Abraham Lincoln on the presidential trail and who later, in collaboration with Mark Twain, helped delimit the moral and cultural vagaries of the 'Gilded Age' in American life. Hamilton was a curious backwater, a German and Scotch-Irish enclave notorious for its heavy industry and brothels, its infrastructural remoteness (no interstate connections) and for its vulnerability to floods. As a place cut off to some degree from metropolitan America, it espoused a particular brand of stoical self-reliance most clearly set out in Howells's famous letter-cum-credo, sent in 1903 to Charles Eliot Norton. 'I am not sorry for having wrought in common, crude material so much; that is the right American stuff; and perhaps hereafter, when my din is done, if anyone is curious to know what that noise was, it will be found to have proceeded from a small insect which was scraping about on the surface of our life and trying to get into its meaning for the sake of all the other insects larger and smaller. That is, such has been my unconscious work ...'. Does this not sit comfortably alongside the locust chatter of 'Bouncer See Bouncer ...', or the other small everyday sounds – 'common, crude material' – that irrupt throughout *Tilt* and its yet darker successor *The Drift*?

Scott Walker is an American artist. *Tilt*'s British provenance is misleading. It is unmistakably the work of an exile. It is as misleading in that regard as all the comfortably assimilated European references that occupy and exercise his listeners: we encounter the doomed Italian film director Pasolini at the very beginning, but in a context that suggests European culture might be on the auction block ... Walker's Americanness is in the line of Benjamin Franklin and Fenimore Cooper, Henry Adams and Henry James, all of whom sustained an attitude to the Old World that was ambivalent at best, opportunistic at worst. If Walker does seem to have a 'European' sensibility, then it is European in the way that Susan Sontag was 'European', which is to say, subject to a distinctively American phenomenology. More than tourists, they nonetheless take in European culture at such an accelerated rate that it fractures and divides into the clouds of epiphenomena one encounters in Walker's lyrics. This is the 'blooming, buzzing confusion' of sense data William James associated with early childhood, but so extended as to have become culturally definitive, quintessentially 'American'. Is 'Psoriatic' on *The Drift*, with its chaotic piling-up of fragmentary speech, physical discomforts (*'Red is patchy/Snows the silver'*) and inchoate sounds (*'Ja-da ja-da/jing jing/jing'*), an attempt to come to terms with this agonising plenum of sensory data?

How does Walker shape a music to convey all this? In the same context, it is worth setting aside some of the artists he resembles only very superficially. Despite a similar cryptic colouration, he has little in common with Michael Mantler's dark Viennese sound-scapes and Samuel Beckett scenarios, or even Nico's *Marble Index* and equally marmoreal *Desertshore*. But nor does he have much in common with the long-form songwriting of Jim Morrison and the Tim Buckley of *Lorca*, for whom songwriting had become a branch of improvisation, both of whom draw their main inspiration from European models. There is perhaps some kinship with David Axelrod's jazz-inspired psychedelia with its half-hidden political references and trance-dictated mismatches of sound and sense. In every respect except methodologically, he might be thought to have something in common with Brian Wilson, but where Wilson adds like a painter, Walker subtracts like a sculptor. Or with Kate Bush, whose rate of production is almost as slow as Walker's but whose aesthetic is maximal, painterly and theatrical, again very different to Walker's. Oddly, perhaps, there is more similarity with the music of Jack Bruce – once the favoured mouthpiece of Mantler's more extreme creations – in which odd metres, clenched and often indecipherable harmonies and Pete Brown's associative lyrics generate a comparable estrangement. Scott's first instrument, taken up in his teens, was also apparently an electric bass, played with enough proficiency to gain session dates, but perhaps more influential in switching the 'natural' hierarchy of clefs.

No Regrets

At bottom, Walker's music is rooted in the pop he would have heard coming out of a Midwest radio station – young Noel Scott Engel reached the age of discretion just as Elvis Presley began to record: he is thus a first-generation rock fan – and in which he served a teenage apprenticeship, pre-Walker Brothers, on Eddie Fisher's influential television show which espoused the star's own brand of cuspy proto-rock 'n' roll, still with a strong Broadway/vaudeville influence. At first hearing, *Tilt*'s opening song 'Farmer In The City' packs an alienating wallop. What's it about? Where's the hook? Time and familiarity haven't softened the impact, or directly answered those questions, though internet wisdom confidently pronounces that some of the material alludes to Pier Paolo Pasolini's 1971 poem 'Uno dei tanti epiloghi' (translated by Norman Macafee as 'One Of The Many Epilogs'), and that the repeated *'21/21/21'* and reference to 'Ninetto' may refer to the age of Pasolini's young lover when he was conscripted into the army. By the same token, 'Farmer In The City' may attempt to capture the flicker and glitch of Pasolini's dying brain as the car goes back and forth (twenty-one times?) over his body on the beach at Ostia. Or it may not. Listen to 'Farmer In The City' back to back with the English group Coil's 'Ostia (The Death Of Pasolini)' from their 1986 album *Horse Rotorvator* and it's clear that Walker doesn't intend any literal or symbolic representation of actual events. In 'significs' terms, the symbolisation only works at ever higher levels of organisation until it is possible to say – indeed, necessary to say – that the song has no meaning beyond its own referential set, which is not to say that it signifies nothing, but merely that it has no reliable point of semantic leverage outside itself. Walker is presumably aware that Pasolini, whom he seems to appreciate as a poet and linguistic philosopher as much as he admires the films, wrote in Friulian, a rare Romance language peculiar to north-eastern Italy, and that he was active in promoting Casarsa Friulian over Udine, the 'official' dialect of the Friuli-Venezia Giulia region. This sense of a language embattled is one that has also appealed to American writers who have struggled with an inherited tension between 'English English' and an array of regional and colonial vernaculars. Hamilton was a town that nourished particularly strong and durable language groups. In the same way, Walker's keening delivery (and here's a 'baritone' who now consistently sings outside his apparently natural range) both takes on and shrugs off significations: bel canto, cantorial, muezzin, the monophonic incipit of Gregorian chant.

All these are persuasive enough as putative sources, but listen to 'Farmer In The City' enough times – even resisters admit to hearing melody, and the internet offers a few 'cover versions' – and it is clear that Walker has not left behind the basic form and contours of conventional pop song. 'Farmer In The City' uses repetition, if not actually a strophic form, and one can readily find the bleached bones of a familiar thirty-two-bar sequence, even down to the ghost of a 'middle eight'. There is also a return to the pervasive three-quarter feel of *Scott 3*, an album cast almost entirely in Walker's idiosyncratic versions of 'perfect' time, a superior record to its more highly regarded numerical successor; in fact, probably Walker's finest recording prior to *Tilt*. Brian Gascoigne's dark arrangement for the Strings Of Sinfonia Of London clearly harks back to Wally Stott's orchestral backgrounds for *Scott 3*, which combine not just lushness of texture but a teetering, continually questioning harmonic trajectory and the same bold use of non-functional sound he had employed as music director on *The Goon Show*. Stott went through a gender reassignment in 1972 and became Angela Morley. In 1999 she told me that Walker's music was 'basically pop, with some jazz and classical things, but then pop has always fed off those things. I never thought his songs were as complicated or as *difficult* as people said, and yes, I think there was a sense of humour there.'

'Farmer In The City', the only later Scott Walker tune you're ever likely to hear a butcher-boy whistling, is bookended on *Tilt* by the stark 'Rosary', a jukebox-proportioned two minutes and forty-one seconds of stark pleading arranged for just voice and anti-virtuosic guitar. It's possibly a song about the making of songs, or about the construction of an album, with individual *'beads'* arranged, or disarranged, along some kind of vague linearity, variously *'thread'*, *'thong'*, *'lines'*, *'hair'*, *'snare'*, *'vein'*, but ultimately *'ribbonless'*, and with bullet-holes kissed in place of the blessed beads. Those who witnessed Walker's rare live performance of the song on the BBC music show *Later With Jools Holland* commented on his palpable discomfort performing before an audience. One wouldn't naturally use the same terms about, say, Johnny Ray or even Ray's latter-day incarnation Morrissey, but the knowledge of Walker's poor performing nerves and 'reclusive' nature stoked a set of reactions which don't quite fit the evidence. Walker's distress is part, surely, of the drama of the song, with its wordless wailed turns, like Wagner's hymn of the river maidens, which is echoed in TS Eliot's *The Waste Land*. But as always with Walker it is difficult to judge whether he is singing as a persona or in his own person, and to some extent the question is unanswerable because self and persona remain cryptic and occluded. The connection with Wagner-via-Eliot is not incidental, because 'Rosary' is perhaps the most 'operatic' track on an album routinely and meaninglessly described as 'operatic', but also its sparest and least impenetrable song. The album ends more resolutely but also more desolately than it begins: *'And I gotta/quit/And I gotta/quit'*, a Beckettian cadence from an artist who doesn't quit, but keeps coming back for ever murkier third and fourth acts. Eliot wrote about dark themes in what were essentially popular forms, music hall tunes and comic turns, jazz, pub talk. It was his contemporary Ezra Pound who minimised that aspect of 'He Do The Police In Different Voices' (*The Waste Land*'s original working title) and, 'better craftsman' or not, it was Pound who turned Eliot from being a great vernacular poet into a more sober academic poet. His motives might well be questioned, not least his need to prove himself in possession of the finer ear.

Walker has gone through a similar translation and redaction. His later career is the perfect illustration of the mythical 'second act' in American creative lives, the second act that F Scott Fitzgerald said American artists were denied and about which he was, of course, crashingly wrong. And so are those who insist on a wholly dark colouration to Walker's musical and lyrical palette. He can scarcely be regroomed as a comic vocalist, but his music is more accessible and more observational (albeit rapidly gated and filtered at the verbal level) than its reputation suggests. If part of that observational element is taken up by Walker's eclectic reading – hence, in 'The Cockfighter' (a song clearly concerned with psychic aspects of the Holocaust), the improbable confluence of Adolf Eichmann, erotica and the trial of Queen Caroline, all set to great train-wreck clusters of sound – it shouldn't be minimised on that score. How do a royal consort and a war criminal happen to come together in a pop song? Any answer must needs be speculative, but existing speculation has tended to run on fairly predictable tramlines. Yes, Caroline of Brunswick (1768–1821) was involved in a messy and vexatious divorce suit from George IV, but she was also the people's champion for political reform in opposition to royal autarky, whose most resounding statement, apart from some good jokes about royal adultery, was to the effect that government could not control the mind any more than it could alter the course of the planets or the rhythm of the tides. By the same token, most people know one or two things about Eichmann: that he provided the 'rolling stock' for the Holocaust and that Hannah Arendt said, following his trial and execution, that he somehow represented 'the banality of evil', a phrase so often quoted out of context that it no longer means anything.[3] Eichmann is also 'The Man in the Glass Booth', the hated, misunderstood pariah figure whose physical separation from us remains ambiguous: who is being protected? Him, from summary justice? Us, from his poisonous vapours? The song has an unmistakable but curious eroticism:

'Do you swear/the breastbone/was bare', *'Do you/have any doubt/ he slept/in that bed'* – but it evokes the strange, cold pornography of the courtroom, where deepest intimacy is forensically permitted but couched only in the most 'acceptable' of terms. If this is a song about love, or love betrayed, it is also a song about violent display, about the manipulation of different kinds of power. And who can say that the figure in the glass booth isn't the musical artist, who is both on trial and pilloried, but also held within in his imaginative cordon sanitaire?

A dispassionate audition of the work suggests an artist whose absolute commitment to the Song is balanced by an alertness to contemporary reality: references on *Scott 3* to Che Guevara and Charles de Gaulle; the whispered *'pow pow'* that, on *The Drift*, apparently registers Walker's shocked but almost exhilarated reaction to the World Trade Center attacks; the fate of South American refugees on one of *Tilt's* best but perhaps least fitting tracks, 'Bolivia '95' (compare Jack Bruce's 'Morning Story', which was apparently inspired by Spanish immigrants around Charing Cross in Glasgow).

'Bolivia '95' begins with a strange invocation to *'Doctorie/give me a C/for this/babaloo'*. It is conceivable that Walker here makes further reference to Guevara, who died in Bolivia and became a bloodied auto-icon of revolution, sponged down for the cameras, sanctified, but still speckling the straw and dirt floor with blood. Is this also hinted at in the kissed bullet-holes of 'Rosary'? Guevara was also a medical doctor and drawn to Marxism through his experience of rural dis-ease throughout Central and Latin America. *'Babaloo'* is puzzling. In Yoruba mythology, Babalu Aye is the name given to the Orisha god of earth and disease, but it is a name that is conventionally not spoken, lest it call up an epidemic. This is entirely consistent with Walker's interest in illness, dismemberment and undefined plague on *Tilt*, but the name has further, more playful associations, too: the song 'Babalou' which Desi Arnaz sang on *The Lucy Show*; but also more intriguingly as the stage and television name of the Filipino comedian Pablito Sarmiento (who, teasingly, appeared in a nineties sitcom called *Oki Doki Doc*), a near-contemporary of Walker's and another ubiquitous televisual presence of the time. He jumps into this prism of associations every bit as comfortably – or uncomfortably – as the juxtaposition of the Holocaust's facilitator and George IV's consort Caroline (whose story Walker apparently plucked at random from the shelf, though he cannot have missed its subtexts of celebrity manipulation *and* democratic populism, two subjects which interest him deeply).

There are similar layers of association in 'Manhattan', which bears the strange subtitle 'flerdele'. This is most obviously a corruption of fleur de lys, a symbol this time of French royalty, used to describe the characteristic branding of slaves in francophone Africa, but it has also been suggested that it is a Danish word[4] for 'branching', in the sense of division, which may hint at the city's sprawl around a riverine estuary and also at New Amsterdam's/New York's early dependence on economic exploitation and indenture. Typically, Walker makes these points, if such is his intention, at a literally sub-liminal level and alongside fairly clear references to 'Dem Bones', a song written by James Weldon Johnson, but apparently inspired by the prophet Ezekiel's vision of the Valley of Dry Bones. Walker may have seen in childhood a television animation of the song, but there were also famous recorded versions by The Deep River Boys (who performed it on *The Ed Sullivan Show* and were wildly successful in Scandinavia) and The Delta Rhythm Boys, among others. 'Manhattan''s other geographies – Bengal, Somalia, Corsica, Burma, Kenya, Havana, Alaska, *'Russo'* – have no single obvious connective logic, but typically multiple possibilities that draw in Rimbaud, Graham Greene, the Taliban and much else . . .

The subtitle and text of 'Patriot (a single)' suggests that the song is concerned with isolated individuality – a theme consistently developed throughout the album – and, in the song's play around good news/bad news/no news, some sense of 'the missing' as a subset of humanity as distinct as the preterite in Calvinist eschatology. Patriot is, of course, also the name of the missile routinely launched against Saddam Hussein's largely ineffective Scuds in the first Gulf War (1990–91) and a symbol of American/Israeli defiance.

This is not to reposition Walker as a political or even as a socially aware songwriter, though elements of both are undoubtedly present and powerfully active. He belongs, to go to a field that would have been familiar to Ezra Pound and which was one of his greatest gifts to American prosody and poetic form, to the complex style of the Occitan trobar clus (and here the root of 'reclusive' at last takes on some significance), the most high-flown and specialised of the troubadour styles. (It's certainly worth remembering that among its other associations, 'tilt' also has a chivalric resonance, associated with jousting, also with courtly love and non-lethal combat according to fixed rules. The expression 'tilting at windmills' is almost worn out with overuse and has blurred what we think really went on in the tiltyard.) Trobar clus was the 'closed form' developed by the elusive twelfth-century troubadour Marcabru, a shadowy figure represented only by some four dozen verses which employ obscurity of language and imagery as well as a certain level of satirical irony. The trobar clus style was knowingly pitched at a specialist audience, but there was a clear continuity between its methods, if not always its subject matter, and those of trobar leu ('light', and effectively the pop music of its day) and trobar ric ('rich', or verbally elaborated).

Walker now stands in the same relationship to the romantic pop of his own youthful heyday as trobar clus stands to the sentimental and formally codified poetry and song of courtly love. One of the elements of Walker's later music, notably, is the absence of erotic charge, and something of the same might be said even of his earlier records, whose romanticism is already detached, elegiac, faintly enervated. Even the apparently surging passion of 'Face On Breast' is ironised by a version of Lauren Bacall's famous lines in *To Have And Have Not*: *'I tried to/show ya/but ya didn't/*

want to go//Ya know/how to whistle/put ya lips/together/and blow'.
Walker processes these references at close to warp speed and the
listener either registers them or not, but with little time to ponder
their placing or significance. There is a certain wilful perversity in
Walker's very precise articulation of highly obscure lyrics. It puts
him in a nicely ambiguous position on a spectrum of vocal clarity
in pop which begins at one end with the muffled, rapid obscen-
ity of 'Louie Louie', the imaginative mishearings of phrases or
lyrics known as 'mondegreens', and even Michael Stipe's Walker
Percy-inspired creative *mis*-hearing, where the wrong word yields a
greater meaning than the right word. Instead, Walker is more like a
performance poet, with every word or sound, however impenetrable, registered with absolute clarity of locution. It is a complex, but
also a highly playful strategy, and part of the delight and strength of
Tilt, once one frees it of weighty associations, is its verbal and musical jouissance. When Walker sings, on 'Patriot (a single)', is he referencing something specific, personal, something that perhaps recalls
the days when American men brought over to Europe both a fresh
new sexuality and consumer desirables ... or is he simply riffing on
the derivation of 'nylon' from New York and London, NY and LON?
It's virtually impossible to say, and the artist himself has always been
sparing with his explanations and privileged readings.

This jouissance is perhaps harder to demonstrate musically than
it is in the album's language, which invites the same kind of refer-
ence-truffling that Thomas Pynchon's work has been victim to in
the graduate schools. Not yet, on *Tilt*, the extreme sonic solutions
of *The Drift*, with sides of meat retasked as percussion, and – almost
as notorious – the huge, cabinet-built gran cassa (or optima cassa)
featured on some of its tracks, but nonetheless a soundworld which
seems out of proportion to the material it is intended to accompany
and convey. Walker's insistence on live, or as-live, recording with
no click or guide tracks – as had apparently been used in places on
Climate Of Hunter – and one-take vocals, impose a certain improvi-

satory strain on the music, which sounds at once predetermined and free, intensely rhythmic but as utterly resistant to 'groove' as Walker intended. His choice of instrumentation contributes substantially to a record which has both a distinctive palette and a quite different sonic profile from one track to the next. 'Single' in this context may refer to the album as a discontinuous sequence of songs rather than as a unified concept with underlying narrative or thematic coherence. No one has ever attempted to describe *Tilt* in terms of an analogy with *Blood On The Tracks*, *What's Going On?*, *SMiLE* or even one of Frank Sinatra's late-night epics (though they might be thought to have an influence on Walker's method). Its aesthetic is curiously atavistic, a throwback to the days when an 'album' was a compilation of pre-existing items. It is perhaps best listened to in that way as well, rather than as a unified experience, which tends to blur the edges of these magnificent songs.

He has over the years, in the words of 'Bouncer See Bouncer ...', been *'spared//all the nickling/all the dimeing'*, but Walker's dogged anti-commercialism is often at odds with the music's extraordinary technical outlay. Whereas 'Face On Breast' uses a Hammond organ, 'Manhattan', 'The Cockfighter' and 'Bouncer See Bouncer ...' all make use of the organ at Methodist Central Hall in Westminster, an instrument which offers some notably full and hard-edged registrations. It also happens to be an instrument formerly played by Andrew Lloyd Webber's father, and it is located in a building that has a curious association with disaster, after all the public inquiries that have been held there, including into various rail crashes and the Bloody Sunday incident in Northern Ireland. Is this part of his game or do these associations simply attach themselves in default of settled 'meaning'? The sound palette also includes chittarone or theorbo, ba-wu flute and Andrew Cronshaw's other ethnomusicological resources, oboe and bass flutes, cimbalom and whistles, a small military ensemble on the sardonic 'Patriot', all these built around an essentially conventional rock group set-up without overt lead instruments. Although Walker's voice is always pushed to the front, foregrounded and often unbearably intimate and intense, not so much performed as overheard, it is the instrumental accompaniment that gives *Tilt* its estranged and estranging quality, one that hovers between fixity of structure and spontaneity, rather more like a written music heard once and incompletely remembered.

'Tilt' is what flashes up when the pinball machine is pushed to the limits, when the motion sensors vibrate and trip out, and when the smooth ur-pop of Eddie Fisher and Bobby Darin (both the elegiac Darin of 'Beyond The Sea' and the almost surreal Darin of 'Splish Splash') are taken to the final degree of abstraction. *Tilt* does not 'deconstruct' pop any more than it satirises it. On the contrary, it is a 'traditional' pop record that lays waste the tradition behind it, an end-of-pop that nonetheless demonstrates the durability of pop's sonic gestures. It is also, of course, a quixotic tilt at a sonic culture of low attention spans and lyrical emptiness.

Who would have thought *The Drift* might follow, and yet who might have thought that *Tilt* exhausted its own possibilities enough to preclude a sequel? The only thing that did, or seemed to, was Walker's reputation as a costive recluse, which it is now possible to say was never more than a myth. Out of the background buzz of popular culture, which suffers not so much from an excess of meaning but rather an excess of interpretation, Walker shaped a work that resisted analysis as confidently as it resisted easy pigeon-holing. The overload of imagery and of sound (but with no easy relation between the two) created a short circuit that locates meaning not in the tracks themselves but in the silences between them. As William Dean Howells predicted a hundred years ago, it is silence that wakens us, that and work which fails to deliver the neatly packaged quanta of information we tend to expect from culture, packed with personal, psychoanalytic, political significance. *Tilt* delivers none of these unambiguously, and its greatest ambiguity relates not to specific meanings but to whether meaning in the conventional sense is present at all. I have tried to suggest here that it does not: that the work is autotelic, self-enclosed, almost puckishly playful in its appropriation of darkness. Not since Miles Davis has an artist so artfully appropriated a public consensus about his nature and made that the basis of his art. Walker is a charlatan, a marketplace ciarlatore or babbler who accepts the logic of the marketplace even if his motive and his meaning are suspected. Walker engages in a game with us, famous for avoiding fame, selling coloured water that acquires virtue only when disbelief and the need to understand are suspended. Fundamentally, though, he has made his art out of good American stuff, and with the immitigable American belief in the principle of 'as above, so below' (or vice versa), the ultimate congruence of art with the world it inhabits, whether that process is top-down (art reflecting life) or bottom-up (life generating art). As American in his way as Twain or Henry James or William Carlos Williams, when his din is eventually done, it is as an American artist that he will be remembered.

1. Howells, William Dean, 'Part IV' in *Pordenone* (*Harper's Magazine*, November 1882).
2. Ogden, CK & Richards, IA, *The Meaning Of Meaning: A Study Of The Influence Of Language Upon Thought And Of The Science Of Symbolism* (Boston, MA: Houghton Mifflin Harcourt, 1923/1989).
3. Arendt, Hannah, *Eichmann In Jerusalem: A Report On The Banality Of Evil* (London: Penguin 1963/2006).
4. Plausible, since Walker's first wife was Danish, and he must have had some familiarity with the language, written and spoken.

Tilting At Windmills
Richard Cook
Interview in *The Wire*, May 1995

Well, I have to ask. Where have you been all this time? 'Who knows, right? Hanging out. Doing a little travelling. Nothing constructive.' An answer to induce despair in the most patient of observers. Scott Walker is, though, his customary charming self. The most singular underachiever in music is a past master at explaining away whatever creative difficulty or business block he's had to labour under. One gets a glimpse of the beguiling manner that he's used to fend off some kind of disaster these past ... oh, twenty-five years or so.

It's that long since the epochal *Scott 4* was released to deafening disregard; eighteen years since the tantalising EP's worth of material on *Nite Flights*; and more than a decade since *Climate Of Hunter* was detonated on the feckless pop surroundings of 1984. Some work rate. No wonder Walker exists as little more than a shadowy half-presence in music.

Tilt, released this month, has a spectral quality about it that derives in part from his elusive, bewildering legend. It's a record of skeletal parts that coheres in the mighty, scarcely diminished voice that acts as its narrator. Just as *Climate Of Hunter* slipped Scott loose, finally, of most of his old associations – the tormented crooner and lovelorn young man of twenty years before – so *Tilt* seems like a bulletin from an outer darkness that is very strange and rare ground for a 'rock' record to tackle. Or: who is this man and what is he doing here?

Now past fifty, he is a veteran in a business that thrives on youthful fizz. At a time when Elastica and Oasis are touted as young radical gods, it might be asked who'll want to hear such a dense, opaque meditation as this hour of music. There isn't much left of the thick romantic swirl that the early Scott Walker records were drenched in.

As finicky and detail-minded as Brian Wilson or Phil Spector, the young Scott Engel used European string writing to finesse a sorely beautiful songwriting style. The grand, sobbing orchestrations of Peter Knight, Wally Stott and Reg Guest on the early Walker Brothers records were a potent backdrop for his looming baritone voice. But now, that music seems as far away and remote from his current work as Beethoven is from Peter Maxwell Davies; as Charley Patton is from Robert Cray.

'I didn't listen to a lot of pop while I was doing this, because you subconsciously reference a lot. I listened to Beethoven's piano sonatas throughout and some Bartók string quartets. And some blues records. After it, I did what I used to do and gathered in every single thing that was going on and listened to all of it, to be sure I was … that the recording was going to be what I wanted. I can't tell you where it comes from. It comes from silence, most of it. I sit around and I'm waiting. I'm waiting and waiting.'

Like the rest of us. Perhaps Scott Engel is just more patient than most. The waiting sits well on him: the famous Walker Brothers mane of hair has receded into a trimmed and thinning top layer, but otherwise he still has the lean, cowboyish physique that he brought with him from Ohio to London when he and John Maus and Gary Leeds set out to become 'bigger than The Beatles' on an exploratory trip to the city in 1965. As The Walker Brothers, they sequenced some huge hits in the summer of that year. It didn't last long, and Maus and Leeds have never made much of an impact outside their few hits together. For Scott Walker, for ever stuck with his adopted name, it was a different if equally star-crossed story.

Five solo records for Philips, cut between 1967 and 1971, were touchstones for a singer-songwriter generation that never knew they existed. While bedsits everywhere hummed to the sound of Al Stewart or Cat Stevens, the deeper draughts of Scott Walker barely registered beyond his original following, which would always prefer him to return to 'The Sun Ain't Gonna Shine Anymore' in any case. By the time *Scott 4* was deleted less than a year after it was made, the pop idol had lost his place and the enigmatic recluse had taken over.

Scott Engel's transition from one rock era to another might seem trudgingly slow. In fact, on the early records, he worked with almost indecent haste by today's standards. After a few compromised MOR records came the Walker Brothers reunion, which seemed like no valuable escapade at all until the four mesmerising pieces which emerged on the *Nite Flights* album of 1978. Scott blueprinted all his subsequent work in those fractured, driven songs, culminating in 'The Electrician', which enumerated many of the issues which have fired him since: the interface of politics and love, societies in flux, and music that bridges classical tradition with some displaced part of rock language.

It took him another seven years to release *Climate Of Hunter*. Frustratingly brief, the record still seems like an interim report: half of it is so powerful that it shames almost everything done in rock before or since, while some of the tracks seem nearly but not quite right. As with *Scott 4*, his other half-baked masterpiece, Engel couldn't seem to see it absolutely through. The best of these records is so extraordinary that anything less seems like failure.

Now, though, eleven years after we last met at the time of the release of *Climate Of Hunter*, we have some catching up to do ...

'I think I said to you before, I don't write until I'm ready to record. It's pointless. If I'm going to sit around in a wilderness because I can't record any songs ... I threw a whole lot of songs away, as many as I could write. Which isn't a lot. Ever.'

Finally, with a deal with Phonogram/Mercury/Fontana having bubbled under for several years, he started work on a new record. 'I'll start an idea, the next part might come up in a couple of months ... Nothing's wasted at all. I'll read something or see something and think, that's where *that* goes ... I'm trying to go for something as carved down as possible. It's unlike a Dylan song or a Neil Young song where everything is moving along. That's not what I want. Everything that way seems too pat to me.'

Nothing on *Tilt* could be described that way. From the aria-like opening of 'Farmer In The City' to the Delta blues threnody of 'Rosary', the record unspools as a sequence of tableaux that abjure both simple interpretation and gratification. This is hard stuff so far removed from rock songwriting that it might as well line up with Franz Schubert as with Van Morrison. How is it put together in the studio?

'By the time I get to the studio, it's all written down. I have to have readers I can work with, because I always want the music to be played together, at once. I don't want any drum machines or click tracks. Nothing like that. Very little overdubbing, if possible. I never try to give them too much indications of what *I'm* going to do. Because then it'll turn into a group thing, which is what I don't want either. I want each piece to have an intensity of its own. So it has a kind of a febrile quality.

'I'll do a couple of tunes on the first day, then take them home and listen to them in the evening, go in and do them again if I don't like them – I don't have any equipment at home except a guitar and an amp and a little five-octave keyboard, so I don't have any fantasy or idea of what it'll be like when I get in there. So I'm surprised, constantly.'

What does Peter Walsh (co-producer of both *Tilt* and *Climate Of Hunter*) do? 'He understands how I work. It's hard for a co-producer to work with me because everything is ... everything comes from the songs. Every single sound in the track is related to the lyric in some way. So there's a security thing there. As it goes along, I give him indications of what I want and he tells me if he can get it. I leave that to him. That's valuable to me, because a lot of guys will feel they have to justify themselves in some kind of way. And then they get in the way.'

Which is what seemed to happen in the lost collaboration with Brian Eno and Daniel Lanois (about whom, Engel confesses, 'I just couldn't get along with that guy'). With another record left on the blocks before it even got started, Scott's contract with Virgin, who only ever had *Climate Of Hunter* to show for their association, was axed. Still, one feels that such superstar collaborations aren't really Engel's forte. One striking aspect of both *Climate Of Hunter* and *Tilt* is the way he coaxes scintillating work from a cast of relative unknowns: such as Brian Gascoigne (Bamber's brother), keyboards and string arrangements, or the almost subliminal bassist John Giblin. Or free-improvising saxophonist Evan Parker, who has so far not been asked to perform on any Peter Gabriel records.

'I've no idea where this record belongs. I'm not making records for that reason.'

Was he disappointed with the commercial failure of *Climate Of Hunter?*

'No, I stopped expecting it years ago. My only thing is I want to make the records. That's where I get off. After it's finished, I'll promote it or whatever, but there's nothing I can do about it then. It's done.'

Surely a musician wants an audience for his or her work?

'I'm trying to get one. But there's all kinds of artists who have different audiences for their work. I know I'm not in the mainstream at all. I'm a marginal artist. But these days so is Lou Reed or John Cale or anyone like that. I don't think I'm unusual in that kind of way.'

The difference, perhaps, is that for all their geopolitical musings and 'adult' preoccupations, the likes of Reed or Cale have never really aspired to the density and weight – at both a lyrical and musical level – that distinguishes the processes of *Tilt*. Cale, for instance, may have done songs about Hedda Gabler and Chinese envoys, but Engel, in the thematic threads of the *Tilt* material, spins together a vista of war criminals, immigrants and displaced persons, Pier Paolo Pasolini, South American despots and a host of unidentified 'personal' matters with a delicacy and intensity that is heartstopping. What, for instance, is 'Tilt' itself about?

'I can only say that it's satirical. It's kind of a black Country music song. I structured the chords very carefully through the whole album and there are new chords, not used before. The chords in 'Tilt' are meant to be like a yin and yang thing. David Rhodes is actually playing a major and a minor at the same time. I'm trying to avoid talking about the material, aren't I? It's a Country song that becomes my own vision of something else during the key change. That's all I can say.'

Do you want people to work at this material?

'Yes. Because otherwise it would have been a dance record or something, something for the background. I don't want to make that kind of record and I'm not the only one. I worked at it and they should work at it as well. More and more, I think, there are people around who'll do that.'

The cult of Scott Walker has persisted through the eighties and into the nineties. After Julian Cope's *Fire Escape In The Sky* compilation and the long-awaited reissue of the first four solo albums on CD, at least people could get their hands on material that was more often talked about than heard, even if its creator still spent most of his time hidden from view. Occasional hints of activity have filtered through, though, such as a project with David Sylvian.

'Nothing really happened. I don't really remember. I was doing something else at the time ...' He furrows his brow. 'All those years of drinking have finally taken their toll! [David] did say that he felt his stuff could use a little more balls. He's much more of an ethereal merchant than I am. I'm a man who struggles with spirituality whereas he's given in to it. My album and the one before it is about struggle in a Dostoyevskian sense. It's a real fight for me in every line. Whereas he's given in to a state of grace. I wouldn't want someone to come along and suggest a collaboration with a record that they thought was like mine. You might as well make your own record. When you can get someone to finance you!'

It might be fanciful to trace the influence of Scott Walker's voice on David Sylvian. In any case, the Engel baritone still has no real precedent elsewhere in music. When his old producer at Philips, John Franz, first heard that voice, he thought he was going to be grooming the greatest ballad singer in the world. One of the fascinating things about the early records is the split between Scott's ambitions as a writer and composer and the inevitable leanings towards territory staked out by Sinatra and his generation. It was a time when the worlds of pop and MOR were still not far apart, when the old-timers of the business had worked in the industry since the days of Glenn Miller. The sleeve photos on *Scott 4* show the besuited Franz and Peter Knight at work in the studio, as if they might have been recording Edmund Hockridge. But that peculiar British elegance gives those records much of their invincible refinement.

The voice was still in magnificent shape on *Climate Of Hunter*. On *Tilt*, there is a stretched quality to some of the singing, and the vibrato that used to bother John Franz can occasionally sound more like a quaver. Engel has also mixed himself further back than he ever has on some tracks. But it's still an astonishing voice.

'I usually sing afterwards, so the musicians don't know what's going on. But I don't do a lot of takes and I don't rehearse it at home. So I'm surprised as well, when I'm doing the vocal. I have the spontaneity. I don't always sing what I've written but I might keep it anyway. In the 'Bouncer' song I didn't sing a line as it was written, but because I felt I couldn't improve on the take, I kept it.

'Singing's always hard for me. Not physically. But to get it neutral, where it's not too emotional and not too deadpan. Somewhere in between is what I'm looking for. It drives me crazy sometimes. In this case, I think it's a little better than some of the shots I've had at it.'

He agrees that an album done all in the style of the closing 'Rosary', a voice virtually alone in the studio, would be an interesting idea. But he laughs at the suggestion that his records are never finished because of a temptation to spend hours brooding alone in the digital silence of the studio.

'No, I'm very confident in the studio! The first day I was a bit edgy, but I don't feel like I'll never come out with anything. I don't work in digital silence, either. I record in analogue. I just hope my option's going to be picked up and I can do more stuff. It's so crazy to me. You get unbelievable, or even believable people being picked up all the time who aren't selling any records. It's puzzled me. People expect a lot more sales out of me than are generated. So they're *vastly* disappointed. Whereas with other artists they'll eke it out.'

Which leaves us with the future.

'I'll do something else, and if I get a positive reaction, I'll do a little tour with the band. Well, I won't *love* the idea. I'll … go and see. You don't think I can do it, do you, Richard?'

I'm waiting, and waiting.

Silence.

Hiding In Plain Sight
David Stubbs
Production, Collaborations, Soundtracks

The reclusiveness of Scott Walker is sometimes a little overstated. Granted, there was his abortive attempt to exile himself to a monastery at the height of his fame. And yes, he 'disappeared' in plain sight during the 1970s, recording a series of anodyne covers albums before his soul could take the strain no more. Similarly, after the remarkable but not quite successful *Climate Of Hunter* (1984), he appeared to lie low for many years until *Tilt* (1995), after which a similar period of apparent inactivity elapsed once more. These lengthy silences have become part of his aura, part of the myth, with his eventual artistic statements assumed to have gone through a far more rigorous process of rumination, fermentation and distillation that sets him apart from the conventional fast-turnover processes of the modern music industry.

There is undoubtedly some truth in all this, but Walker is not necessarily as Salinger-esque a figure as he is often made out to be. Granted, if he makes a record now, he'll record on his own singular and fastidious terms, but like a great many leftfield artists, his 'silences' are often enforced by apathy and lack of investment by the commercial powers-that-be. Talk to artists like Suicide and Robert Wyatt and you realise that the intermittent nature of their output is more usually down to logistical or financial reasons rather than enigmatic ones. 'I've become the Orson Welles of the record indus-try,' Walker himself has said. 'People want to take me to lunch, but nobody wants to finance the picture ... I keep hoping that when I make a record, I'll be asked to make another one.'[1]

Furthermore, it frequently has to be pointed out that since the release of *Tilt* in particular, Walker has kept his hand in the music making business in a variety of projects and collaborations, whether curating London's Meltdown Festival in 2000, producing, co-composing or working across a variety of other media. He has always had to protest as much to interviewers who ask him to account for his supposed years of inactivity when he eventually does release prod-uct under his own name. You might say that over the last couple of decades, he has become rock music's most ubiquitous recluse.

Scott Walker has become a touchstone – a process which began when the tireless Julian Cope rescued him from the mists of critical oblivion with his compilation of Walker's late-sixties solo output, *Fire Escape In The Sky: The Godlike Genius Of Scott Walker* (Zoo Records, 1981). Since then, he has released albums regularly – one per decade – but his permanence and constant presence as a sig-nifier has been sealed. It's no coincidence that all of this occurred in the immediate aftermath of punk, which ushered in a new con-sciousness about rock's legendary past, and was as much concerned with restoring neglected figures as demolishing overpraised icons. By invoking Scott Walker, 'celebrity fans' like Nick Cave and Jarvis Cocker aren't just paying due homage, but saying something about themselves, contextualising their own cultural efforts and adding to a comprehension of what they themselves are about.

Scott Walker's value is that, unlike the studious likes of Cope, Cocker, Cave, he arose in an era of innocence and unstudied authen-ticity. He was a pop star, at a time when the selfconscious notion of the distinctions between pop and showbiz had barely developed, even when the Beatles, Stones and Dylan were in full swing. (As an example of how advanced rock discourse was in, say, 1967, the review of The Beatles' *Sgt. Pepper's Lonely Hearts Club Band* in the *New Musical Express* concluded along the following, Pathé Newsworthy lines: 'The Beatles have provided us with an album that not only makes you tap your toes, but also gives us something to think about.'[2] In such a climate, without the vast apparatus of hipness, received wisdom, back catalogue and overall cognitive framework we take for granted nowadays, Scott Walker's lonely drift leftwards, the siren lure of Brel that teased him from the clutches of American-born MOR convention, is remarkable, convincingly, instinctively soulful, a great deal more so than some modern indie group listening to a Can record and deciding to take on a Krautrock element, for example. The only similar journeys made in pop (and both travelled less far, in later times) are David Sylvian post-Japan, and Mark Hollis with Talk Talk.

In terms of his arrangements and instrumentation, Scott Walker has wandered far and wide over the course of many decades, but his voice has remained steadfastly, assuredly constant – a fixed point, a touchstone again. Gothic and tremulous; affected yet nervously, profoundly sincere; vulnerable and lost in its own cavernousness: it would probably sound a little preposterous if it wasn't emanating from his own mouth and his own, particular history. With Walker, we know that this is a voice that has traversed a vast cultural distance, from Innocence to Experience, from LA teen idol to the outer reaches of Bartók country; one alternatively thinks of Matt Monro lost in space. It seems to me crucial to the Walker experience that those self-same, sonorous tones which nowadays reverberate with epic, cryptic portent were once, we know, a keystone of the masonry of the overall sixties Wall of Sound. Scott Walker tells us something about the ability to extend the very idea of what can legitimately be said and done by someone who is ostensibly pop, as well as setting a precedent in showing how artists can subvert pop, as well as be themselves subverted, or damaged, by the pop experience.

All of this may sound as though Scott Walker appreciation is itself calculated and effective, self-serving even. Certainly he is a figure who is seen to carry a certain cultural cachet, the go-to figure who can to deliver a certain effect. However, it would be churlish to overstate 'signification' and overlook not just the value and content of what Walker delivers, but the value in which he is held, and therefore sought after. The very fact that he is such a source of inspiration has kept his name justly in the frame, kept him active in that uncertain terrain beyond music, hovering on the edges of art.

Production

Scott Walker was first offered the opportunity to produce other artists in the late 1960s, as a sideline to his activities under the spotlight. However, he didn't immediately seize the opportunity to be a producer/mentor or even producer/auteur. In 1968, he was at the controls for *Fall Out*, a solo album cut for Philips by his friend and musical director, the guitarist Terry Smith, who would go on to work with Blood, Sweat And Tears and Chicago. Although it's a precursor of a later, more self-indulgent era of jazz rock, it does however signal that despite the almost resolute jazzlessness with which one immediately associates Scott Walker's music, it was, and is, a part of his background and make-up, and a discreet string in his bow. In 1969, he also produced Ray Warleigh's *First Album* (Philips), a solo debut by a jazz saxophonist/flautist and prolific session man who would later appear on records by everyone from Alexis Korner, Mike Gibbs and Mike Westbrook to Nick Drake, Donovan and Gavin Bryars. On this purely instrumental album, Warleigh unassumingly confines himself to conventionally sumptuous big band covers of standards such as Bacharach/David's 'The Look Of Love' and songs by Antonio Carlos Jobim and Dory Previn. Both albums are efficient and attractive enough period pieces, but while Walker was doubtless able to draw on his already vast experience of music making, he doesn't exactly stamp his identity or authority on these recordings.

Just over thirty years later, however, with much troubled water having run under numerous bridges of rock history, Scott Walker met Jarvis Cocker at the 2000 Meltdown Festival, which Walker had been invited to curate. Alongside Cocker were the likes of Mark-Anthony Turnage, Asian Dub Foundation, Blur, Clinic, Jim O'Rourke, Radiohead, Elliott Smith and Smog, many, if certainly not all of whom, existed in the long shadows of what you might call a post-Walker landscape. Cocker and Walker struck up a friendship. Having scrapped an original set of recordings with British producer Chris Thomas, whose long pedigree included working with The Sex Pistols, Roxy Music and John Cale, as well as on Pulp's *Different Class* and *This Is Hardcore*, Pulp decided to take a chance with Walker and invited him to produce 2001's *We Love Life*.

It was an apt choice. Much as Walker had survived the sixties, albeit somewhat charred and disillusioned by the experience of pop adulation, so Cocker and Pulp had come through the bright blue pseudo-sixties of the nineties as the beneficiaries of a long-sought fame which, once achieved, Cocker in particular had greeted with deep ambivalence, especially some of its hedonistic excesses – to which he himself (like Walker, something of a bibulous fellow in his time) was not immune. *This Is Hardcore* (1998), thick with gravitas and pitch-black in places, had garnered praise for 'mad for it' retro-poptimism of the Britpop years. It felt quite Walkerian, in the magnificent descent of its comedown.

The songs already written for the album did, however, contain within them a seed of potential awkwardness. The song 'Bad Cover Version', written, Cocker insisted, long before there had been any talk of Walker producing Pulp, contained a reference to his seventies album *'Til The Band Comes In*, whose second side, as if admitting some sort of creative defeat, lapses into covers mode. Pulp cite the album in a series of pop-cultural comparisons with which the lyrical protagonist tries to taunt an ex-lover who has replaced him with another. These include *'the later Tom And Jerry when the two of them could talk'*, the TV version of *Planet Of The Apes* and own-brand supermarket cornflakes. Fortunately, Walker did not hurl his cloak about his shoulders and storm out of the studio in disgust when he finally heard the nervously delivered lyric, but laughed instead.

We Love Life may just be Pulp's finest album, the more so for being after their supposed 'time' had passed. It's a supreme act of sustained maturity, less deliberately wallowing than *This Is Hard-core*, a cleverer matter of light and shade, even a life-affirmativeness that feels worked-for and earned, rather than induced chemically or by peer pressure to be sanguine. Although it is the group's achieve-ment, the arrangements, with their blackened, eventful skies, and the choppy strings of 'The Trees' are full of the organised turbu-lence and melancholic grandeur which is Walker's bequest to the pop climate. You sense Walker's involvement, as well as influence, on tracks like 'Roadkill', in the very feng shui of the piece, the isola-tion of the instruments from one another, the judicious alterations he effects in the space in which Pulp play.

Walker also had some pertinent and practical advice for Cocker in his vocal approach. When asked by journalist John Earls what he had learned from being produced by Scott Walker, as well as congratulating him on his 'sarky sense of humour', Cocker added, 'Personally, how to make my vocals much better. I'd always needed a drink to calm myself before I did my vocals. I don't think I've got a great voice, I felt a bit of a cheat doing vocals. It was doubly bad singing to Scott, who has a great voice. But he'd make me compare vocal takes when I was sober and after a drink, and the sober ones were much better.'[3]

Walker and Cocker have a similar, chins-buried-in-chest approach to vocalising, but lyrically they are quite different. Walk-er's style is oblique, full of segmented and surreal juxtapositions, whereas Cocker, although capable of pitches of intensity, does so by deadpan, almost anti-poetic means, often resorting to spoken word passages, affecting to undermine the grand, lyrical rock 'n' roll manner, even as he rises to it.

However, the friendship the pair struck up clearly had much to do with their common experiences as labourers in the hit factory, and of the realities of fame. Asked by *Pitchfork* if he and Walker had discussed this at all, Cocker replied, 'We live in an age where people are kind of a bit obsessed with celebrity and stuff. You can't help but be curious about it ... but I think there comes a point where you have to think to yourself, "Well, am I doing this because I want to go to a party and meet Britney Spears? Or am I doing it because I want to create something that excites me?" And that's what he talked about in a way, that he just – you can kind of experience that fame thing for a bit, but eventually you have to decide why you're doing something. Are you going for the Duran Duran lifestyle, in which case fair enough, do it, or are you trying to create something a bit more than that? I don't think that necessarily means you have to become Mr Serious, Mr Every-Word-I-Say-Is-The-Truth or whatever, but you do have to check your motives, I think.'[4]

This approach, when applied by Walker, was nonetheless considered evidence of eccentricity and reclusiveness, rather than helpless, deep-seated sanity.

Cinema

There has always been a broad, cinemascopic scale to Scott Walker's music. *Scott 4*'s 'The Seventh Seal', his retelling of the great Ingmar Bergman movie of the same name in a parched, brassy, Morricone-esque setting of his own, is one of the more obvious examples. However, it's also to do with the vivid, illustrative potential of his arrangement skills, as well as the way his voice fills a theatre, an expansive presence rather than an intimate murmur.

During the 1990s, before and after *Tilt*, Walker obligingly broke his recording silences to help out on a number of film soundtracks.

No Regrets

The first of these was in 1993, guesting on a song written with the Serbian Goran Bregovic for the movie *Toxic Affair*, directed by Philomène Esposito. Bregovic has had a colourful musical history, having written for Iggy Pop, as well as the Serbian entry in the 2010 Eurovision Song Contest. His style has ranged from conventional mainstream rock to full orchestral ensemble, while he has written original soundtracks for movies by Emir Kusturica, as well as being sampled heavily in Sacha Baron Cohen's film *Borat*.

Despite its morbid title, *Toxic Affair* is a feelgood comedy, a showcase for Isabelle Adjani to do a self-deprecating turn as the hysterically self-absorbed hypochondriac would-be writer Penelope, who is dumped by her boyfriend, and is despaired-of by her friend Sophie. How tolerable you find the film depends on your patience for a character who chronically tries the patience of all those close to her, but whose antics, such as jumping in the Seine, self-medicating and getting into arguments with strangers, afford some entertainment. Inevitably and thankfully, Penelope finds redemption in the forest (a recurring terrain in Scott Walker's mindscape, as it happens) and at last comes to understand the meaning of selflessness.

The film is topped and tailed, not unlike a TV theme tune, by Walker's rendition of 'Man From Reno', credited as a Walker/Bregovic composition, but which was first performed in an earlier incarnation by Bregovic's old group Bijelo Dugme back in 1979. It's strange to hear lyrics such as, *'I ain't no pussy with the blues/Just step out on the floor and see'*, emerge from Walker's mouth, but the distant, allusive echo of Johnny Cash is more familiarly disquieting. The effect of the song in the movie, however, especially when Bregovic kicks in with his somewhat earthy, rhythmical guitars, is warm rather than portentous. Walker's velvet, avuncular vocals offer an assurance that everything will ultimately work out for the lost soul Penelope, with Walker as not so much Dark Angel as Guardian Angel. This is affirmed at the movie's conclusion, when the song strikes up for the last time. (It was later covered by The Walkabouts.)

In 1996, Nick Cave worked with longtime collaborator, the film director John Hillcoat (with whom he had co-written 1988's *Ghosts ... Of The Civil Dead*, an ambitious effort of debatable quality in which he also co-starred) on *To Have And To Hold*, for which he put together the soundtrack with the help of Mick Harvey and Blixa Bargeld, among others. A humid, psychological thriller with echoes of *Vertigo*, *Apocalypse Now* and *The Mosquito Coast*, it's set in the tropics of Papua New Guinea and tells the story of Jack (Toheky Karyo), a tragedy-stricken drunkard, who meets romantic novelist Kate (Rachel Griffith) and strikes up a relationship with her. It soon becomes clear, however, as they head upriver to his home, that the reason Jack is fixated on Kate is because she reminds him of his late wife Rose, videos of whom he plays over and over behind closed doors. Cave and co's soundtrack evokes the enveloping heart of darkness and insanity, but the soundtrack concludes with Scott Walker's rendition of Bob Dylan's regretful 'I Threw It All Away', which first appeared on 1969's *Nashville Skyline*, Dylan's affecting, slightly out of character Country music outing.

The Dylan original is held in great affection by his fans, perhaps because it's a departure from his normal scabrous and embittered tone when addressing failed romance. In wistful rather than scathing tones, and in unambiguous lyrical terms, Dylan takes full responsibility for the breakdown between himself and his loved one, which, it has been speculated, might have been Joan Baez, though it could easily have been about any of his paramours.

Although Nick Cave's regard for Scott Walker is high, in a 1997 interview he suggested that it had been Hillcoat who had suggested covering the Dylan song. Moreover, it had been a choice between Walker and PJ Proby as to who they would ask to sing it. This perhaps indicates more of a desire for a certain shrewd bit of pop-cultural placement, bordering even on a kind of kitsch, rather than a desire to avail themselves of Walker's full artistic depths. They agreed on

Walker, and Cave, in a five-minute meeting with the great man, says that he 'tried to explain how I wanted him to sing it, which was a reasonably arrogant thing for me to say, to suggest the thought. And I asked if I could come into the studio with him, and he said "no". He didn't wanna have anything to do with that. He just went in and did the song and kinda posted it to us and ... that was kinda our involvement with Scott Walker.'[5]

Although the song, as rendered, has a certain effect within the grim context of the movie, as a standalone performance, it suffers from the sentimental triteness not just of the original but of the chamber arrangement, as mauve and as gaudy as a grandmother's wallpaper.

By 1999, British musician and composer David Arnold was well settled into his neo-John Barry role soundtracking the James Bond series. In interviews, Arnold was always deeply conscious of the Bond brand as it stood in the 1990s – how he could update, but how necessary it was to observe certain traditions – that, for all their state-of-the-art trimmings and contemporary touches, Bond movies are, in a sense, all about previous Bond movies. For all that, his grander ambitions were often undercut by the producers' incessant demands that he incorporate the original Bond theme as often as possible into the soundtracks. *The World Is Not Enough* was the third to star Pierce Brosnan, and displayed some of the flaws that would be most evident in Brosnan's final outing as 007 (*Die Another Day*) – far-fetched plot devices, distracting celebrity guest appearances (here, Goldie and John Cleese), and Robert Carlyle ill-advisedly bringing a touch of nuance and self-loathing to his Bond villain, ignoring the golden rule that Bond villains should be unabashedly and breezily rotten to the core.

Scott Walker was invited to sing one of Arnold's own compositions, written with lyricist Don Black. Entitled 'Only Myself To Blame', it's another paean to lost love, with Walker bringing class, pedigree and shades of Matt Monro (who sang the theme to *From*

Russia With Love), walking through the song as if he had his tuxedo slung Sinatra-like over his shoulder, against Arnold's fine-cut, Gil Evans-style arrangement. It had been considered for use over the closing credits; after all, unlike most recent Bond songs, its title at least makes sense. However, although it appeared on the soundtrack album, it was discarded in the movie in favour of a Techno version of the James Bond theme.

For *Pola X* (1999), Walker played far more than a cameo role. Not merely lending his trademark vocals, he produced the entire soundtrack, which includes contributions from Sonic Youth and Bill Callahan (aka Smog) as well as several purely instrumental contributions of his own. Directed by Leos Carax and based on Herman Melville's novel *Pierre: Or, The Ambiguities* (1852), *Pola X* tells the story of a young novelist Pierre (played by the late Guillaume Depardieu), whose idyllic life and near-incestuous relationship with his mother are abruptly jolted while en route to announcing the date of their wedding to his fiancée. He encounters a woman in the forest who claims to be his lost sister and they began a relationship, choosing to live in a derelict, post-industrial compound. Pierre willingly plunges into this abject, dystopian environment for the sake of his art and his new love.

The film was notorious for its scenes of unsimulated sex and as an example of French extremist cinema, and its heightened anti-realism will be a little rich for some. However, it's attuned to Walker's own epic, nightmarish visions of freefall into the underworld; not just the inevitable forest, but also the scenes featuring the compound's house band of Glenn Branca Orchestra-like zombies. These are seen hammering out primitive, solemnly atonal fare on anvils and guitars in a setting that anticipates the studio scenes depicted in the *30 Century Man* documentary, which showed how Walker achieved some of his effects on *The Drift* using a giant box and a pig carcass. As for his contributions to the soundtrack, they demonstrate all the flourishes of a man who has fully absorbed some of the darker, larger-scale composers of the twentieth century, including Bartók, Lutoslawski and Penderecki, and found a way of codifying their turbulent, ominous orchestration in a more populist setting.

Cross-media

Shortly after the release of *The Drift* in 2006, Scott Walker was commissioned to score a dance work choreographed by Rafael Bonachela for CandCo, a company featuring both disabled and non-disabled dancers. Attuned to the language of contemporary art and its preoccupation with space and physical relations, Walker declared that he wanted the piece to reflect 'how we cut up the world around us as a consequence of the shape of our bodies'. He further mused on how such physical sociability is relevant or required 'in an age of increasing AI'.[6] Whether this is a reference to the still-faraway contingency of machines matching human intelligence, or simply the remoteness that is now part of everyday life, is unclear. However, whatever its conceptual implications, *And Who Shall Go To The Ball? And What Shall Go To The Ball?* – scored for cello, percussion, alto saxophone and flute with added effects and sound manipulation – is viscerally stunning, both visually and as a standalone Ambient (and decidedly anti-Ambient) piece. It would be glib to suggest that it can 'mean whatever you want it to mean' – but it's certainly an open-ended, as well as imposing and compelling experience.

Onstage, the CandCo troupe hurled themselves at each other in a prolonged ritual of brief, angular, violent physical engagements – at one point, a wheelchair-bound dancer was manhandled out of his chair. All this was enacted to Walker's orchestration, courtesy of The London Sinfonietta. The first movement is couched the low hiss of near-silence save for an air-conditioner-style hum, against which strings tab tersely, like sudden, illuminating bolts of lightning, or brief phrases, like unfinished sentences. The second movement explodes in a Bar Mitzvah-style riot of agony and delirium, before the oppressive stabbing recurs, like multiple, personal space-invading prods to the chest. In the third movement, black blocks of sound ooze, with a force far greater than sadness, as if on the point of evolving into a slow Stravinsky movement, but never quite emerging from the cello quagmire. The final movement of the piece, barely twenty-five minutes long overall, gathers all the musical elements on display hitherto into a final frenzy, with some backwards taping added to the mix. Again, it's an example of a popular artist steeped in the twentieth-century avant-garde but academically uninhibited and unintimidated, free to twist and sculpt its tropes and tendencies to his own ends.

Songs

Throughout the first decade of the twenty-first century, Scott Walker agreed to write and/or perform a number of original songs for inclusion in works outside of his own oeuvre. Having been signed to 4AD – one of that independent label's great coups in recent times – Walker contributed to a specially curated compilation entitled *Plague Songs*, in which a variety of artists of varying stature, both on and off the label, were invited to write tunes themed around the biblical plagues. These included Cody Chestnutt ('Boils'), Laurie Anderson ('The Fifth Plague') and The Tiger Lillies ('Hailstones'). Brian Eno's 'Flies' is probably the best thing on the album, sampling Robert Wyatt's insect vocalisations to such poignantly comic and anthropomorphic effect that you end up in a sort of sympathy for the buzzy little nuisances. Walker runs it very close, however, chiming in, not uncharacteristically but wittily, with 'Darkness'. To the unnervingly jaunty, minimal beat of a tambourine, Walker masses a chorus similar to that on Einstürzende Neubauten's 'Halber Mensch'. The choir's fiendish, hysterical, gospel-like shrieks flash with thunderous brevity across blackening skies of apocalyptic gloom – a darkness that can be physically felt – building to an orgiastic climax:

'And when do we go? And when do we go?', before Walker punctures it with a surly, cool murmur: *'Get your coat.'*

Brighton-based Natasha Khan, aka Bat For Lashes, is one of the more deceptively formidable new breed of female singer-songwriters. Her penchant for bodypainting, mysticism, headbands and a fondness for late-sixties Aquarian Age trappings may not be to everyone's taste, but she has effectively absorbed the best of all who precede her, including Stevie Nicks, Kate Bush, PJ Harvey and Tori Amos, into a synthesis of her own, underpinned by a highly developed musical sensibility which includes an understanding of the pulse minimalism Steve Reich.

For her 2009 album *Two Suns*, Khan travelled to California to sit beneath the Joshua Tree for inspiration and devised an evil, party-going alter-ego named Pearl, who sounded rather more fun than her 'more mystical, desert-born spiritual self'. The album sought to explore her duality as well as lament a recent, failed relation-ship, and Walker was invited to contribute a guest vocal. For all the condescension towards this 'Goth hippy chick', it's a finely realised album, deserving of Walker's involvement. After the sparkle and Sturm, colour and Drang of what precedes it, closer 'The Big Sleep', Khan's own composition, unfolds over a distressed trickle of piano chords, with her vocals, pained and straining as she reaches for the upper register (*'Not even out of my dress/And already my voice is fading'*), weaving in and out of Walker's echoing responses. He acts as a kind of hologram, briefly conjured up; a patron saint and living icon summoned from the legendary dimension of rock history. It's as if Khan herself is experiencing a little death of sorts as the song (and the album) expires, and Walker's is the first voice she hears as an afterlife glimmers into being.

Finally, fast rewind to 2000. The German singer Ute Lemper is a great student of the Brecht/Weill tradition, marketed perhaps too consciously, in a manner that's perhaps too on the nose at times, as a Lotte Lenya de nos jours. With her highly photogenic, platinum and angular looks, she seems like the physical embodiment of her emphatic, dramatic, precisely enunciated vocal style. On her 2000 album *Punishing Kiss*, she performs specially commissioned songs written by a range of artists including Elvis Costello, Neil Hannon, Tom Waits and Kurt Weill (naturally), as well as two compositions by Scott Walker (though one of them, 'Lullaby (By-By-By)', initially only appeared on a Japanese edition of the album).

If much of *Punishing Kiss* feels a little too polished and over-determined, more suited to fans of cabaret and musicals than those with fuzzier, leftfield rock tastes, then thankfully, Walker's pieces lift the whole exercise on to another level, extending Lemper in a manner to which she proves equal.

'Scope J' is no Walker cast-off but quintessential, as the opening lines, delivered over the measured intonation of a piano, instantly, soberly affirm: *'The Russians are going/The Russians are going/Departing like merchants/Dragging the contours/Into the never settling snow.'* Suddenly, a hailstorm of siren guitars breaks out, as strings flurry back and forth, and we are on our way. *'The sun will never rise/But I will see it'*, shrieks Lemper, raging against the blinding light. The strangest segment of this Midnight Sun-soaked trek across this imaginary, disorienting Northern European plain is the quote from 'The Sleeping Bag', a piece of verse intended as humorous by Herbert George Ponting, a photographer who chronicled the early stages of Captain Scott's ill-fated Antarctic expedition in 1911. *'On the outside/Grows the furside/On the inside/Grows the skinside/So the furside/Is the outside/And the skinside/Is the inside …'* The poem was featured in the film *Scott Of The Antarctic*, and Walker is alive to the contrast between its jaunty whimsicality and Scott's cruel fate, with Lemper intoning the words with a restrained shudder, as Walker's orchestral arrangement is reduced to a single, bleak ticking, like rain dropping from a drainpipe after a heavy storm, as residual dark clouds of strings continue to flit and threaten.

'Lullaby (By-By-By)' is equally strong, though its inclusion on the album may have put *Punishing Kiss* further out of kilter, given its more conventional fare. A series of abrupt woodwind chirrups over a woodpecker-style pulse gives way to the mournful peals of some ancient, bagpipe-style bladder instrument, as Lemper intones, *'Tonight, my assistant will pass among you/This cap will be empty'*, before wondering, *'Why don't minstrels go from house to house/Howling songs the way they used to?'* Walker's lyrics supply no specific answer to this quandary, this apparent lamentation of the detachment between artist and audience in an ever more mediated age. A later verse ponders similarly about painters. *'Because... because'*, cries Lemper, over a rising squall of electronics. All is disjointed, some former unity lost – perhaps a mythical unity, the loss of which modern music is often lamenting, rather than celebrating. This inkling is exacerbated by the allusions here to 'My Sweet Little Baby', a lullaby written by the Elizabethan composer William Byrd, in more wholesome, pre-postmodern, fractured times.

1. Cook, Richard, interview with Scott Walker in *The Independent* (April 1995).
2. Evans, Allen, review of The Beatles, *Sgt. Pepper's Lonely Hearts Club Band* in *New Musical Express* (20 May 1967).
3. Earls, John, interview with Jarvis Cocker on Channel 4 Teletext (13 April 2002).
4. Plagenhoef, Scott, interview with Jarvis Cocker in *Pitchfork* (2 April 2007).
5. Cross, Steve, interview with Nick Cave in *Sadness Is In The Sky* (August 1997).
6. Walker, Scott, 4AD press release (September 2007).

Against The Clock

Chris Sharp

Making *The Drift*, 2004–05

Scott Walker is colour blind. He can't distinguish between green and red.

He's sitting in a living room in West London with the graphic designer Vaughan Oliver. Vaughan is ebullient, eccentric; he has twenty-five years of dealing with artists and their inarticulate desires under his steadily expanding belt. I have never seen him disconcerted – disconcerting is something that he does to other people – but he's disconcerted now.

In silence, Scott draws a square on a sheet of A4. He shades it in with diagonal pencil strokes, pressing lightly in the top left corner and heavily in the bottom right. Carefully, using a child's block capitals, he writes across the top of the square: SCOTT WALKER THE DRIFT. Then, finally, he speaks. 'Down there', he says, indicating the darkest corner, 'I'd like a deep red, like blood.' His finger moves across the paper. 'And up here, it needs to be green. A really nauseous green.' He pauses. 'You see what I mean?'

This episode is an oblique glimpse into Scott Walker's driven imagination. The colour scheme seems deliberately, methodically chosen to confront one of his own weaknesses. He is seeking to bring into being something that he can't see, something summoned wilfully and quixotically from beyond the borders of his own experience. And he knows from the outset that he will never be able to confirm for himself that the artwork achieves what he wants. It's an absurd, instinctive battle with his own limitations, an unswerving quest for an end result which many people will find either baffling, or disagreeable, or both. All of which, of course, you could say about *The Drift* itself.

True to form, Vaughan chooses to interpret his instructions loosely. When the artwork is delivered, Scott barely comments on the cover image; instead, his concentration is focused fiercely on the long, narrow and precisely arranged columns of lyrics in the booklet.

A former church at the top of Haverstock Hill in Hampstead houses AIR Studios. Sir George Martin no longer owns this august institution, but there's still an indefinable weightiness to the atmosphere, as if the high-ceilinged and elegantly domed Lyndhurst Hall is permanently haunted by the dying falls of Mahler or the lyrical flights of Vaughan Williams. This is not a facility that 4AD uses very often, to say the least, but today, shrouded by rain in late 2004, it's the venue for the single most crucial day in the making of *The Drift*. We are recording all the string parts, using a thirty-six-piece orchestra over the course of two three-hour-long sessions. Musicians' Union rules will be rigidly observed; the players are entitled, and expected, to get up and leave the moment that the six hours are up. And today's activity will consume, at a stroke, one third of the budget for the whole record – if it doesn't work out, there's no way we can afford to do it again.

None of the musicians have seen the arrangements beforehand. Neither of the arrangers (Mark Warman and Philip Sheppard) have heard their work played in unison before. This is the first chance that anyone will have to find out whether what they have written matches the sounds in Scott's imagination. Not surprisingly, there is a certain amount of apprehension in the air.

This tension is amplified by the strange, skeletal extracts from the as-yet-untitled work in progress which emerge from the monitors piecemeal; multitrack tape spools whipping backwards and forwards as the engineers hunt for the right places to drop in the orchestral material. The tracks are incomplete at this stage, gaunt rhythm sections garlanded by skeins of spectral texture. None of the vocals have been recorded, so guide melodies have been laid down in their place, a staccato synthesized harpsichord which sits high and naked in the mix. Over the course of the day, this awkward, disorienting sound seeps implacably into all our skulls.

The slight man in the denim jacket at the centre of it all seems oblivious. In Walker mythology, tales of eccentric and temperamental studio behaviour are legion. But today there is no evidence of anything other than brisk, good-humoured professionalism. It's impossible not to be reminded that Scott is a graduate of the 1960s music industry, when albums were routinely bashed out in a matter of days and released almost immediately; unlimited time is a luxury that he's never really been in a position to demand.

The hands on the studio clock accelerate remorselessly. The piece that will become 'Clara' absorbs almost all of the first three hour session. As the second gets underway, discussion moves from the leisurely and ruminative to the telegraphic and terse. The arrangers dart in and out, conveying comments and amendments from the control room to the musicians. Scott remains relaxed, cracking the occasional well-timed joke to diffuse the tension, but things get unnervingly tight. With quarter of an hour remaining, there is still one six-minute piece to be recorded. There's no time even for a run-through – the musicians play it straight from the score, the final chord ebbing to silence with literally seconds to spare. Within minutes, the studio is deserted.

In the studio, everyone's looking at Scott. Slowly, he looks up from the mixing desk. With relief, we see a broad smile spread across his face. He's happy. Later, I thank him for letting me sit in on the session. 'Hey man,' he says, 'it's your show.'

A year passes. My mobile phone rings towards the end of a blustery November Sunday afternoon. It's Charles Negus-Fancey, Scott's manager of many years, and the owner of the living room in which we will discuss artwork a few weeks later. There is no preamble. 'I'm just calling to say that the record is finished,' Charles announces. 'Scott wonders if you could come to the studio tomorrow to listen to it?' Yes, Charles, I think I can find the time.

This time, 'the studio' is Metropolis, a labyrinthine and unapologetically high-end complex in Chiswick. Scott likes working here for various reasons, but the main one is that it's a straightforward cycle ride from home. None of the Metropolis live rooms were big enough for the orchestra, but the rest of *The Drift* has taken shape here, in unpredictable bursts of intensive activity. Tracking of the instrumental parts was completed earlier in the year; the drawn-out final act has been the recording of the vocals, delayed first by the arrival of the hayfever season (Scott is a confirmed sufferer) and then by the fact that he likes to deliver these performances as the impulse takes him, confirming sessions at the last possible moment. One song, one take, more often than not, and then he's gone.

We climb a succession of metal staircases and find ourselves in a control room. Behind the mixing desk is the gentle and genial producer Pete Walsh, who also worked on *Climate Of Hunter* and *Tilt*. Next to him, complete with his two signature artefacts (baseball cap worn low over the eyes, half-consumed packet of oatcakes), is Scott. Both men seem to be suppressing smiles; faintly, I sense a mood of conspiratorial mischief.

But the lightheartedness evaporates the moment that Pete presses 'play' and the glowering, restless guitars of 'Cossacks Are' start to circle at high volume around this anechoic, claustrophobic space. Time can blunt the impact of the most startling recordings, and even work as harrowing as *The Drift* can be assimilated. But I can look back beyond my current familiarity to summon the sheer sensory overload of that afternoon, my breathless, adrenalised attempts to grapple with the dread enormity of what I was hearing. Record company apparatchiks like I was at the time become adept at producing cheery, non-committal enthusiasm on occasions like this – 'great middle eight', 'love the backing vocals', 'that guitar sound is fantastic'. But faced with the remorseless reality of *The Drift*, such banalities are out of the question. For much of the time, I am speechless, my nervous tension winding tighter with each successive track. When I hear a rasping, satanic Donald Duck intoning *'What's up Doc?'* during 'The Escape', I genuinely think that I have started hallucinating.

Between songs, Scott offers tantalising snippets of information. He points out the murky scraping that opens 'Psoriatic', explaining how they built a wooden box in the studio and placed a mic underneath it to get the sound. A light dawns – I'd paid an invoice from a joiner a few months previously without having the faintest idea what it was for. The intention, Scott says, was to create the sensation of being a pea beneath a thimble shuffled around a table, a helpless pawn in a carny man's confidence trick.

After playing the epic, horrifying 'Clara', Scott fills our fraught, palpitating silence by recalling the newsreel footage of the Mussolini/Petacci lynching that he saw as a child, an experience which provoked a succession of nightmares. Later, he explains that the *faces of the grass* passage in 'Buzzers' refers to the evolution of horses and the way that the shape of their skulls changed over the millennia. And he confesses that the Donald Duck impression was in fact perpetrated by Pete Walsh, who, it turned out, was much better at it than he was.

About some songs – notably 'Jolson And Jones', possibly the most cryptic of them all – he remains resolutely silent. About others, he is almost voluble. 'Jesse', of course, is about Elvis Presley's stillborn identical twin brother. But it's also a response to the loss of two more twins – the twin towers of the World Trade Center. So, the baritone guitar arpeggios are a deliberate, pitched-down echo of 'Jailhouse Rock', while the drone that hovers threateningly beneath them is intended to evoke the approaching jet engines of the hijacked aircraft. Scott's hushed *'pow pow'* is a deliberate, sepulchral substitute for DJ Fontana's jaunty snare hits – and also a whispered echo of those two seismic impacts on 11 September 2001. But of the aching, lonely lament that closes the song – that part-anguished, part-resigned incantation – *'I'm the only one left alive'* – he says nothing.

High harmonics trail behind the last, awkward chord of 'A Lover Loves', and fade into silence. There's a pause, then Scott murmurs, 'That's it, man'. Within the simplicity of the phrase I hear something else: a reluctant resignation, a sense of laying down arms and walking away from a struggle. Charles produces a bottle of champagne, a scrap of celebratory gentility which seems absurdly flimsy in the wake of the holocaust. Mine barely touches the sides, but by the time I set the glass down Scott has slipped out, the hydraulically controlled door closing softly behind him. I've just heard *The Drift* for the first of many times. Scott Walker will never listen to it again.

Silence, Cooked Like Gold, In Charred Hands

David Toop

The Drift (2006)

With a variable key

A solitary witness in the crypt of St Bavo Cathedral, Ghent, I view an ancient drawing of the Holy Spirit's gift of tongues, breath issuing from mouth in a schematised funnel of triangular energy. A dove hovers above the head of the glossolalist. Also in the crypt I find a relic, monstrances, a vast manuscript of notation for Gregorian chant. In a bookshop nearby, images from the Belgian Congo: a man holds up a large bat for display, its wings stretched apart like a winged black fox that has flown out of the mouth or chest of this man who spreads its death with such indignity for the colonial camera.

you unlock the house in which

A report from the 2010 public inquiry into the death of Baha Mousa, an Iraqi hotel worker who died while in the custody of British forces in Iraq. Mousa and other prisoners were subjected to inhumane treatment. This included hooding, stress techniques, verbal abuse, physical violence and the use of sticks to 'orchestrate' their cries of pain into a choir, much, I imagine, like the arcade game called Whac-A-Mole, in which plastic moles pop up from holes at random and must be struck with a mallet.

drifts the snow of that left unspoken

Auditory anecdotes from the Normandy landings of 6 June 1944 (in which, incidentally, my father took part): when paratroops became separated from their units in thick-hedged countryside, they tried without success to communicate with each other by sounding hunters' duck-calls and children's 'clickers'; those who survived the low altitude night drop heard the nauseating sound of bodies hitting the ground before their parachutes opened, a noise likened to watermelons falling from the back of a truck. Another story of that war, from air raids on Glasgow in 1941: the shrapnel from anti-aircraft guns falling on slate roofs like handfuls of pebbles thrown into a pond, night filled with the banshee howling of bombs whistling through the air, the terror eased by a folk belief that the bomb that killed you would be the bomb that fell unheard.

What snowball will form round the word

Alfredo Stroessner, the dictator who ruled Paraguay for three and a half decades until 1989, was said to enjoy a very particular form of music, whereby opponents of his regime were dismembered with chainsaws by his secret police, the Technical Service as some have called them, to the accompaniment of traditional Paraguayan harps. Stroessner ensured that the 'symphony' was relayed to colleagues through the telephone lines.

In a Baghdad press briefing by the Coalition Provisional Authority in Iraq, 25 February 2004, an Iraqi journalist asked the following question: 'General Kimmitt, the sound of helicopters which fly so low to the ground is terrifying young children, especially at night. Why do you insist on flying so low and scaring the Iraqi people?' General Kimmitt's reply was as follows: 'What we would tell the children of Iraq is that the noise they hear is the sound of freedom.'

depends on the wind that rebuffs you.

What, if anything, do these memories and images (and lines from Paul Celan, the German Jewish poet whose parents died – typhus and a bullet – in an internment camp in Romanian-occupied Transnistria) have to do with Scott Walker? Nothing, of course nothing, yet they rose into my mind as I listened again to Scott Walker's *The Drift*. Released in 2006, *The Drift* provoked dismissals, circumspect and nervous admiration, derision, a degree of shock compounded by anguished excavations for meaning, all concealed under a shell of superior amusement. We live in a time when the growing crisis afflicting closed or narrative forms – book, film, music album, newspaper – has thrown up a corresponding backlash against modernist experiment. Contrary to this trend, Scott Walker could be described as a neo-modernist. Like so many of the pioneers of modernism, a century ago now, his work refuses easy ingress, repels interpretation, decomposes familiar forms, spreads discomfort, makes us question who we are and how the universe is constituted, all deeply unfashionable strategies in the age of economic expediency.

> *The night is calm; multitudes of stars are palpitating; only the crackling noise made by the tarantulas is audible.*
>
> **From Gustave Flaubert, *The Temptation Of Saint Anthony* (1874)**

Is this truly a violent record or simply a night at the opera? I am not entirely exempt from those reactions listed above. At times he repels me, pushes me out on to thin branches, abandons me in wet mud-chutes and dark holes. Sometimes the sound is too glossy; sometimes too raw. Its convulsions are too sharp, its anguish too considered. Sometimes the impression of exposure in the voice induces shameful squeamishness of the soul, as if confronted by the sight of aged parents in disarray. A voice mannered or simply unadorned, pushed to a place beyond the edge of its tessitura? The first line – *'A moving aria for a vanishing state of mind'* – proposes some connection with opera and yet the comparison is unfortunate, if only because it brings to mind baritone voices that are trained and perfected to be capable of extreme technical demands – a Bryn Terfel or Dietrich Fischer-Dieskau.

But while these latter voices may represent the pinnacle of vocal art within a specific tradition, they are by their nature creatures of artifice. Listeners unfamiliar with the oeuvre or unsympathetic to it may find its power and enunciative precision (those rolling rrr's) comical, so the naive listener to Schubert's *Winterreise* hears not so much a soul in torment as the final reaches of technical refinement now so mannered as to be unaware of its own absurdity.

This *Drift* voice is also comical but in its untrained way it falls open into believable humanity, no more human than the baritone singers mentioned above because humans are capable of remarkable achievements (a cruelty to the self, perhaps) but human in a way that is more easily identifiable. This is a voice that cries with fear and growing self-knowledge into a well of intolerable black silence and cursed memory, a voice of fear unafraid to sound itself out in all its tremulous anguish. That quality that critics of a certain vocabulary may once have described as the rich, creamy depths of the Scott Walker voice has now been put aside, leaving a man who seems cold, alone, naked.

In his own words, a baritone can tranquilise people. Think of Billy Eckstine, Johnny Hartman, Nat 'King' Cole, Dean Martin, Lou Rawls, Teddy Pendergrass, Larry Graham, their gentle embrace. Then here he is, haggard in the virtual space of a winter nightmare. 'Now all speech calls for a response,' said Jacques Lacan, '… there is no speech without a response, even if speech meets only with silence, provided it has an auditor, and this is the heart of its function in analysis.'[1] He is under duress, alone in wild seas of history, in a state of emergency, bent and twisted under the effort of it all. Think of what Gilles Deleuze wrote about Francis Bacon: 'The entire series of spasms in Bacon is of this type: scenes of love, of vomiting and excreting, in which the body attempts to escape from itself through one of its organs in order to rejoin the field or material structure.'[2]

AS THOUGH THERE COULD BE OTHERS MORE NOCTURNAL

He sings and I think of extraordinary paintings: *St Jerome At Prayer* by Hieronymus Bosch and the clamorous mouths of *Christ Carrying the Cross*, also by Bosch; *Saint Francis In Meditation* by Zurbarán; *The Fall Of The Rebel Angels* by Pieter Brueghel the Elder; Francis Bacon's *Man In Blue IV*. Male flesh in a jacket, the man in blue leans over a desk or from within a vitrine within a blue field of nothingness. Dressed in suit, tie, white shirt, his face is swelling, peeling, fissured, as if a transformation is taking place, a shapeshift from businessman to zoo freak. This is from 1954, a sense of cool moving into anti-cool, into the hot.

Outside human time, an angel gazes down from the rooftops on to battered Europe. Death comes soon enough. Look at Rembrandt's self-portrait of 1661, aged in his own eyes, think of Samuel Beckett's late plays, *Nacht Und Träume* and *What Where*; James Joyce's monumental struggle in his last years with *Finnegans Wake*; and Bacon's final works in which a nude melts into a black screen, the torso vanishes, bodies are cut-up meat.

'Wouldn't it be better if we could just forget all the places,' says Jack Nicholson in Antonioni's film *The Passenger*, 'forget everything that happens, just throw it all away day by day.'

How does he grow old? So many pop careers are short, snuffed or resuscitated to serve afterlife terms of perpetual adolescence and nostalgia; the rest are mostly incapable of passing beyond the early middle years. The star is a carapace, a concealment, sometimes a liberation. 'It was as if he [Elvis Presley] were a different person,'

Peter Guralnick wrote in *Last Train To Memphis*, 'he could create a whole new image for himself and never have anyone bring up the old one.'[3] He is two people, three people or more among many. One is the secret self, the Engel who is angel barely glimpsed by those hypnotised by that other self, the dead self who could have been the most beautiful blue-eyed blond survivor but who chose burial instead. There is something of Dirk Bogarde about it, another beautiful young object of desire who then withdrew into a private self of unreliable autobiography, emerging in person only to make darker, more difficult films with directors like Visconti, Cavani, Tavernier, Fassbinder.

'I'm just trying to make images as accurately off my nervous system as I can,' Francis Bacon told David Sylvester. 'I don't even know what half of them mean. I'm not trying to say anything.'[4] Deleuze wrote of 'capturing forces', of painting as a medium that can make invisible forces visible; of music as a medium that can make unheard forces audible.

In 'Jesse (September Song)' he sings of the Twin Towers, collapsing steles, the presence of one having mirrored and sustained the continuation of the other; he sings of Jesse Garon Presley, stillborn, and Elvis Aron Presley (for a songwriter, the internal rhyme of their names is pleasing). Guralnick again: 'As a child Elvis was said to have frequently visited his brother's grave; as an adult he referred to his twin again and again, reinforced by Gladys' belief that "when one twin died, the one that lived got all the strength of both."'[5] The survivor is always guilty.

Is he an archaeologist from a city in denial of its own angels, an LA private eye digging through his own past, the ruins of Europe, the far echoes of Dixie? The world is a drift of displaced persons, protected from persecution by new names, new shells. *But the days grow short when you reach September ...*' Listening to 'September Song' by The Ravens, a vocal quartet led from 1945 by the caressing bass voice of Jimmy Ricks, you can hear the beginnings of something, fifties rhythm 'n' blues first of all, then a maquette for the monumentality of The Righteous Brothers and so, of course, The Walker Brothers. Listen to 'Deep Purple' by The Ravens, or 'Ebb Tide' by The Righteous Brothers, both of them as viscous and inexorable as warm dark treacle flowing slowly over a table.

Warchild, he has been here before. Buried within a fraught history there was a cunning strategy, circumstantial maybe, whereby blacks and Jews of America combined their considerable talents (at times with unhappy extra-musical consequences) to make a hitherto unknown music that would overwhelm even those who held blacks and Jews as less than human, even though they are themselves displaced. I am thinking of Phil Spector and Darlene Love, Burt Bacharach and Dionne Warwick, Leiber & Stoller with The Coasters and Big Mama Thornton, Jerry Ragovoy with Erma Franklin and Lorraine Ellison, Jerry Wexler with Ray Charles and Aretha Franklin. If I ever listened to my vinyl copy of *Looking Back With Scott Walker* (demos from 1958, one of which ended up with Elvis's contemporary, the singer Tommy Sands), I would hear a singer with a potentially different career trajectory. Had he been a little older or a little more convinced by the flimsy material written by J Baird, aka Bernie Solomon, he might have become the next Bobby Vinton, Bobby Rydell or Bobby Vee, building a fleeting career on what Burt Bacharach has described as 'vanilla songs'. But Scott was a fan of jazz, particularly West Coast jazz which at the time possessed an aura of cool detachment. As a teenager he listened to Barney Kessel, even studying guitar in the hope of being so capable. A young singer could learn a lot about time and timing from listening to Barney Kessel play, for example, a Bacharach & David song, 'The Look Of Love' (released in 1968, by which time, I am aware, *Scott* and *Scott 2* had been recorded). Kessel holds back so far from the beat that he threatens to stumble backwards into the next chord. It's a trick you couldn't manage unless you knew exactly what you were doing and where you were. This is what he aspired to, for a while at least.

He listened to Gregorian chant, taking it seriously enough to attempt a short retreat in Quarr Abbey, a Benedictine monastery on the Isle of Wight. Part of the Solesmes Congregation group, the monks continue with work that began in the nineteenth century, a restoration of the chant to its original simplicity. When I listen to recordings of monks from the Abbey Saint-Pierre de Solesmes in western France, I hear voices moving in procession, gliding weightless and substantive above the abyss. 'The solitary voice reading aloud seems to issue from an inner silence even greater than the silence that surrounds them,' wrote Patrick Leigh Fermor in an account of retreats in monasteries in France and Turkey. 'The reading comes to an end; the single light is extinguished; and the chanted psalms follow one another in total darkness. The whole service is a kind of precautionary exorcism of the terrors of the night, a warding-off of the powers of darkness, each word throwing up a barrier or shooting home a bolt against the prowling regions of the Evil One.'[6]

NOTHING IS RINGING ITS SEAS

Now in autumn (or fall, as they say in America, which brings to mind the fall of angels in apocalyptic Jewish tradition, or Lucifer himself) he has fallen further from grace to make a record which at the very least is evasive, elusive and bitter to the taste.

He drops clues, sings in discrete blocks of thought or image. Time itself is challenged in the combination of sound and word and this throws the listener into confusion, perhaps all listeners, because I have only read or heard reflections from listeners who seek to restore time, or the problems of time that narrative is intended to solve, moving forward, straining for closure, for happy endings, or endings at least, a solving of crimes (even though, in Raymond Chandler, for example, we never really understood the crime in the first place). To paraphrase Frank Kermode, discussing time and the novel: '... it would never occur to us that a [song] written to such a recipe, a set of discontinuous epiphanies, should be called a [song]'.[7]

Despite his helpful clues which may not be helpful at all, my instinct is to resist meaning in order to listen. Do we have to go all the way back to Susan Sontag? 'Real art has the capacity to make us nervous,' she wrote in 1966. 'By reducing the work of art to its content and then interpreting that, one tames the work of art. Interpretation makes art manageable, comfortable.'[8]

Don't take them so hard. They are postcards (I won't say from the edge but from some place of silence, exile and cunning), flakes of recollection, old news still pungent, interior struggle. Mysterious objects from a very private past are held up into light, just to see if they implode or melt. In the singing there are tremors and some vibrato but little elaboration, extemporisation or melisma (despite his youthful enthusiasm for Gregorian chant); no roughing up the edges of the voices, no workings inside the mouth and certainly none of the artifice of his inspiration, Jack Jones, whose Kennedy-era smoothness and clarity summed up that era that we might now frame within the aesthetic and moral universe of *Mad Men*. They are scripted drama delivered with the utmost sincerity, a form of music theatre or radio opera, even cinema in which there is nothing to see other than the shadows of sound blocks and fragmented visions flaring in the lesser darkness of imaginative space. Language is no longer 'on the page' or in 'conversation' or even 'in the head'; it drifts across a space that can be envisaged. There is no time. All of it happens at once.

Tarkovsky spoke with some dismay about the reaction to his film *Mirror*, autobiographical, overpoweringly beautiful, yet cryptic: 'I had the greatest difficulty in explaining to people that there is no hidden, coded meaning in the film, nothing beyond the desire to tell the truth. Often my assurances provoked incredulity and even disappointment. Some people evidently wanted more: they needed arcane symbols, secret meanings. They were not accustomed to the poetics of the cinema image.'[9]

You could say that he sings of the disparate flotsam, lagan and

233

derelict rattling around in the head of a man in his sixties. As a man also in my sixties, I recognise some of this debris. I hear streaks of the past, allusions to odd cultural artefacts and events, resonances only barely recalled. Like a fragment of sound poetry, the syllabic nonsense of *'ja-da ja-da jing jing jing'* is intoned on one note, as if Jackson Mac Low had broken into a poem by Gary Snyder or Robert Creeley. Did you think you were getting somewhere in this thicket of medieval shawm and Tibetan tubax? For me, 'Ja-Da' is a song from 1961, a B-side recorded by Alma Cogan. A song with a smile, you might say, it memorialises a dying era in its conflation of upbeat crooning and Dixieland jazz. In fact Sidney Bechet had recorded a version of the song with typical vigour in the 1930s but I doubt that is the record that came into his mind; maybe a trace memory of Basie, Bob Brookmeyer or Louis Armstrong, some childhood encounter with radio and the meaning of meaning which suggests dada or Freud's 'fort–da', here and gone, who knows?

Look at his face, his eyes; his papers are in order. He can pass.

America itself, a haunting presence illuminated by dispossessed drifters like Al Jolson, the Lithuanian Jew originally named Asa Yoelson who took blackface on to the American cinema screen and through a minstrel tradition that stretched back to the eighteenth century, more or less invented the concept of celebrity in the electrical age. 'And that which is reflected,' wrote Nick Tosches in *Where Dead Voices Gather*, 'no matter how radically its reflection changes, remains as deeply enigmatic today as it was in the days of minstrelsy. Beneath the singer, beneath the song. It goes on.'[10]

'I wish I was/in Dixie', he sings in 'The Escape', and there it is again, revenant, a song that came out of blackface entertainment in the late nineteenth century as a valorisation of the institution of slavery. Nostalgia is a toxin of history that perpetually draws humans back into the violence of the past – 'Some of the incidents revealed an almost medieval savagery and calculated cruelty', said the chief

prosecutor at the Hague during the trial of Slobodan Milosevic. At the same time, nostalgia can be the glue that holds those who are dispossessed and otherwise rootless within a-temporal geographies of emotional sustenance and belonging.

Borders are drawn on a map, borderlines then erased from this map to make another but not erased from atavistic memory; ethnic and religious groups drift like dust across territories, settle, regroup; then the lines are drawn again and the killing begins in earnest. Music yearns to be formless. Eras and genres of music are bags of skin, tightening, flexing, sagging, cracking, breathing, stretched over bloody fluidity.

Meditating on time, Tarkovsky quoted Dostoyevsky, from *The Possessed*: '... in the Apocalypse the angel swears there'll be no time ... Time isn't a thing, it's an idea. It'll die out in the mind.'[11] Music is said to mark time, yet nothing is marked, only given new forms; in the same way, music marks ritual and so mythical time. Revelation of the Angel Gabriel and call to prayer, the Angelus bell is rung three times daily, and each time three times. James Joyce rings the Angelus bell – evenchime, BENK BANK BONK, Pingpong and Pang – as a hypnotic sonorous motif in *Finnegans Wake*. In the month preceding Rosh Hashanah, when combs of honey will be eaten to sweeten the coming year, the shofar is blown as a reminder to those within earshot that judgment day is coming:

> *World about*
> *to end*
> *World about*
> *to end*
> *World about*
> *To end*

But eschatology is not so much ending as beginning, as Joyce made clear in the *Wake* and its story of Finnegan who fell, who died and was born again: 'Wring out the clothes! Wring in the dew!'.[12] Alain Corbin's book, *Village Bells*, describes the tolling of the Angelus as a restoration of religious intensity to everyday time: 'The morning Angelus, if one follows the symbolism of bell ringing, evokes at once the Annunciation, the Incarnation, and Jesus's triumph on Easter morning. The bell invites one to treat awakening as a rising up, recalling that of Christ from the tomb; it calls for the consecration of the new time it announces.'[13]

STILL SONGS TO BE SUNG ON THE OTHER SIDE OF MANKIND

'Now it begins ...' but how does he begin? Images glow out of the dark, white text on black ground, like the rushes of an incomplete film projected on to the sky at a drive-in movie theatre. I can visualise JR Eyerman's famous 1956 photograph for *Life* magazine, Charlton Heston's Moses spreading his arms wide across a sulphurous horizon, watched by a congregation of cars blue and silent in the gathering dusk.

Angels move silently through the library, incognito, eavesdropping on streams of thought.

Sometimes he begins with a fragment snipped from some other music, then cuts across it, the way a body cuts across space, 'reflecting how we cut up the world around us as a consequence of the shape of our bodies', as he wrote in his notes for *And Who Shall Go To The Ball? And What Shall Go To The Ball?*

May 1957, Elvis Presley's 'Jailhouse Rock' sessions: as if opening a door and each time stepping into the unknown, Scotty Moore slides a major chord up one fret, marking the start-stop structure of the song's verses. On 'Jesse', over strings that glower and threaten like the approach of incoming bomber squadrons, guitarist Hugh Burns echoes Scotty through the slow surf filter of Duane Eddy, Vic Flick with John Barry, and Morricone, *Once Upon A Time In The West*.

'The Escape': another fragment, over an indeterminate chord for strings an ascending glissando on slide guitar, another crumb of clue to send us delving into Carl Stalling's music for Warner Brothers cartoons, after which the doleful descent of his vocal loosely follows the cello part written for Frances-Marie Uitti and her two-bow technique by the Hungarian composer György Kurtág in his 1989 piece, *Ligatura – Message To Frances-Marie, Op 31b (The Answered Unanswered Question)*. Thanks are given to 'Mr K' by Scott Walker, but Kurtág was also quoting by adapting the slowly descending strings of Charles Ives's *The Unanswered Question* (1906). Is this enough quotation? Probably not (Gregorian chant is buried in here as well). Aside from passing references to the Kabbalistic Sephirot, the ten emanations through which God is revealed, and the Kellipot, those husks said to imprison the sparks of divine light exiled from God and bind the soul of each individual, there is also the brief harmonica part, an alternating two-note wail taken from another hanging. This is the one gloated over by Henry Fonda in *Once Upon A Time In The West*, a coup de cinéma in which a harmonica pushed into the mouth of a boy plays a two-note theme (by Morricone) at the same time as registering his desperation. After all, he is supporting his father on his shoulders and if he falls, well, his father has a noose around his neck.

Finally, there is the nightmare voice that quacks out Bugs Bunny's catchphrase, *'What's up Doc?'*, somehow conflating Daffy Duck and Donald Duck into one chilling hybrid that *'waddles into the afternoon'*. As Bugs Bunny once said, caught on the end of Elmer Fudd's gun: 'You're gonna hurt someone with that old shotgun.'

Now there is what looks a lynching, *'like what happen in America'*, though appearances are deceptive. Two bodies hang upside down. After being led into disaster and defeat by Benito Mussolini, the Italian people took savage revenge on him and his lover, Clara Petacci, just as the Romanian people took revenge on their hated dictator, Nicolae Ceausescu and his wife Elena.

'Clara (Benito's Dream)' begins as documentary, quiet footsteps, a click, tape spooling quickly as two souls depart, male and female, then a steady tom-tom and doubled ocarina, one either side of the stereo picture. '*This is not a cornhusk doll*,' he sings. The pastiche of Native American music is not a huge improvement over Dimitri Tiomkin's 'adaptation' of Kiowa flute magic in John Huston's *The Unforgiven* (a disturbing and confused Western from 1960 that can't seem to decide whether racism is a necessary evil or just stone cold evil), but then its point is not to be authentic but to send out another haunted intimation through which America's foundations in genocide and slavery connect to more recent eruptions of barbarism.

As I read his words I am looking at a photograph of an Iroquois doll (faceless, as always, as a protection against vanity, and made in response to a dream) fashioned from cornhusk, beads, cotton and wool, collected in 1865, and at the same time listening to a recording of Sioux Sun Dance music, recorded probably just after World War Two. The Sun Dance had been prohibited by the US government in 1881, leaving a spiritual void to be only partially filled by so-called crisis cults – the messianic Ghost Dance religion, the peyote cult and Christianity. The sound is raw, its vocal textures as urgent and abrasive as the rhythm of drum and piercing eagle-bone whistle. How striking it is to think that *The Drift* will repel many listeners with its apparent difficulty, but then compare its polished, machine-tooled motion with the fraught energy and rudimentary means of a Sioux ceremony that can no longer be practised. As the doll is buried, so the malevolence of the dream is buried also.

In all but two of the songs, the introductions are restrained, pensive, quietly ominous; the lack of conventional song structure sets up a mood of going who knows where in which shocks, when they happen and they will happen at least once in every song, punch the listener with maximum force. He was said to be a boxing fan in 1960s London. Amid the exultant mob, two fists slamming into a standing object: 'Hit him in the slats, Bob,' Rose Fitzsimmons shouted from the corner during her husband's fight with Jim Corbett in 1897.[14]

The percussion is visceral, meat and bone: the voice, *'Pow! Pow!'* as planes hit the Twin Towers; metal pipe, masonry slammed down on to a huge wooden box constructed in the studio because nothing bought from a shop or collected from a percussionist's kit would do the same job. 'The noise was a violent staccato knocking,' Don DeLillo wrote in *Falling Man*, 'a metallic clamour that made him feel he was deep inside the core of a science-fiction city about to come undone.'[15]

Knuckles punch into dead flesh, a carcass is struck with fists, not for the first time in a recording session. Akira Kurosawa felt that the sword cuts in his samurai films should have a sound, so Ichiro Minawa (the sound technician who worked with Kurosawa for many years, as well as inventing the stomping and roaring sounds of Godzilla) experimented by slashing large cuts of pork and beef while recording the sound. Eventually he found that the most satisfying of all these aural woundings came from assaulting a whole chicken stuffed with chopsticks.

'There's a song in the air.' A donkey cries out its serenade, hee-haw, comic and persecuted, the laughable scream of humans at their limits, *'... stick the fork in him ...'*, cannibalism, torture, the nightmare of extreme nationalism and fascism unleashed from years of containment. Listening to 'Jolson And Jones', I can only think of Goya, his *Cannibals Contemplating Human Remains*, the bewitchings, the madhouse, the stabbings and rapes, the firing squad, *Saturn Devouring His Son* and the horrors of *Los Caprichos* and their satire: a man carrying a donkey on his back, a donkey taking the pulse of a dying man. Is our only redemption the dream that humans might eventually evolve from this state of squalor whereby meaning is found through barbarity, become another sort of animal altogether?

The *'face is a dream, like an angel I saw, but all that my darlin' can scream is "e-e-aw".'*

MY MOST BITTER DREAM

He speaks of blocks of sound, recalling composer Edgard Varèse who articulated his approach to sound as a massing of forces, sudden stops, sharply broken intensities. According to his supporters, Varèse was a primitive, a description that in 1959 at least was complimentary in certain limited circles.

'Each of my works discovers its own form,' Varèse (the displaced French-American) explained in a 1959 lecture at Princeton University. 'There is an idea, the basis of an internal structure, expanded or split into different groups or shapes of sound, constantly changing in shape, direction and speed, attracted and repulsed by various forces.'[16] Varèse 'looks upon chords as objects,' wrote Canadian composer François Morel, 'as bodies of sound similar to superimpositions of frequencies and not as vertical coagulations above the harmonic functions proper.'[17]

The sound of *The Drift* is simple, voice against turbulent backdrop (often a chord on one note that might as well be bees or airships) that threatens to engulf this vulnerable human within a field that is ominous and present, against which the voice struggles to hold itself separate, but then the field gives way and the voice is left alone, crying out to whoever or whatever is out there among the ruins and the darkness, whoever other than itself. He has been here before. Listen to 'It's Raining Today', from *Scott 3*, a Wally Stott arrangement from 1969, an eerie quivering cloud that hovers around one pitch for nearly two minutes as the guitar works its way more conventionally through the chords.

These hermetic words that loom out of silence; a dark voice drowned in the glacial drift of enveloping strings; a complicated ancestry that is Spector and Kurtág but also the forgotten genre of light music. Stott himself worked in this hybrid of jazz, pop and light orchestral programme music, composing intricate, jaunty melodies typical of the genre along with music for comedy shows such as *The Goon Show* and *Hancock's Half Hour*, fertile ground for a musical innovator in the 1950s. Working as a writer and researcher for a

Channel 4 television series in the first half of the 1980s, I interviewed Angela Morley (the name taken by Stott after his sex change in 1972). I had wanted to interview Scott Walker as well but in those days you couldn't even get close. Perhaps unaware of the cult that was developing, Morley talked about Walker with a degree of disdain, a boy who sat on the floor and strummed a few chords on an acoustic guitar and then expected Delius and Sibelius to materialise, and if we listen to that wonderful opening chord of 'Big Louise' or the sumptuous drama of 'Montague Terrace (In Blue)' then it seems that the boy who sat on the floor knew how to make something happen even though he needed others to realise the details.

Memories and present realities knocked unconscious by necessity, post-war chaos and the atmosphere of the Cold War lie underneath the icy perfection of light music. Think of Mantovani, described by Ryoji Ikeda as 'radical Easy Listening', Trevor Duncan's music used to soundtrack Chris Marker's *La Jetée* or John Addison's score for Carol Reed's Cold War thriller of 1953, *The Man Between*, a forsaken saxophone bleating over baleful tympani, then high strings so drenched in echo that they sound synthesized. Wally Stott tried the formula himself with his score for *The Looking Glass War*, a flawed adaptation of a John Le Carré novel, but John Barry had made the territory his own years before with his music for *The Ipcress File* (1965), a scintillating mix of West Coast jazz, exotic percussion and instruments like zither and cimbalom, reminiscent of Vienna and what lay to the east, the new Soviet republics and, of course, Anton Kara's theme for Carol Reed's *The Third Man*. In all this music there was a feeling of fear and alienation in which a voice that spoke in riddles yet in its true voice would be singing on the other side of mankind.

I also think of Eduard Artemyev, his luminescent drones for Tarkovsky's *Solaris*, the clanking undertow of *Stalker*, the sombre weight of basses and cellos that open *Symphony No 4* by Sibelius, the threnodies of Penderecki, the alien atmospheres of Ligeti and Arvo

Pärt, the uncanny electronics, the steam, industrial racket and radio emanations of Michelangelo Antonioni's *Red Desert* against which a solitary female voice drifts, just as humans were now drifting across landscapes ruined by war and encroaching industry, breathing air so toxic that God himself had taken up James Joyce's formula of silence, exile and cunning.

In a world in which Snoop Dogg records a duet with Willie Nelson, science fiction no longer exists. I can imagine Scott Walker singing with King Crimson, taking lead vocals on *Starless And Bible Black*, then withdrawing from public life; I can imagine one week of *The X Factor* being given over to the songs of Scott Walker, Scott on hand to give inspirational guidance to the season's representative of unorthodoxy who must accept the poisoned chalice of singing 'Cossacks Are' and so be voted off the show; I can imagine the formation of a group of four singers – Scott Walker, Bryan Ferry, David Bowie and David Sylvian, who name themselves The Billion Dollar Quartet, or The Four Baritones; I can imagine a world in which *Big Louise: The Musical* is a greater success than *We Will Rock You*; I can imagine him performing a nostalgic set to great acclaim on the Pyramid Stage at Glastonbury; I can imagine him acting the lead role in a straight-to-VOD film by Nicolas Roeg, Werner Herzog or David Lynch; I can imagine him singing an early James Bond theme composed by John Barry and Anthony Newley; I can imagine him taking the role of Serge Carrefax in a radio play based on Tom McCarthy's *C*; I can imagine trawling YouTube to discover a grainy black and white clip of Scott Walker singing 'Days Of Wine And Roses' accompanied by Derek Bailey; I can imagine him drafted into the army during the Vietnam War, then on return starring in a series of mediocre films; I can imagine the PSYOP technical service discontinuing usage of *The Drift* in Guantánamo Bay because its sincerity and self-belief, its assault on time, only intensified the convictions of its target audience, reinforced their resistance to interrogation, aligned them with other victims of persecution and imbued them with an obscure but palpable strength, a resistance that flew at the facts. They may as well have been listening to Millie Jackson singing '(If Loving You Is Wrong) I Don't Want To Be Right' and converting its message to their own ends.

PERHAPS THERE'S NO ONE THERE

'And when the Lamb opened the Seventh Seal, there was in heaven a silence which lasted about the space of half an hour. And the seven angels who had the seven trumpets prepared themselves to sound.' Steeped in Gary Snyder, Henry Miller, general beatnik lore, and no doubt wondering what it all means, this life of disappointment, brutality and displacement, he is sitting in a movie theatre somewhere in America, experiencing some of the emotions that every introspective young person feels when they are ready for a director like Ingmar Bergman. The film is *The Seventh Seal*, released in 1957. I imagine he saw it at some repertory cinema, a few years after release. The film begins on a beach of stones. Antonius Block, a knight returning from the crusades, plays chess with Death. As the knight and his squire ride towards Block's home, they encounter the plague, the Black Death, looting and chaos, the burning of a young woman accused of witchcraft. Everywhere cruelty, venality, suffering, and God offers no response.

'Now I live in a ghost world enclosed in my dreams and imaginings,' says Block. 'But he remains silent,' Death replies. 'I call out to him in the darkness ... but one day you stand at the edge of life and face darkness ... faith is a heavy burden ... it's like loving someone in the dark who never comes, no matter how you call ... is it the angels of God or Satan or just emptiness?' Block finds some scrap of meaning for himself at the last moment with an act of sincere good will. And Death itself, who occasions all these questions and perplexity by his determination to disallow any time beyond an allotted span, the angel of death has nothing to offer other than inexorable neutrality: 'I am unknowing.'

No Regrets

1. Lacan, Jacques (trans Bruce Fink), *Ecrits* (London: Routledge, 1966/2004).
2. Deleuze, Gilles (trans Daniel W. Smith), *Francis Bacon: The Logic Of Sensation* (London: Continuum, 1981/2005).
3. Guralnick, Peter, *Last Train To Memphis: The Rise Of Elvis Presley* (London: Abacus, 1994).
4. Sylvester, David, *Interviews With Francis Bacon 1962–1979* (London: Thames And Hudson, 1980).
5. Guralnick, *Last Train To Memphis*.
6. Fermor, Patrick Leigh, *A Time To Keep Silence* (London: John Murray, 1957/2004).
7. Kermode, Frank, *The Sense Of An Ending: Studies In The Theory Of Fiction* (Oxford: Oxford University Press, 1966/2000).
8. Sontag, Susan, 'Against Interpretation' in *A Susan Sontag Reader* (Harmondsworth: Penguin, 1982).
9. Tarkovsky, Andrey (trans Kitty Hunter-Blair), *Sculpting In Time* (Austin, TX: University Of Texas Press, 1989).
10. Tosches, Nick, *Where Dead Voices Gather* (London: Jonathan Cape, 2002).
11. Tarkovsky, *Sculpting In Time*.
12. Joyce, James, *Finnegans Wake* (Harmondsworth: Penguin, 1975).
13. Corbin, Alain, *Village Bells: Sound And Meaning In The 19th Century French Countryside* (London: MacMillan, 1999).
14. Mullan, Harry, *The Book Of Boxing Quotations* (London: Hutchinson, 1988).
15. DeLillo, Don, *Falling Man* (London: Picador, 2007).
16. Ouellette, Fernand, *Edgard Varèse: A Musical Biography* (London: Marion Boyars, 1973).
17. Quoted in Ouellette, *Edgard Varèse*.

'Singing Is A Great Terror'

Rob Young

**Transcript of interview with
Scott Walker, 23 March 2006[1]**

*Scott is hunched on a sofa across from me at the Notting Hill abode
of his manager, Charles Negus-Fancey. Hoping to put him at ease, I
begin by telling him I think* The Drift *is an incredible achievement.*

Scott Walker: Well, thank you – it's so unusual for people to just
   say that out to me, I [usually] feel like I brought in the plague or
   something. If people just said they liked it upfront, it would make
   me feel so much better [laughs].

Rob Young: The studio seems to be where your creativity is focused
   these days – I'm not sure I'd want to see *The Drift* performed live,
   it would reduce the impact so much ...

SW: [Laughs] *I* wouldn't want to see it! No, it would be nigh impossible. It would be financially prohibitive, there's no way you could
   tour it because you couldn't take a force like that out every night.
   And if you did it for one night, you'd have a nervous breakdown,
   you know? There's no way. I've been asked that, so now I'm toying
   with writing something I could actually do some gigs with ... but
   it would have to be scaled down. A lot. I'd have to take four or five
   players. But the problem with me is that I'm an either/or man. My
   imagination either gets very big, or it ends with a whimper, like all
   the end songs on all my records. It's very small or it's very big, but

245

somewhere in between – you know, like a band – always sounds too normal to me.

RY: Even *Tilt* had recognisable rock structures here and there, but on the new one you've really unlocked the songs from that reliance on familiar coordinates.

SW: It's true, of course, all the stuff that I have, all the basic tracks are rock structured – it rocks, but it's only because I came from that. I started as a rock musician so that's always there … I don't particularly want to go into a strictly avant-garde position or a rock position or anything else.

RY: Since virtually all the tracks involve these knife-edge arrangements, I assume you never really hear it until you're right there putting it together in the studio – so it must be a little like being deaf to the entirety of the song until that moment.

SW: Well, it usually is. I mean, it's a question of keeping it all in my head until I get in there, and that includes drum parts and everything else. But [for] this one, I actually bought a keyboard and I've been able to program the drum parts in, so I could actually hear what it would be, and I was actually able to take a lot of the stuff in and say, 'This is the part, you have to play this.' And of course, they play it, and they play it beautifully, and sometimes they'll add something that's wonderful as well. I'm lucky, 'cause I work with great players, I've worked with them for years. They're used to all the stuff that's going in there [laughs], they're not surprised. We could run a herd of cattle through there and nobody would blink.

RY: Where did you pick up your core group?

SW: I can't really remember now, it's been so many years. I remember how I got [producer] Pete Walsh, 'cause he worked on *Sparkle In The Rain* [1984] with Simple Minds, and of all the guys I had sent to me, his sound I identified with. And the others came through various demos and tapes and whatever. And slowly but surely that sound was created …

RY: Do you rehearse together before you go into the studio?

SW: No, not a lot, 'cause they get it together very quickly. It also helps that they're readers, because I don't have that luxury of rehearsing guys over and over again in band rooms, you know? I have to be able to get guys who can get it together quickly. I like to record very quickly but this time it didn't work out that way. All the time is taken writing – writing the words which will inform the rest of it. Getting the words exactly right. So that tells you everything you're going to do. Then, when you get in the studio it should take … well, for this kind of record it's fast – a couple of months, month and a half, for mixing everything. But this went on for a year, and guys were sick, we couldn't get studio time, people were on tour … So sometimes we were only in the studio only two days a month. But in a sense that added tension, because we knew we had to get it then – and everybody was really down to it.

One of the prerequisites of working on one of my records is that everybody's got to have a sense of humour. 'Cause we would all die if we didn't, in that situation. I've always said, I don't want a lot of guys in black, brooding around the studio noodling on things. It goes past that … So, it's always good to work with those guys because of that.

RY: When the orchestral players come in, do you give them any sense of what's going to be required for each song?

SW: In this case, I had to get special people who I felt … because the string part on something like 'Cue (Flugleman)' was so dense, and it couldn't sound 'stringy', they had to play it all kinds of ways. The first section of it, even before it gets to the middle screaming string thing, it took nearly a whole session just for them to get … 'cause they had to play it in one continuous take and keep everything under control. It was very difficult. So I used [orchestrator/ conductor] Philip Sheppard, who was a string player himself, who could actually give them technical reasons why it was sounding too stringy, why I had to have less of that, or whatever. Mostly it's just a question of getting the guys in the rhythm to get it all as shaved down as they can.

Each album I've cut down more and more and more. This album has no beautiful string arrangements or anything like that. It's about big blocks of sound and noises. You always have to keep matching it to the lyric: there's no excess, or anything at all much left any more. I've been doing it for so long, it sounds normal. Somebody said to me the other day that it's not songs any more, it's something else. I don't know what it is; to me it's songs, but I can understand what they mean. I decided to try a couple of narrative things to see if I could do that again. But I also kept breaking it up with the other thing as well, so there wasn't too much of it. Some guy strumming away, telling you the story of his life …

RY: What kind of stuff were you listening to in the build-up? Before *Tilt* you said you'd been listening to Beethoven and Bartók. Was there anything that informed this one?

SW: I think all my listening days are pretty well cemented, you know what I mean? And also, while I'm working on a record I hardly listen to any other music, especially while I'm recording, 'cause you might have a terrible day, and you'll hear a fabulous record and you'll want to ditch everything. So I hadn't been listening to a lot of music. So I can't say on this one there had been any particular influences.

RY: At what point did the idea of building this percussion box come in?

SW: The big box? Well, I know pretty much everything that can be used in percussion, but I couldn't hear in my head anything that was gonna create that noise. So I realised we had to build … I just gave the guy the specifications. It's a five-by-five-foot box, and we put it on cinder blocks, and then Alasdair Malloy eventually began beating it with a big cinder block, so we got that real sound … Because with all my things, they take on nightmare proportions, so everything's out of proportion. It's usually very big, it's like a dream, so this had to fall into line with that. And later we used it for this song, 'Psoriatic'. We drilled a hole in the top, and the mics were all inside the box underneath, and stuck a mic in the middle, and we got these big dustbins and moved them around to get ... you know, it's about the shell game. And of course the pea became a giant bowling ball that was slowed down.

RY: What was your brief for the sleeve artwork?

SW: Basically I just gave [Vaughan Oliver] some information about it, that's what it should do. Because that's the idea of the album: the idea is that it starts with something we know – a political issue, and then it drifts into another world, and into something else. So all kinds of disparate elements then take place. So I just sketched something out, and then he perfected it.

RY: There are multiple resonances around the word 'drift' – random movement; or a snowdrift, which is the opposite because there things coagulate and become a larger mass; or meaning itself, the sense of 'I get your drift'.

SW: [Smiling] That's it, yeah. I'm glad you did, because that's the idea of listening to something like this, is that you bring your own interpretation. And nine times out of ten it's probably better. So those are good thoughts about it.

RY: Do you surprise yourself with the lyrics sometimes, as they come through?

SW: Of course. Always. I always surprise myself with the music, or the lyrics. You hear that from writers all the time, especially novelists, they'll say, 'God, I don't know how this happened, how I did it.' And I have that all the time. But you have to wait for that – that's what takes the time. You gotta wait till that next piece fits, and it requires a lot of patience and frustration. If you rush it, it always sounds wrong. It never rings true.

You might get a run of lyrics, but generally, you might get a 'paragraph' or a sentence, and then suddenly down the line you get … Like for instance, the song 'Buzzers'. I started writing it during the Milosevic thing that was going on, and I left it for a while. But then I came across this little news thing in the paper or a magazine, which eventually the newsreader [in the song] reads out, but it was actually a news clip – and then I started thinking about the horse, the evolution of the horse, and brought that element into it.

RY: And is that meant to contrast with what was going on with ethnic cleansing, which you could call an enforced version of evolution?

SW: There are some images from that … no, it's essentially a plea for love, really. The horses' faces lengthen, so it's more about longing for the time a spiritual face can stay with us … So it isn't actually about the lengthening in that sense, it's about lengthening of time, that you can hold that. Most of my stuff is about frustration, of being unable to hold on to a spiritual moment, always losing it. And it's the frustration of not understanding what it is. So in this case that's how that relates: *they* lengthen, why can't I have *this* face lengthen for me. *Their* faces lengthen, only in another way. [Claps hands while speaking last part]

RY: Has that sense of frustration increased as time goes on?

SW: Yes, because it's an impossible thing, you can't hang on to it. You just get glimpses of it, and so you have to desperately try and give an idea of it, and that's all you can do.

RY: I wanted to talk about some of the other songs. The whole album seems to drift toward death, blackness, and silence, and a lot of individual songs have that movement. There's also a powerful undercurrent of disease …

SW: Well, ['Cue (Flugleman)'] was maybe the toughest song I ever wrote, for ages. You did pick up on that, at the beginning of it was rather a meditation on all these plagues that are coming that we have no answer for. We put it out of our minds. But they are coming, and they're there. It started out that way, and then it became something else, as with all my songs, it all comes back to the self in some way – not the ego self, but the other self. So, yeah, you're on the right track on that one – to start with, anyway.

RY: 'Jesse' seems like the centrepiece of the record, with its complex image of the Twin Towers and Elvis's twin brother ... how that image came up, it reminded me of Dalí's 'paranoia-critical method', his way of seeing one image mapped on to another ...

SW: That seeing one image in another has a great spiritual force, but with something of the hubris of the Twin Towers – that's just American muscle. Those skyscrapers: that's pumping yourself up. So I was looking for something that also didn't have any reflexive quality. It came down to Elvis's dead twin brother – we've never seen him, [it's] something he imagines, but he can't really have it. It's once again a frustration – he can't have it. Then it moves into the other American image, the prairie, so you have a horizontal and then a vertical image going on as well. And finally it zeroes back in to the existential moment – the self – for the very end of it.

RY: What's your relationship with America at the moment? I gather you don't go back there very much ...

SW: No [laughs], I don't. I would say if I could compound all the time I've been back there in the last forty years, it might reach to three months. So it's hard for me, I'm as fascinated as anyone when they come over here ... I curated the Meltdown Festival a few years ago, and I had people like Elliott Smith coming over, and I was standing with the Brits looking over at them, thinking, 'they're kind of like from outer space, you know?' That's not a negative thing, it's just an observation. A cousin of mine wrote me a few years ago, and she'd been in Los Angeles and went to one of those big megastores, Tower Records or something, and went to W, couldn't find me there. Went up to the counter, and

said, 'I'm looking for a Scott Walker CD, can you help me?' And
he says, 'Hmm, Scott Walker', calls his assistant over, says, 'Do we
have any Scott Walker CDs?' And the guy says, 'Oh, yeah, he's the
English singer, he's in the international section.' So that kind of
sums up my relationship with the United States.

RY: Did you feel galvanized, artistically, after September 2001?

SW: It was astounding, because a lot of people started writing things
after it, but a lot of people said, I have to digest it for a few years
… Usually I suppose I would have had that reaction, but I actually
wrote this about a month after it happened. And it came together
pretty quickly, so obviously it had a dramatic effect on me. As for
what transpired afterwards, I mean, I just couldn't believe what
was going on. I never actually believed, even the night before,
when they said they were going to do Iraq, I never believed it. I
thought, well, Saddam will stand down, and this is a big bluff, and
then they did it, and everybody just watched.

RY: Does that kind of thing make you feel even more alienated from
the States?

SW: Well, definitely from this regime. It's something I don't really
get. But whenever that happens, I never really think of it relating to me [as an American] particularly. I've been here so long, it
doesn't register in any way that I'm part of it, an American part of
it. So that's probably another indication of the split.

RY: A lot of your focus seems to have been on the European atrocities, in any case. Have you been travelling in the Balkans?

SW: Oh no, I haven't travelled to those places, though I've lived
in Europe … But the European thing has always been with me.
That's why I came here, because of European cinema. I tend to
think that way anyway.

RY: With European cinema, does anything do it for you now? When
you first arrived it was the heyday of Godard, Pasolini, Tarkovsky,
Bresson – that pantheon. Now that that's a gone era, has anything
replaced it?

SW: Well, there isn't a lot. But funnily enough, in the last year, I've seen two great French films and a great Belgian one recently. I saw [Jean-Pierre & Luc Dardenne's] *The Child, L'Enfant* ... I've seen [Michael Haneke's] *Hidden* – fantastic film – and I've seen [Jacques Audiard's] *The Beat That My Heart Skipped*. You get a run, fantastic run, suddenly. *Hidden*'s like an old-fashioned art movie, it's almost back there with those guys. So they do surprise you now and then, just when you've given up. 'Cause the French make, what is it, like two hundred films or something a year, and some of them are shocking, compared with what they used to do.

RY: Have you seen *The Werckmeister Harmonies*, the Béla Tarr movie?

SW: I've seen it, with the big whale [laughs] ...

RY: Somehow that came to mind listening to the new album ...

SW: Yes, I've seen that one. It's funny you should mention that, because the [American journalist] I was on the phone with earlier, he's seen the latest one, he said the title [*The Man From London*], I said, I don't know that. Maybe it's not here yet. He was very excited about that director. But yeah, he's interesting, it's a very Eastern European sense that he has. I like that.

RY: Slow pace, a lot of space unresolved, and then big startling gestures ...

SW: That's an appealing thing.

RY: If you don't mind, I'd like to ask you for some clues to some of the songs on *The Drift*. Does 'Cue' contain references to AIDS?

SW: I mentioned before how that started off, with plagues ... I don't want to get too specific about those things. But it really is a song that is so odd, so strange, in all the turns it takes, that I'm kind of loath to talk about it, because it started off as one thing, then it became something rather personal ... So I'm kind of loath to deconstruct that ... That one really is the kind of song that almost resists deconstruction.

RY: I know you also didn't want to say too much about 'Jolson And Jones', but I had to ask about the line about the donkey in the streets of Galway...

SW: Well, it's only 'cause ... Allan Jones ... You probably don't know the song 'Donkey Serenade', do you? It's a very famous song, it's like the song 'Ja-Da', a very famous old song from the twenties and thirties, even before I was born. And Allan Jones was Jack Jones's father. Did you ever see *Night At The Opera*, the Marx Brothers? He's the romantic tenor in there. And he had a big hit with 'Donkey Serenade'. So you ought to try and hear it, 'cause it's a funny song. So, there are quotes from 'Donkey Serenade' in there. And of course, that spurred all the other donkey stuff that went on ... And there are quotes from ... I can't remember now, an Al Jolson song – so that's why it's called 'Jolson And Jones'.

RY: Some lines in 'Cossacks Are' sound like they're sampled from reviews.

SW: They are! They're not reviews of me. They're cribbed from reviews – most of them are backhanded compliments, sort of, one of the ongoing things. There's also a quote from George Bush in the middle. I remember when Chirac was over in America recently, somebody said in the press conference, 'Are you going to take him out to your ranch, Mr President?' And he said, 'Well, I'm looking for a good cowboy', and I thought, I'll put that in, 'cause that's a real backhanded compliment. Chirac took it that way, too.

RY: In 'Escape', with the Looney Tunes references ... is that you doing the Donald Duck voice?

SW: [Cheeky grin] Well, we'll never know, will we?

RY: That is a creepy moment ... so, what's Donald Duck doing in there, saying 'What's up Doc?'

SW: [Startled] You got that? Fantastic! You're the only one who's been able to understand what he was saying – it's interesting. Well, I'll leave it at that. I'm duly impressed. I had a guy who just couldn't understand it, and the more he drank, the less he understood it...

RY: What's Donald doing in that song?

SW: I don't know … [mumbles] Give that a week, just play with that one for a while … 'Cause, you know, Donald doesn't say that …

RY: I know, it's Bugs says that …

SW: Bugs says that.

RY: Who's the dedicatee, 'Mr K'?

SW: Oh, it's because there's a composer called [György] Kurtág that had that chord sequence, and I thought, well, I'll thank him 'cause I love the chord sequence, but then I discovered he took it from Charles Ives, *The Unanswered Question*, so I should have said 'Thank you Mr I' [laughs]. 'Cause, you know, he's famous for quoting people. So that was a missed opportunity.

RY: And there's a couple of references to the Kabbala in that song too, what's that about?

SW: Yes, I honestly forget what a lot of that is; I think it had to do with just the secretive society business, and conspiracy theory – I think I was trying to match those two together.

RY: Zionism?

SW: Well, I mean, I don't for one minute believe there's a Zionist threat, but … you know.

RY: I looked up the kelippot, and apparently they're little shells containing sparks of divine light; some can be redeemed and some are irretrievably blackened … seems appropriate for this record.

SW: Yeah. You've done some good work, you been diggin' away. You and Madonna, I guess [laughs]. Let's really hope that it's not associated with *that*.

RY: And the last, 'A Lover Loves', a deathbed song?

SW: All my albums tend to end with whimpers. Yeah, all the people named in there either don't exist, or they're dead, and if they are dead, they don't exist any more, in reality.

RY: Is this someone's life, and the things they loved, flashing before their eyes?

SW: Well that's another good interpretation, you see, as good as mine [chuckles].

RY: Clara is heavily theatrical, with the wind machine sound, and the meat punching ...

SW: You mean the basses? That's purely great string playing. And until it gets to the crowd section, that's the first time we use a machine, where the narration starts. So it's purely just great playing. Yeah, the meat punching, that's an idea that came to me because she was going, especially in her section, you sing quite a beautiful melody, and I needed an undercurrent of evil. 'Cause it is a fascist love song, essentially. I didn't want to do some clichéd thing with strings. That came to me, so we got the side of pork in, and made poor Alasdair [Malloy] punch it. It's pathetic – this guy, he's one of the greatest percussionists in Europe, and he not only does rock sessions, he plays with Boulez, Stockhausen, all these people, and I always subject him to some kind of awful thing, you know. He's been working with me so long that it's OK, he just ignores me [laughs], but the thing about him is, he's such a fantastic actor/percussionist.

I remember when we were doing 'The Cockfighter' [on *Tilt*], and I was looking for something at the beginning for this thing clawing its way inside a shell, the nails inside a shell. So we were looking at all the stuff he'd brought in, and there was this big gourd with coarse beads on the outside, a Brazilian instrument. And I said, 'That's perfect.' So I explained what I wanted, and he went out into the studio, said 'Turn out all the lights', and he did this movement and it was fantastic. He gets so involved with it, you can hear him scream and shout at the end of it, when he's finished punching it so hard and with such involvement. And many of them are like that, the guys I work with. Great actors, actor-musicians.

RY: In 'Hand Me Ups', you wrote about a TV celebrity and his children.

SW: Yeah, he takes it too far, he's jealous of his children. And he wants to be the child himself, and a celebrity. I wrote that during the first *Big Brother*, one of those awful things. That's why you hear the children's screams. And there's some quotes from *The Iliad*.

RY: Was the song based on anyone specific?

SW: [Emphatically] No. I just thought of this guy, this man who probably ... it's easy to imagine, took it too far. In fact I was talking to Jarvis Cocker the other day, and it happened to be a day when this guy, this awful thing, he had murdered his little baby, because he was jealous of it, because of the affection of the wife. We were talking about this song, and he said, you'll never guess what I read today ... ['Hand Me Ups'] at least has some comedy aspect, but that had nothing, you know, to save it ...

RY: You said earlier that you need to wait for the right words to form. How then do you place them in relation to the music: is it like staring at the words, rotating them in your head, seeing what structures come up around them?

SW: That's right, I mean you have the spaces too, you gotta consider the spaces. I have this mad analogy, and people look at me like I'm crazier than I am when I talk about it. But it's like: I actually see the words as soldiers in a field – that's my thing. So I can move them around, they have a certain space and everything else. So, after I've done that for a while, it starts to come to me, what each thing needs. It's a very abstract way to talk about it, but it's how I see it.

RY: How is it, living with that music? Is it difficult with that intensity?

SW: Well, the horrible thing about it is that it's become normal for me. To me, I hear it as just normal, you know? [Laughs] I guess I've been working that way so long, that it's become a part of how I see or hear things. But the album is [also] quite funny, because if you don't have that, you don't have any balance. So you have to always remember that it's absurdist, funny, but the people who

257

are making it are all engaged with that as well. So we have Donald Duck impersonations to the extreme! [Laughs]

RY: Punching a pig is funny ... and gruesome.

SW: Yeah, that's funny as well ...

RY: What about your voice? Do you have to look after it in the intervals when you're not singing?

SW: Well, I just don't use it, I look after it great! [Laughs] I only start singing maybe a couple of months before I start. I'll sing the blues or something. I'm not a trained singer, so I get it in shape by instinct. But the one thing I do know is that – you don't always hear it with this kind of material – but it stays pretty fresh because you don't use it a lot. If you're touring and touring and touring, you can really wreck your voice. But if you just take it out of its case every now and then ...

But singing is a great terror for me anyway, so it's something that I've never wholly looked forward to. When I'm home, I'm just singing for myself, it's OK, it's relaxing sometimes. But if I'm actually going to do it, especially for things like this, it's very worrying, it really gets on my nerves. But I have to capture that as well, 'cause that's part of it, part of what it is.

RY: Why is it terrifying?

SW: It's always been that way, you know, unless I've had a lot of drinks under my belt, which I used to do in the old days ... It's so ... so difficult to get it right. It seems such an incredible thing when the singing comes out of your mouth, but if you're doing paragraphs or sentences or whatever, you have to catch the phrasing right, it has to sound really right and real. And I'm just afraid I'm never gonna get it. And in my mind I never do. But at least I try. I get glimpses of it, but I never get it.

RY: You're often disappointed with the finished recordings?

SW: Sometimes I'm not, I get a day when I'm fine. No, no, we're getting better and better at getting this picture together. This picture of what this is. But because I never listen to my records once I've made them, I spent how many years writing it, then I'm producing it and mixing it with Pete, then I'm arranging it and singing on it ... and I never want to see it again, basically. I'll let someone else live with it for ten years. I mean, you couldn't want to go hear it again, 'cause you would just hear mistakes.

We're a bit purist in the sense that we don't use a lot of compression on our records – it seems to cramp up the space and everything sounds very flat. There's so much compression on everything today, just to make it loud. Everybody wants to be louder than everybody else. Then when they get it to the radio station, they add more compression on it, the disc jockeys, 'cause they want to be loud and the station wants to be loud. So you have this flat, cramped digi-noise. When you listen to our records the best thing to do is really crank them up loud, 'cause then you'll hear everything. You'll hear all the space and it'll be comfortable.

RY: In the first four or five years after *Tilt*, before the *Pola X* soundtrack came out, what were you doing?

SW: Oh yeah, I think I waited a couple of years before I started again. I'm always aware of the time, and I'm always aware now that I have to speed up. But I think I took some time off, and then I must have started, probably started 'Flugleman' around then. And maybe I started 'Clara', I'm not sure. Part of the reason for completing 'Clara' was because, uh, we have all this fascism in the air now, coming from all kinds of directions. And I'm never a fan of out-and-out protest songs – someone preaching to me and strumming – so my idea is to sneak up on it. It's a love song and it's a very, um, interesting relationship – she was besotted by [Mussolini], and had posters of him in her room and was a real fan. She didn't need to die with him. In a way it's funny, but it's kind of moving. So it's really his dream that he's having about it all, and then of course it ends with me, or you, or anyone else talking at the end. But I digressed again ...

Oh yes, the time it took. So I probably started, but then I wouldn't have completed it until all this stuff started. Two years, I probably started with Leos [Carax] then. And that went on for a couple of years. The music was easy – but it was him, calling me over to Paris, 'cause he's really fanatical about how he works, so I had to give him a lot of time, going back and forth watching him film ...

RY: You just mentioned needing to speed up a bit – what do you mean?

SW: Well, I do, it's ridiculous, this whole last thing – 'cause like I said, it wasn't only all these things that I was doing; there were other things that were going on, a couple of deaths in the family and stuff like that. And then the record company changed regimes about five times: some were favourable, some weren't, and the next guy was favourable – it was like, he loves me, he loves me not ... And then, when it got to the last people, they were favourable as long as they could marry you up with somebody who was going to produce you, and basically give them a middle-of-the-road record of, I don't know what, standards, or something. Something they could market. And of course I wasn't willing to go back there. So we had to ... So that took time.

RY: What about for the future – when you say you need to speed things up, do you have goals in your sights?

SW: Well, it's only what I've said earlier, having to write an album that I could probably gig with or tour with. So I have an excellent idea for a starting point for an album like that, as far as the concept goes. I just have to find a way to do it with about five people. So that I can get it out, manageable, on the road. So we'll see what happens ... I'll probably wind up with a two-hundred- piece orchestra again. [Laughs]

RY: Are you still comfortable with the identity of Scott Walker? The alias was created a long time ago under very different circumstances, and I'm curious how that feels now ...

SW: I toyed with idea round my fourth album, of getting rid of it. Putting only songs in the name Engel. But after a while I started to think – during that hiatus I had, you know, where I became the great leper – that that wasn't the thing that would stop people or start them buying records. I don't think when people hear my name now they associate it so much with that as with this new stuff, which is ... either more horrifying to them or not, I don't know. But I don't think it's going to make any difference now. It would just confuse issues even more, and it's hard enough.

RY: But in terms of your own identity? Doesn't it feel like a dead weight?

SW: No, I never think about it. Probably, like the English singer, I've become it. It's attached to me: a permanent appendage.

1. An article based on this interview was published in *The Wire* 267 (May 2006).

Just A Man Singing
Stephen Kijak
Scott Walker – 30 Century Man (2006)

20 July 2001 (Re-faxed: 6 September 2001)

Dear Mr Negus-Fancey,

I'm writing to introduce myself to you and to tell you about
a project I am developing relating to your esteemed client,
Scott Walker. I'm a New York based film maker and I have
started to develop a unique documentary project about the
music of Scott Walker, as told through musicians who have
been inspired and influenced by him.

Inspired myself by Bruce Weber's great film about jazz
legend Chet Baker, *Let's Get Lost*, I have set about to create a
somewhat unconventional documentary to explore how Scott
Walker's music has, through the last few decades of music,
continued to amaze people, and continued to be a force of
inspiration for many singer/songwriters.

I am currently working independently, and really, it is in its
infancy as an idea. I am doing some exploratory interviews
with some musicians in September when I'll be in the UK.
These include Marc Almond, Brendan Perry and Cousteau.
I am currently working with Winstar Worldwide on another
project – Winstar as you know released *Pola X* in the US –

and they may come in as a partner once I develop the project further.

I'm contacting you for several reasons, the first of which is that I would love to meet you while I'm in London to tell you more about the film and if at all possible, communicate the idea to Scott himself. Knowing his love of privacy, I can imagine the last thing he would want is a film to be made about him – and in conceiving the idea I am trying to be as sensitive to that as possible. I'm not trying to do some invasive biographical film about his life – on the contrary, the subject really is the music. I figured he should at least be aware of the project if possible, and it would also be wonderful if he wasn't actually opposed to the idea.

Your guidance through these issues would be invaluable. I will be in London 17–21 September and, like I said, I would be very keen to meet with you, even briefly.

Most sincerely,

Stephen Kijak

I can't actually remember how I got Charles's fax number. But I do know that, when after a few days I didn't get a reply, I dialled the fax number on the phone, changing a digit each time until I got a phone to ring. Charles answered and we had a pleasant chat. Can't remember if he asked me how the hell I got his phone number.

It's amazing how little changed from this initial pitch (except for the inclusion of the Scott-influenced British group Cousteau. Brendan Perry is on the DVD extras). Also amazing how long it took to really get the ball rolling, but not so amazing, actually, once I realised my entire life would now adjust itself to Scott-time. An hour becomes a day, a day becomes a year, just as one song can orbit the imagination for a decade until it is finally executed in the studio, over the course of several days (months perhaps), piece by excruciating but necessary piece. Bam bam bam bam.

No one wanted to fund this film. A discussion with someone at the BBC ended with them telling me, 'Frankly, I feel like I've been down this road before.' Meaning – we tried and we failed. Scott will not cooperate. Hell, at this rate, he may never finish the record.

I meet a fellow Scott obsessive at the Tribeca Film Festival in 2003. Over many whiskies he has me believing he will give me some money to make the film. Three days and two hangovers later, he kicks in the seed money and we are off. Sort of. If anyone is going to take this film seriously, I have to film some significant interviews and gain the all-important access to Scott Walker himself. I am told that access to the studio might be possible. I want a week. They say one day. And then we wait ... a year.

I found the following 'production diary' that I started writing once we actually started shooting, over a year after the initial investment had been made. The diary is all of three entries long. I couldn't bear to chronicle the agonising pace at which we were working after that.

25 November 2004

Three months of waiting in London – one day in the studio with Scott. Worth the wait. In the meantime, sifting through Scott quotes to drop into film at points – signposts along the long road: 'We are entering into silence, the most noisy, chaotic silence.' The waiting. The silence. I can hardly get with the notion of a 'production diary' in this headspace – the waiting is part of the process, has been since the first communiqué was sent to the Negus-Fancey's in 2001 while I was working on Cinemania.

In the studio – two small cameras – we try to become as invisible as possible, as silent as possible. An amazing day. Percussion. The incredible Alasdair Malloy arrives to make some beautiful noise. We have begun ...

The 'beautiful noise' Alasdair made that day included the now legendary 'meat punching' sequence; a percussive side of pork, pummelled for use on the track 'Clara'.

This was the first day we 'met' Scott. We were in the studio for hours before he showed up, watching Pete Walsh, Scott's producer, and Pete's brother-in-law Tim build an enormous wooden cube in the centre of the studio. This is for the song 'Cue'. Pete explained to us that the idea is to replicate the sound of a guy banging an empty pint glass on a bar. (Bam bam bam bam.) But loud. Nightmarishly loud.

The album, we had learned, had been in production for months but recording happens sporadically, a day here, a day there. The first attempt to get this sound started over a month ago with a much, much smaller wooden box. It was more 'ping ping ping ping' than 'bam bam bam bam', so they chucked it. Pete recalled that once, during the recording of *Tilt*, timpani were delivered to the studio for a particular track and Scott was more impressed with the large wooden crate the timpani came in than the drum itself. They filed that idea away and then, ten years later, an enormous custom-made wooden box is built for 'Cue'.

Alasdair Malloy arrives to warm up. Alasdair played on *Tilt*, is a brilliant percussionist, willing and able to do anything Scott asks of him, and always seems keen to tackle a challenge. This is the first of many presented to him today. Pete mikes up the box as Alasdair starts to thwack it with a wooden orchestral brick. Grant Gee has rigged up a stationary camera in the corner of the studio to capture the action in a geometrical wide shot and I roam around with the B camera.

At some point, a man in a green anorak walks in and stands in front of me as I'm trying to get a shot. I move right and catch

Alasdair turn and face the man. 'Hiya Scott!' I try not to drop the camera. As instructed, we hang back, keep filming, but just don't get in his way. We will be introduced when the time is right. He seems aware of the cameras – not annoyed, but he definitely finds ways to keep his back to us as much as possible. But we carry on.

The little wooden brick is not working. Again, too much like a Ping. Not a Bam. A variety of objects are tested before Scott looks down at the large concrete breezeblocks the wooden cube is propped up on. 'Do we have any more of these?' he asks. A spare breezeblock is brought in and with a mighty swing, Alasdair hammers the cube with the concrete block unleashing a cloud of dust and concrete pebbles all over the studio. They all laugh. Bam! That's it.

It was the first example that day of what resembled Foley work on a film. The search for a specific sound that connected to a narrative (and in this case, also a musical) idea. It is not just a sound effect. It is an idea made concrete. And it has to be real. Occasionally, Scott suggests putting a sound in 'the digital thing' to possibly alter its brightness or placement, but often, it is the raw, real noise he is after. It was and is one of the high points of my career to date. In a perfect world, the whole film would have been a vérité observation of this incredible album being built, but we did feel like we had the world in a day by the end of that session.

Despite Alasdair's arsenal of mallets, sticks, bells, brushes and other assorted professional percussive noise makers he had on hand, he rarely used them. He might try every single one of the hundreds of sticks and mallets he brought to find a specific sound, only to find that an old spoon might actually be the right thing.

We were filming him making the most fantastic sound. He was striking a rectangular bell (a key from a xylophone strung on a string) and then dipping it into a bucket of water to bend the pitch. (This sequence can be seen as a special DVD extra on the US edition of the film.) Scott has already exhausted every xylophone mallet ('It's too musical. It can't be too beautiful. It has to sound like what it is, a piece of metal.') Then came the spoon. ('That's a very good spoon.') But it ends up having too much attack. Metal on metal. When it should just be ... metal. It ends up being a hard rubber hammer. 'And Ally, just let it hang there, hang back, it should just be wafting out there.' The bell is used on 'Buzzers (Faces Of The Grass)'. *'Polish the fork and stick the fork in him ...'*

It must be noted that as they are working, there is no real backing track to work against, simply a guide track which is essentially Scott plinking out a melody line on a keyboard, sometimes accompanied by a click-track. Parts are recorded in isolation. So after a few hours, you're left with a simple line of notes dancing in your head, joined by Alasdair's wafting, pitchshifting bell tone, and wondering how this will all resolve itself into a song. *'He's done boys ... he's done boys ...'*

Then came the meat. In the song 'Clara', the sound of fists punching raw flesh evokes the horrific image of the dead bodies of Mussolini and his mistress Clara Petacci hanging in Piazza Loretto in Milan while being beaten and defiled by the angry mob.

In the studio, Scott turns to Pete Walsh with a devilish grin at one point and asks, 'Should we do the meat now?' He likes to save the best for last, and they cannot wait to see Alasdair's face when they present him with a side of pork Scott picked up at his local Chinese takeaway on the way in. A bit tricky to carry it while cycling in from Chiswick, but he made it and he can hardly contain his delight at what is about to unfold. Nor can we. I recall seeing an actual chart written out with the title, 'Meat Part'.

The prankish fun gives way to a concentrated effort to get the best sound out of the meat as possible, and then to get Alasdair into the right rhythmic head-space. This is a typical rhythm, actually, to the whole day – there is so much goodwill and camaraderie on display – everyone wants to help Scott find exactly what he is sonically questing for. It's hard work, but it's a hell of a lot of fun. And they always nail it.

When Alasdair gives the meat one final punch after several

gruelling, greasy takes, he puts all his weight behind it and ends with an audible grunt. Scott is delighted. 'We'll keep that in!' (And he did!)

10 December 2004

Radiohead interview in the can. Johnny Marr in the can. Sitting across from Jonny, Colin and Ed, I didn't realise I was nervous until we were rolling for about five minutes – 'So what do you want to ask us?' Um ...

Trying not to conduct the typical interview – I travel with stacks of Scott LPs and singles – I want the experience to be tactile, and they get right into it, never having seen Scott's albums on vinyl – the gate-fold sleeves, the notes, the lyrics. They've never heard the Nite Flights *tracks so we start there – amazing to see these guys grooving on an old Scott track for the first time.*

Johnny Marr a few weeks later at the Night And Day Cafe in Manchester. Waiting for the word from Scott's camp that we're cleared to shoot him in the studio, I spend afternoons at my friend's flat in London flipping through magazines – there's the Smiths special edition of Q that I read from cover to cover. There's a bit about Strangeways Here We Come *... 'I wanted a real Scott Walker vibe on this one,' Johnny is quoted as saying. I call Tanya, my Dublin based-music supervisor. 'Get me Johnny Marr!' He wasn't on our original hit list for some inexplicable reason – but can't imagine the project without his input now – so incredibly thoughtful and deeply into the music – we listen to 'The Seventh Seal' and he picks apart the arrangement instrument by instrument – it's one of his all-time favourite songs. We tell him we were not allowed to shoot a recent session Scott did with a guitar player because Scott had invented some new impossible-to-play chords and it was a very intense session in a very small room. 'They should have called me!'*

17 December 2004

We're nearly out of funds. I've been here since October. We got some good stuff but it's not enough. All at once, we finally get word that Alison Goldfrapp is available, as are Simon Raymonde and Rob Ellis – all on the same day. So we've arranged to have them all driven over to the flat in Bermondsey to shoot all three interviews. No matter that the number one bus rumbles by the front window every ten minutes ... we need to cut a solid promo before I go home for the holidays and really need more material to work with. The car that's sent to pick up Simon goes to the wrong neighbourhood entirely – so we're already an hour behind – but once we get the Scott spinning, it's all good ... Simon is moved to tears by 'Two Ragged Soldiers'; Rob wants to listen to 'Patriot (A Single)' from Tilt *(the first Scott Walker album he had ever heard). About halfway through Alison's interview she asks (with a roll of her eyes), 'So, you've been listening to Scott Walker songs ALL DAY?' I top up her Pinot Gris and off we go.*

Now we've got about four days to log it all and cut the promo ...

The 'listening heads' came about sort of by accident, more as an ice-breaker, because at that time I was not very experienced in conducting interviews. And partly because, after we chucked the idea of having other people cover Scott songs, this was a way to create a more intimate experience with the music. It was essentially what the whole film was meant to be; a chance to sit down with someone and turn them on to Scott's music. It put the interviews into an immediately reflective place. You see a range of reactions, unlocked memories, and emotions.

Marc Almond chooses 'Mrs Murphy' and immediately conjures visions of British kitchen-sink dramas, suggesting that if this song were set in America it would be a Tennessee Williams play.

Jarvis wants to be chronological – 'Let's have a listen to "Always

Coming Back To You" from *Scott.'* And is reminded that he first heard Scott when he had the flu and once he recovered he thought that maybe he had imagined the music.

Johnny Marr is interested in contextualising The Walker Brothers, noting how long after their release the songs were still played on the radio, and how their beautiful gloom fitted the atmosphere of life in the North of England in a way the Swinging London set might never have understood.

Simon Raymonde, former Cocteau Twin, Bella Union label boss, and son of Walker Brothers conductor/arranger Ivor Raymonde, simply basks in the multifold memory of turning on to Scott only after his father had passed and recalling how in their youth Scott and Dusty would swing by the flat, and the bittersweet moment when you realise, only after the fact, how cool your Dad actually was.

Richard Hawley, like Jarvis, got to work with Scott when Scott produced Pulp's swansong *We Love Life*. Richard played some guitar on the album. He took a break during the session 'and cheekily nipped off to the local record shop'. When he returned, Scott asked him what he had bought. He showed him an old Eddie Cochran record. 'Shake my hand,' Scott demanded. Richard complied. 'When I was fourteen I met Eddie Cochran and he shook my hand. So you're shaking Eddie Cochran's hand through me.'

We interviewed a great many more admirers including some of the gents from Radiohead, Dot Allison, Cathal Coughlan (who has a handwritten note somewhere from Scott telling how much he likes The Fatima Mansions' cover of 'Nite Flights'), Gavin Friday, Sting, Bowie and Damon Albarn.

We interviewed collaborators like keyboardist/arranger Brian Gascoigne ('The strategy is to get this great seesaw going back and forth and the pivot for it is to get the musicians into the no-man's land between melody and harmony, conventionally, and the squeaks and grunts of the avant-garde'), and improvising saxophonist Evan

Parker ('The first thing he said is, "This is not a funk session. I know your work, I'm thinking about clouds of, clouds of saxophone, and I'm thinking more about Ligeti than anything else"').

Rhythm section Mo Foster (bass) and Peter Van Hook (drums), who played on *Nite Flights*, *Climate Of Hunter*, and the never-completed follow-up that was to be produced by Brian Eno and Daniel Lanois, were interviewed but sadly never made the final film. As much as I enjoyed interviewing famous fans, it was the insiders who really provide that rare insight into Scott's methods, even though they are considered closely guarded secrets. Peter and Mo needed to be reassured that they wouldn't be hunted down or blacklisted for sharing inside information ...

Van Hook: The one I remember is one that didn't come out. 'Cause I was playing well.
Foster: It was just the three of us, Brian [Gascoigne], Peter and I, and I remember in one song achieving incredible intensity. So powerful. No vocals, just three guys playing – bass, drums and keyboards.
Van Hook: He asked some bizarre stuff, like play things backwards. 'Can you play that backwards?'
Foster: Yeah. The on beat and off beat would be swapped round.
Van Hook: So, quite technically difficult, but it was really good, and then Brian Eno and Daniel Lanois, they kind of messed it up really, I thought. They had a totally different view on what Scott wanted to do ... I don't think he wants people to impose their musicality on him.

Rumour has it that Scott pitched the master tapes into the Thames.

After *The Drift* is finished, mastered, pressed and ready to go – once Scott has had some time to reflect on the experience – we are finally granted The Interview. It is the very last thing we shoot for the film, which by now is almost completely edited.

No Regrets

In the middle of the interview, manager Charles pops into the room. 'Sorry to interrupt – *The Observer* just called. It's album of the week!' Scott is visibly pleased, turns to the camera, 'I hope you got that!'

We've been talking for about thirty minutes. About two hours ago I was downing my second Boddingtons at the corner pub. We are going to have about one hour with Scott. It's not much time to try to explore such a long and complex career, but at least we know we will not be talking about sex, drugs, girls, family, or any topic that strays too close to the well-guarded self, the inner sanctum, the private life that is just that: private. This is part of the deal. You can read a biography about Scott[1] that delves into the slightly salacious details, tracks down ex-girlfriends, discusses a possible suicide attempt, and seems to come to the ridiculous conclusion that a good deal of what followed the sixties was a bit of a waste of talent. The one person not interviewed in that book is Scott. 'Ultimately your work is your self,' he tells me. To me that more or less says it all.

It was a fascinating hour that did manage to cover a good deal of ground. It was less terrifying after the Boddingtons kicked in. When we reached a topic that Scott wasn't keen to discuss (like his pre-teen turn as a Broadway actor in Rodgers & Hammerstein's short-lived musical *Pipe Dream*), he would simply pause and say, 'I don't really recall anything about that.' Years later, sitting in the audience of the Drifting & Tilting event at London's Barbican (a staging of Scott's later works with full group, orchestra and guest vocalists – Scott sat in the back at the mixing desk), I couldn't help but think of that twelve-year-old Scott and marvel at the alternative universe of sound that he has now created over his decades-long career, yet still amazed by how deeply theatrical and grandiose it all is, in the best possible terms.

To date, as far as I know, Scott has never seen the film. He doesn't listen to his own records so I can't imagine he would want to watch himself in a film. His management, on the other hand, have seen it. They were at our world premiere at the London Film Festival in 2006 and have been supportive champions of the film ever since, and we all have become quite good friends. I was shocked that night when Cathy Negus-Fancey pulled me aside and, in a hushed whisper lest any circling Scott fans were in earshot, introduced me to Scott's daughter. We spoke for a few seconds before we had to take our seats for the film. In typical Walker fashion, she vanished just before the lights came up. But Cathy told me later that the film made her 'very proud' of her father.

From the transcript of Scott's interview: 'There's less and less personality as the years have gone by, in the singing. Ultimately it's just a man singing now. There are no soul inflections … I just want to get to a man singing, and when it has to have emotion … hopefully it's real emotion.'

1. Watkinson, Mike & Anderson, Pete, *Scott Walker: A Deep Shade Of Blue* (London: Virgin Books, 1994).

Contributors

Richard Cook was a British jazz writer, magazine editor, radio presenter and former record company executive. A former *NME* contributor, he was jazz critic for the *Sunday Times* and *New Statesman* before taking over as editor of *The Wire* in 1984. After leaving the title in 1991, he took over the jazz catalogue at PolyGram/Verve and, with Brian Morton, began co-editing *The Penguin Guide To Jazz Recordings*. His other books include a *Jazz Encyclopedia* and a history of Blue Note Records. He edited *Jazz Review* from 1998 until his death, aged 50, in 2007.

Stephen Kijak is a director of fiction and non-fiction films. His credits include the critically acclaimed BAFTA-nominated feature doc *Scott Walker – 30 Century Man*, the celebrated cult documentary *Cinemania*, and the platinum-selling *Stones In Exile*, a documentary commissioned by The Rolling Stones, and produced by Oscar-winning producer John Battsek/Passion Pictures, about the making of the Stones' classic 1972 album *Exile On Main Street*. He has recently teamed with Passion Pictures again and Rob Trujillo from Metallica (making his debut as a film producer) on a feature doc about the late, great legend of bass, Jaco Pastorius. Kijak was born and raised in Massachusetts, attended Boston University's

College of Communication, and currently lives in Los Angeles.

Biba Kopf (real name Chris Bohn) has been working for *The Wire* since 1997. Before then, under his own name or as Kopf, he wrote about music and film for *Melody Maker, New Musical Express* (for which he reviewed *Climate of Hunter*), *The Wire*, London's City *Limits* magazine, Berlin's *Tip* and *Zitty* magazines and more.

Damon Krukowski is a musician (Damon & Naomi, Galaxie 500) and poet (*Afterimage, The Memory Theater Burned*). He has also been a frequent contributor of articles about sound to *Artforum*.

Brian Morton has been an academic, a *Times* journalist and BBC broadcaster. His Radio 3 jazz programme *Impressions* ran for eight years and his daily live arts programme on BBC Scotland for ten, some of them overlapping, which led to some interesting commutes. University teaching led him to Tromsø in Norway, Pau in southern France, and Berlin. Instinct led him to the country; he has farmed in Norfolk and Argyll and currently lives on Kintyre with his wife, landscape photographer Sarah MacDonald, and assorted children. He owns many saxophones but rarely plays them nowadays, and is cheerfully agoraphobic, rarely leaving the disused monastery that is the family home. On St Andrews Day 2000 he was awarded an honorary doctorate by St Andrews University for services to Scottish culture.

Ian Penman began writing for the *NME* in 1977 and later contributed to a wide range of publications including *The Wire, Uncut, Sight & Sound, The Face, Arena, The Times, The Independent, New Statesman, Esquire* and *Dazed And Confused*. A collection of his writings on music and film was published in 1998 as *Vital Signs*.

Amanda Petrusich is the author of *It Still Moves: Lost Songs, Lost*

No Regrets

Highways, And The Search For The Next American Music and *Pink Moon*, an instalment in Continuum's 33 1/3 series. Her music and culture writing have appeared in the *New York Times, Pitchfork, Spin, Entertainment Weekly, Salon*, the *Oxford American* and elsewhere, and she currently teaches creative writing at New York University. She's working on a new book – forthcoming from Scribner and titled *Do Not Sell At Any Price* – about collectors of rare 78rpm records.

Nina Power teaches Philosophy at Roehampton University and Critical Writing in Art & Design at the RCA. She is the author of *One-Dimensional Woman* (Zero Books, 2009) and has since written about policing and protest for *The Guardian* and about many other things for many other places.

Anthony Reynolds was born in South Wales in the early seventies. Between 1993 and 2004 he was founding member of the groups Jack and Jacques, releasing five albums. Jack's debut *Pioneer Soundtracks* (1996) was produced by long-term Scott Walker producer Peter Walsh. Since 2004 he has released two solo albums and also worked as a writer, publishing three biographies and two volumes of poetry. His first book, *The Impossible Dream: The Story Of Scott Walker And The Walker Brothers* was published in 2009. *Life's Too Long – 1995–2011*, a double CD anthology of songs, was released in early 2012. He lives in Wales, where he is working on the screenplay of his first film, *A Small Spit Of Land*.

Chris Sharp is a Music Programmer at the Barbican Centre in London. Between 2000 and 2008 he was Managing Director of 4AD, in which capacity he signed Scott Walker and worked on the release of *The Drift*. He has been a contributor to *The Wire* magazine since 1995.

David Stubbs is an author and music journalist. His youth was mis-spent exploring and illegally taping the cache of deleted musique concrète LPs at Leeds Record Library, as well as spending his dinner money on Cabaret Voltaire and funk import twelve-inches. He first joined *Melody Maker* in 1986, joining the staff a year later. He has since worked for *NME*, *Uncut* and was Reviews Editor at *The Wire*. He is also a regular contributor to *The Guardian*, *The Sunday Times* and *The Independent*. He has written, among other books, a full-length study of the work of Jimi Hendrix, the Ace record label (Black Dog Publishing) as well as *Fear Of Music: Why People Get Rothko But Don't Get Stockhausen* (Zero Books). He is currently working on a history of Krautrock for Faber And Faber.

David Toop is a composer, author and sound curator. He has pub-lished five books, including *Ocean Of Sound*, *Haunted Weather* and *Sinister Resonance*. In 2000 he curated Sonic Boom for the Hayward Gallery, and in 2005 curated Playing John Cage for Arnolfini Bristol. His first album, *New And Rediscovered Musical Instruments*, was released on Brian Eno's Obscure label in 1975; since 1995 he has released eight solo albums, including *Screen Ceremonies*, *Black Chamber* and *Sound Body*. Musicians he has worked with include Max Eastley, Paul Burwell, Evan Parker, Derek Bailey, John Zorn, Talvin Singh, Scanner, Ivor Cutler, Steve Beresford, Jon Hassell and Jin Hi Kim. As a critic and column-ist he has written for many publications, including *The Wire*, *The Face* and *Bookforum*. His recent compositions include *FLAT TIME/sounding* for improvisors, pieces for video and live voice – *Tambourina* and *Of Leonardo Da Vinci*, and a chamber opera entitled *Star-shaped Biscuit*.

Derek Walmsley moved to London in 1997 in search of Jungle but found only drum 'n' bass. He worked for a chain of second-hand record shops for several years before starting the blogs *Pop-*

life and *Blocked Synapse*, both of which concentrated primarily on London's burgeoning Grime scene. He began contributing to *The Wire* in 2004 and has since written features on figures ranging from Wiley to Bonnie 'Prince' Billy. He became *The Wire*'s Reviews Editor in 2007, and has also contributed to *The Quietus* and *Resident Advisor*.

Rob Young joined *The Wire* in 1993 and was the magazine's editor 2000–04. His books include *Electric Eden: Unearthing Britain's Visionary Music*, *Rough Trade* and *Warp*. His blog is at electriceden.net.

Established in 1982, and now based in East London, *The Wire* is an internationally acclaimed magazine specialising in editorial coverage of all manner of alternative, experimental and underground sound and music. In addition to publishing a monthly print magazine, its operations include maintaining various online platforms, hosting a brace of radio shows, and curating a range of live events. 2012 marked *The Wire*'s 30th anniversary.